# Investigating Adolescent Health Communication

# Corpus and Discourse

**Series editors:** Wolfgang Teubert, University of Birmingham, and Michaela Mahlberg, University of Nottingham.

**Editorial Board:** Paul Baker (Lancaster), Frantisek Čermák (Prague), Susan Conrad (Portland), Geoffrey Leech (Lancaster), Dominique Maingueneau (Paris XII), Christian Mair (Freiburg), Alan Partington (Bologna), Elena Tognini-Bonelli (Siena and TWC), Ruth Wodak (Lancaster), Feng Zhiwei (Beijing).

Corpus linguistics provides the methodology to extract meaning from texts. Taking as its starting point the fact that language is not a mirror of reality but lets us share what we know, believe and think about reality, it focuses on language as a social phenomenon, and makes visible the attitudes and beliefs expressed by the members of a discourse community.

Consisting of both spoken and written language, discourse always has historical, social, functional and regional dimensions. Discourse can be monolingual or multilingual, interconnected by translations. Discourse is where language and social studies meet.

The *Corpus and Discourse* series consists of two strands. The first, *Research in Corpus and Discourse*, features innovative contributions to various aspects of corpus linguistics and a wide range of applications, from language technology via the teaching of a second language to a history of mentalities. The second strand, *Studies in Corpus and Discourse*, is comprised of key texts bridging the gap between social studies and linguistics. Although equally academically rigorous, this strand will be aimed at a wider audience of academics and postgraduate students working in both disciplines.

***Research in Corpus and Discourse***

*Conversation in Context*
A Corpus-driven Approach
With a preface by Michael McCarthy
Christoph Rühlemann

*Corpus-Based Approaches to English Language Teaching*
Edited by Mari Carmen Campoy, Begona Bellés-Fortuno and Mª Lluïsa
 Gea-Valor

*Corpus Linguistics and World Englishes*
An Analysis of Xhosa English
Vivian de Klerk

*Evaluation and Stance in War News*
A Linguistic Analysis of American, British and Italian television news reporting
 of the 2003 Iraqi war
Edited by Louann Haarman and Linda Lombardo

*Evaluation in Media Discourse*
Analysis of a Newspaper Corpus
Monika Bednarek

*Historical Corpus Stylistics*
Media, Technology and Change
Patrick Studer

*Idioms and Collocations*
Corpus-based Linguistic and Lexicographic Studies
Edited by Christiane Fellbaum

# Investigating Adolescent Health Communication

## A Corpus Linguistics Approach

Kevin Harvey

B L O O M S B U R Y

LONDON • NEW DELHI • NEW YORK • SYDNEY

**Bloomsbury Academic**

An imprint of Bloomsbury Publishing Plc

50 Bedford Square
London
WC1B 3DP
UK

1385 Broadway
New York
NY 10018
USA

www.bloomsbury.com

**Bloomsbury is a registered trade mark of Bloomsbury Publishing Plc**

First published 2013

© Kevin Harvey, 2013

**British Library Cataloguing-in-Publication Data**
A catalogue record for this book is available from the British Library.

ISBN: HB: 978-1-4411-3070-9
ePDF: 978-1-4411-4671-7
ePub: 978-1-4411-3688-6

**Library of Congress Cataloging-in-Publication Data**
Harvey, Kevin (Sociolinguist)
Investigating adolescent health communication: a corpus
linguistics approach/Kevin Harvey.
pages cm. – (Corpus and discourse)
Includes bibliographical references and indexes.
ISBN 978-1-4411-3070-9 (hardback) – ISBN 978-1-4411-4671-7 (pdf) –
ISBN 978-1-4411-3688-6 (epub) 1. Teenagers–Health and hygiene. 2. Communication in pediatrics.
3. Corpora (Linguistics) 4. Interpersonal communication. I. Title.
RJ101.H25 2013
618.92′855–dc23
2013021715

Typeset by Deanta Global Publishing Services, Chennai, India
Printed and bound in Great Britain

*This book is dedicated to Ann McPherson (1945–2011) and Aidan Macfarlane. Tireless champions of adolescent health.*

# Contents

# Preface

This is a groundbreaking book. It is groundbreaking in the field of applied linguistics and groundbreaking too in the field of health communication research. The book challenges a number of assumptions about the role of language in communication while at the same time challenging conventional paradigms of where, why and how language should and can be studied.

In the field of applied linguistics there is one definition provided some time ago by Christopher Brumfit which serves as a statement to which most applied linguists would subscribe.

> The theoretical and empirical investigation of real-world problems in which language is a central issue. (Brumfit, 1995: 27)

Since the 1960s in the field of applied linguistics the main focus of real-world problems has been the language classroom and the broad issue of teaching and learning a language. While this focus will always remain a valuable one, the scope of the field is expanding fast and a wider range of applications are now developing. *Investigating Adolescent Health Communication* is a rich example of paradigm-shifting with a move to the medical world and to the centrality of language and communication within that world. This book breaks important new ground in showing the relevance of language investigation in a domain where few applied linguists have ventured. Kevin Harvey is concerned here not simply with describing language and communication in the medical domain, nor with simply showing its relevance to medical communication; instead he prioritizes a problem-oriented view identifying specific real-world problems in an important part of that domain and developing the means by which they can be addressed linguistically. In the terms of Brumfit's definition his approach is indeed empirical. He is not interested in broad sweep examples but in an empirical engagement with real data that also importantly helps us reformulate theories of applied linguistics as a research practice.

But how is the book groundbreaking in the field of health communication. Here Kevin Harvey moves us beyond the worlds of adults and child health which figure so prominently in medical health and medical communication research to the world of adolescent health. More significantly still, the locus of investigation is language and communication to which professionals do not have regular or consistent access: emails sent by adolescents to a website to which doctors then send composite replies. This is a world away from a surgery in a health centre with its inevitably rather uneasy interchanges between adolescent and healthcare professional. What is communicated through the emails (a remarkable collection of over 2 million words) reveals much about health concerns that is normally difficult, if not impossible, to access.

Kevin Harvey analyses this data and identifies for us recurring vocabularies and patterns of language that in turn reveal personal concerns that have not previously been seen to be voiced in this way – covertly and anonymously, of course – but accessed here in ways that reveal dominant concerns and anxieties in a population, thus making available to health practitioners information to help them both with diagnosis and, initially, support through effective communication.

Methodologically, the use of corpus linguistics methodology, described illuminatingly in this book, provides substantial quantitative evidence of a kind that is accepted in the evidence-based and scientific world of medicine; but there are also crucial qualitative complements to this analysis driven by the latest approaches in discourse analysis that allow a sharply focused lens to be directed on individual instances and particular examples. The mixed-methods approach adopted makes for a rich tapestry of research with numerous individual threads subtly sewn into the larger-scale picture.

Linguists learn much both from this encounter with the data as health language usage can then be illuminatingly benchmarked against standard corpora and different degrees of variation and patterning analysed in a domain of English usage that has not been extensively described. Linguists also see how research from other disciplines such as medical sociology, psychology and health science can be integrated in a better understanding of how young people linguistically construct and account in their own discourses for how they feel. And health professionals get to understand better the needs and concerns of patients uniquely accented in their own idiom and with the texture and feel of their own point of view; and it may also be that health educators benefit further from a data-rich and investigative environment that may complement the more hypothetical, staged and role play exemplifications that are currently more common in health education.

*Investigating Adolescent Health Communication* does indeed therefore push back boundaries: in applied linguistic research practice, in methodology, in its rich interdisciplinarity and in its potential for impact on a key and hitherto relatively neglected area of social life. It is model of applied linguistics in action and it brings to the arena a use of corpus linguistics which is distinctive, richly nuanced, and exemplary.

Professor Ronald Carter
School of English,
University of Nottingham, UK

September 2012.

# Acknowledgements

First off, I would like to thank the series editors, Michaela Mahlberg and Wolfgang Teubert, for their commissioning this book and for their support and helpful insights during its preparation. I also received invaluable support from Louise Mullany, Paul Crawford and Ronald Carter, all of whom offered many perceptive and constructive comments on earlier drafts of this book.

Svenja Adolphs and Catherine Smith, fellow corpus investigators, and Ana Jolly, fellow traveller, assisted me with tricky technical matters which were beyond my range of computational linguistic proficiency, blissfully saving me hours of needless manual drudgery. Thank you.

I would also like to thank Nicola Gray who first introduced me to the *Teenage Health Freak* website and its creators Ann Mcpherson and Aidan Macfarlane with whom I have subsequently collaborated on research in adolescent communication. I have learnt so much from Nicola, Ann and Aidan about adolescent health, and their wonderful work in this area has been continually enlightening and motivating. I have also learnt much from Brian Brown and Dick Churchill, health communication researchers extraordinaire.

Finally I wish to thank the following copyright holders for permission to reprint the following materials:

- Fig 4.1 Homepage of Teenage Health Freak website: courtesy of Aidan Macfarlane (*Teenage Health Websites*).
- How to use corpus linguistics in the study of health communication. In M. McCarthy and A. O'Keeffe (eds), *The Routledge Handbook of Corpus Linguistics*. Routledge, UK, 2010 (co-authored with Sarah Atkins).
- Disclosures of depression: Using corpus linguistics methods to examine young people's online health concerns'. *International Journal of Corpus Linguistics*, 17: 349–79. John Benjamins, 2012.
- Harvey, Kevin, and Brian Brown. "Health Communication and Psychological Distress: Exploring the Language of Self-harm." *Canadian Modern Language Review/La Revue canadienne des langues vivantes*, 68, 3: 316–40. University of Toronto Press, 2012.

# Introduction: Why Study Adolescent Health Communication?

Health communication research has, without doubt, privileged the discursive routines of adults. Theories of, and practical insights into, health communication have typically been founded on the discursive routines of adults, with relatively little consideration for the communicative repertoires of younger users of health services. Consequently, we know comparatively little about the linguistic choices with which adolescents voice their health concerns, and hence little about what such choices reveal about their subjective experiences and perceptions of health and illness. Even if adolescents are generally a healthy group, young people nevertheless have many questions and concerns about their health which they wish to discuss with professionals (Klein and Wilson 2002a).

This book aims to address the neglected area of adolescent health communication. Using the tools of corpus linguistics, I have conducted an analysis of a two million word collection of emails submitted to a doctor-operated website dedicated to adolescent health provision. The corpus approach to research in health discourse constitutes a novel yet rigorous mixed-methodology, combining both quantitative and qualitative techniques to linguistic analysis. By examining the common ways in which adolescents discursively construct their concerns to professionals online, this study aims to identify and describe patterns and commonalities in young people's accounts of health, specifically sexual and mental health. In doing so the research aims to give voice to an age group whose subjective experiences of health and illness have often been marginalized or simply overlooked in favour of the concerns of older populations.

This is the first book-length study to use corpus linguistics to interrogate a substantial dataset of naturally-occurring adolescent health discourse. Corpus analysis affords a systematic means of identifying the 'incremental effect' (Baker 2006: 13) of discursive patterns, facilitating the discovery of recurring (and exceptional) patterns of communication which might be overlooked by health professionals and policymakers unaccustomed to exploring the significance of language in determining health interventions, and, more generally, the discursive practice of advice-seeking itself. This study demonstrates the utility and relevance of interrogating the linguistic routines of adolescents, and how, by extension, it is important for practitioners to pay close attention to such patterns of discourse if they are to appreciate the 'richness of everyday communication about health care issues' (Brown et al. 2006: 139). Accordingly, as well as being of interest to health communication researchers, my hope is that this study will also be of value to professionals and educators concerned with the health of young people.

## 1.1  Contemporary adolescent health issues

The focus on adolescent sexual and mental health is timely. As we will see shortly, concerns about sexual and mental health feature prominently in the young people's requests for online professional advice. The emphasis on these particular health themes reflects some of the key health problems that currently face adolescents in western societies: although today's teenagers experience a broad range of health problems, sexual and mental health are some of the most common, and pressing, among them (British Medical Association 2003, 2005, 2006). For instance, with regard to emotional well-being, one in ten of British adolescents is liable to have some clinically recognized psychological disorder (British Medical Association 2006). Mental health problems which develop during childhood and the teenage years are, moreover, not simply confined to these periods: they are liable to persist into adulthood and can deteriorate over time (British Medical Association 2003). For instance, a study in the *British Journal of Psychiatry* (Maughan and Kim-Cohen 2005) reports that for people experiencing mental health problems at the age of 26, half of them will have the clinical criteria for their condition by the age of 15. Mental health problems in children and adolescents are thus of great importance to public health.

Problems relating to young people's sexual health are also a significant western health concern. The prevalence of sexually transmitted infections (STIs) among teenagers, for example, is high and has increased in recent decades (British Medical Association 2003). Indeed adolescents and young people under 25 have the highest rates of curable STIs (Advocates for Youth 2010). With regard to HIV/ AIDS (the most serious of all STIs), health agencies warn that too many young people are at risk of HIV infection (Centre for Disease Control 2011). In 2009, for example, young people accounted for 39 per cent of all new HIV infections in the United States (ibid.). Similarly, in the United Kingdom, a Health Protection Agency (2011) report noted that higher proportions of HIV infection were also seen among younger people aged 15–24. As with mental health disorders, sexual health problems, such as teenage pregnancy, can adversely influence adolescents' education and social development (British Medical Association 2003).

Despite some researchers thinking otherwise (or simply overlooking the fact), adolescents are not small adults: they are a specific client group at a unique stage of emotional, neurological, physical and social development (McPherson 2005) and thus require policies, services and support tailored to reflect these differences (Aynsley-Green et al. 2000). Thus if we are to develop a culture where young people can take responsibility for and promote their health, it is vital to access and understand the perspectives of adolescents themselves. Although, as the British Medical Association (2005) argues, improved education to empower teenagers to make decisions that meet their unique requirements is essential to improving adolescent health, it needs to be recognized that individuals (whether adolescents or adults) do not straightforwardly process and adopt official health education messages. Such information is liable to be filtered through subjective experience and popular beliefs about health (Herzlich and Pierret 1986; Helman 2007), reinterpreted through existing belief systems to suit young people's personal requirements (Aggleton and Homans 1987).

Consequently, it is ever important to first explore the perspectives of adolescents, to ascertain their beliefs and understanding about health and so describe the attitudes which influence their health and help-seeking behaviours. As Peremans et al. (2000: 134) comment, health education initiatives are 'developed by "adults" and are based on the "assumed" needs of adolescents'. Thus, if educational interventions and policy initiatives are to be successful, they need, first and foremost, to be delivered in accordance with young people's pre-existing health beliefs and conceptions, and tailored appropriately in light of them.

## 1.2 The Teenage Health Freak website

The demand for health provision tailored to the need of adolescents has resulted in a rise of health websites designed for young people (Jones et al. 1997;

Aynsley-Green et al. 2000). These sites typically provide interactive advice and information in accessible, non-technical language, affording young people the opportunity of freely expressing their health questions to professionals, as well as sharing their concerns with fellow teenagers. Consequently the internet has become a popular provider of health advice and information for adolescents, with the electronic gateway offering confidential advice and information that might be otherwise hard or compromising to obtain from more traditional health services (Suzuki and Calzo 2004).

The focus of this study is on one such specialist internet service, the UK-based website, the Teenage Health Freak. The corpus of health emails from the site constitutes a rich source of linguistic data for exploring the personal perspectives and communicative routines of adolescents, complementing data derived from more traditional methodological approaches to adolescent health communication, such as questionnaires and interviews. The emails originate from the adolescents themselves, meaning that their questions are motivated by what they deem to be personally relevant to them, rather than being solicited by the problem-focused agendas dictated by health practitioners or researchers.

A further distinctive feature of the messages explored in this study is that they are free from external linguistic filtering. Unlike the postings appearing on some other health websites, they are neither simplified nor edited for the sake of clarity and convenience by the website operators. The linguistic material interrogated in this study retains its textual integrity, preserving the exact words and grammatical forms employed by the contributors (including typographical and spelling errors and other non-standard features of language). The emails submitted to the Teenage Health Freak website thus constitute a unique and novel vantage point from which to survey adolescent health and, in particular, how young people communicate their experiences of, and attitudes and beliefs about, sexual and mental health.

## 1.3 Discourse and the study of health communication

In examining the situated, naturally-occurring linguistic routines of young people, this study is concerned with discourse. Language in use is essential to the way in which people constitute their experiences of health and illness. Individuals' experiences of health and illness are not simply based in the biological 'realities' of their bodies, but, crucially, in the discourse they use to communicate them (Atkins and Harvey 2010). If we take the view that language in use constitutes people's understandings of themselves and the world around them, then analysing discourse offers a means of making sense of the social experience of health. As Fox (1993: 6) puts it:

> illness cannot be just illness, for the simple reason that human culture is constituted in language . . . and that health and illness, being things which fundamentally concern humans, and hence need to be 'explained', enter into language and are constituted in language, regardless of whether or not they have some independent reality in nature.

It is certainly true that we are constantly presented with the need to 'explain' illness. In an increasingly medicalized society, discourses surrounding the body permeate the texts people consume on a daily basis, such as in news media and advertising. Thus when individuals fall sick, they find out about their illnesses through the language of health professionals, through conversations with family and friends, through books and internet media, and so forth. The central importance of discourse in our experience of illness cannot be underestimated.

This far, I have used the term 'discourse' rather glibly, as though its meaning were glaringly clear to the reader and did not need unpacking in any way. But what exactly is discourse, and in what sense am I using it in this book? It has become a truism to say that discourse is a nebulous term and a commonly contested concept. Indeed it goes without saying nowadays that discourse has been harnessed in numerous, diverse studies with an almost insouciant disregard for consistency. Indeed definitional variety and instability is, paradoxically, perhaps its one stable defining, characteristic feature.

At the risk of simplifying (in point of fact, I am simplifying), 'discourse' can be defined in the linguistic sense of organized stretches of spoken and written (including computer-mediated) language 'above the sentence or above the clause' (Stubbs 1983: 1). This formal, linguistic approach to discourse analysis involves the study of larger linguistic units, such as spoken exchanges or written texts, and, as such, is concerned with analysing language in use in certain social contexts (ibid.). In this realm of linguistic analysis, discourse is studied in order to explicate its structural properties, for example, looking at how cohesion is achieved (or otherwise) across clauses and utterances, and how discourse is organized and managed through features such as turn-taking, topic management and narratives (Thornbury 2010: 271). In examining discourse in this way, it is possible to discover more about the communicative context in which discourse is produced (such as service encounters, media interviews, doctor-patient encounters, etc.), and the ways in which discourse is used to achieve specific purposes (obtaining goods and services, disclosing and diagnosing medical problems, and so forth).

Another approach to discourse and discourse analysis comes from a social theoretical perspective, research which draws in particular on the work of the philosopher Michel Foucault (1972) (for an accessible introduction to this line of discourse study see Parker (1992)). According to this socially oriented approach, discourse is a particular way of thinking and talking about aspects of reality (Cheek 2004: 1142) or, as Parker (1992: 5) defines it, 'a system of statements which constructs an object'. A discourse is a framework for understanding the world, a set of ideas and assumptions which inform and shape people's perception of reality. The point to note here is that the sets of ideas and assumptions which comprise a discourse are typically taken for granted, unquestioned, and hence tend to remain invisible (Cheek 2004: 1142). The workings of discourses are quite insidious; people are liable to draw on them unconsciously or least pay them little, if any, critical attention.

As the reader will have noticed, discourse, from this social theoretical standpoint, is not a singular but a plural entity: discourses are multiple, various, countable. It is thus possible to identify and speak of, among an inexhaustible amount of others, a 'discourse of capitalism', a 'discourse of socialism', a 'discourse of medicine', a 'discourse of homeopathy', a 'discourse of racism', a 'discourse of sexism', and so forth, all of which incorporate unique underpinning networks of values and meanings (Gwyn 2002: 26). The fact that discourses are manifold means that, evidently, there are various discursive frames for talking, writing and thinking about the world (Cheek 2004: 1143). As Baker puts it, 'around any given object or concept there are likely to be multiple ways of constructing it, reflecting the fact humans are diverse creatures' (2006: 4).

Yet despite the plurality of discourses on which people draw in order to make sense of and order reality, not all discourses are equal; some carry significantly more weight and influence than others, and thus some discourses exclude or marginalize others, particularly at a given moment in history (what might be called dominant discourses). For example, in contemporary western society, scientific and medical discourses presently dominate understandings of health and illness and the body, having achieved a 'truth status' denied to other 'non-scientific' ways of thinking about health and health care practices (such as alternative medicine). Consequently the authority and dominance of professional medicine, derived in no small part from its scientific value, is liable to influence the way people make sense of, experience and respond to health care concerns.

One way of illustrating this is to consider how people account for and relate their personal experiences of illness to others. For example, with regard to subjective accounts of low mood, people are liable to utilize a range of discourses and reasonings to explain their problems. They may, for instance, perceive their emotional distress as simply being part of the stresses and strains of everyday life, thus drawing on a normalizing discourse which construes depression in non-pathological terms (i.e. low mood is something that happens to everyone; it doesn't necessarily mean that one is ill). A potential consequence of cleaving to this particular set of beliefs (this normalizing discourse) is that people may well shun professional medical help, instead taking personal responsibility for their recovery, adopting what Switzer et al. (2006) refer to as the 'pull yourself up by your bootstraps' approach to depression. Alternatively, people might situate their distress in a medical discourse of depression which constructs the depressive state as illness. Such a discourse privileges the voices of health professionals and deems depression a medical problem for which people are licensed to seek professional medical assistance (Bennett et al. 2003: 292).

These two discourses (normalizing and medicalizing) offer two interpretative resources for explaining and responding to psychological distress. It should be noted, though, that they are not, by any means, the only discourses available to people trying to make sense of depression. Moreover, people are liable to draw on aspects of a number of discourses, not just affirming one particular set of beliefs. However, such is the dominance of the medical discourse of depression that it has virtually become the orthodox way of thinking about low mood and sadness. Consequently, as a number of researchers have demonstrated, people are liable to privilege medical versions of psychological distress over explanations which normalize the experience (a theme I expand on in this book).

As the social theoretical perspective approach to discourse demonstrates, discourses have important consequences for how people talk about and perceive illness. Yet for all their insights into people's sense making processes and systems of beliefs, it is important to realize that discourses are, as Cameron (2001: 17) argues, not just pure content but windows into people's social and mental worlds. Discourses are inscribed and realized in texts – be it in speech, writing or non-verbal behaviour – and thus are dictated by the way language and communication work (ibid.). The lexical and grammatical choices which language users make encode discourses or traces of discourses (Baker 2006: 5). Thus in order to discover and interrogate discourse one needs to not only consider the content of a text but also the form it takes – in other words, not just what is communicated by it but how it is communicated (Cameron 2001: 17).

It is therefore possible to see the two aforesaid (linguistic and social theoretical) takes on discourse as respectively adopting micro and macro approaches to textual analysis. The micro, or linguistic, approach emphasizes the close analysis of specific spoken, written or multimodal textual practices (Gwyn 2002: 26), while the macro approach is not so much concerned with the specific formal features of texts as with the social and cultural meanings they communicate. Despite the different vantage points they offer, the micro and macro senses of discourse can be usefully combined in order to conduct fruitful analyses of texts, exposing the underlying discourse(s) within them. Indeed it is in this complementary sense that I approach discourse analysis in this book. Following Gwyn, I treat discourse as both a 'generic style of representation' or way of 'thinking and talking within a given sociocultural orbit', as well as in the more explicit sense of spoken or written discourse, 'the particular means by which people express themselves in language' (2002: 27).

## 1.4  Structure of this book: Research aims and questions

Although adolescents submit a variety of questions to the Teenage Health Freak website, reflecting the broad range of concerns that teenagers are liable to have about health and illness, questions relating to sexual and mental health are particularly prominent, constituting the two most common health themes in the corpus. Given the saliency of these two topics in the data, along with the significant challenge they present to public health, this study focuses on adolescent sexual and mental health communication.

Against the backdrop of contemporary adolescent health described above, the general aim of the study is

- to explore the subjective experiences and perceptions of adolescents regarding sexual and mental health, and the common ways in which their concerns are discursively constructed;
- to identify and explicate the dominant discourses which adolescents draw upon to make sense of their health concerns.

Given the potential significance of the research to professionals working with young people, the secondary aim is

- to outline, where appropriate, some practical implications of the study, namely, how certain findings may be of relevance to professionals and educationalists concerned with adolescent health.

This research will contribute to an increased appreciation and validation of the various health problems that young people commonly encounter, along with their attitudes towards and beliefs about these problems and the discursive routines through which they construct them. Given its unique and sustained attention to the insider perspective, that is, the individual views and experiences of adolescents themselves, this study affords a greater understanding of teenage subjectivities in relation to issues of sexual and mental health and, in the process, helps to raise the profile of adolescent health more generally. In addition, the study adds original data to the previously under-investigated field of adolescent health discourse, as well as providing, in an age of new information technologies, new linguistic material to research in the rapidly expanding field of computer-mediated communication.

In order to investigate adolescent health communication, it is necessary to harness a range of theoretical perspectives. Accordingly this book adopts an interdisciplinary approach to the subject of adolescent health, drawing on insights from medical sociology, social policy, psychology, psychiatry and health science in order to analyse and help make sense of the health emails. The early part of this book (Chapters 2–3) brings together many of these various multidisciplinary strands, outlining a number of key issues germane to adolescent health communication and internet health provision. Specifically, Chapter 2 focuses on the doctor-adolescent patient relationship, identifying some of the issues that young people are liable to encounter when seeking advice from health professionals, as well describing the promise and challenges of electronic communication as a form of health provision. The chapter also provides a linguistic assessment of the character of email, including a review of its potential for personal self-disclosure in the context of health care.

Chapter 3 contextualizes young people's sexual and mental health, detailing in particular how research into teenagers' accounts of health and illness have tended to neglect the perspectives of the adolescents themselves. Much of this research, especially psychiatric and epidemiological studies, which have tended to rely principally on relatively quantitatively intense evidence, privileges, I argue, the voices of health experts and academics at the expense of their adolescent subjects. In this chapter I also explore the linguistic dilemma of communicating sexual and mental health problems, examining the language of delicacy and taboo and how it constrains people from expressing themselves freely and accurately.

In Chapter 4, I outline the corpus approach to linguistic research, describing some of the conceptual underpinnings of corpora, as well as pointing out its quantitative and qualitative utility for interrogating health discourse. The reader is then provided with a detailed description of the Teenage Health Freak website, including details concerning the site's ethos, routine functions and the interactive virtual surgery through which users are able to submit their health questions to the virtual general practitioner (GP), Dr Ann. In this chapter I also describe the adolescent health email corpus (AHEC), providing details of the construction of the corpus, spelling variation and issues regarding its size and representativeness.

Chapters 5–9 present the corpus analysis of the adolescent health messages, with Chapters 5 and 6 first outlining the corpus techniques and procedures employed throughout the analysis before presenting the main analysis itself. In Chapter 5, using frequency and keyword measures, I survey the key concerns appearing across the health emails, while describing some of the general linguistic properties of the adolescents' discourse. Having quantitatively described the landscape of the health email corpus, Chapters 6–9 are dedicated to a more qualitative, contextual examination of the health emails, investigating, through the use of collocation and concordance analyses, the recurring themes and discourses evident in the texts. Chapters 6 and 7 are dedicated to the topic of sexual health and the following research questions:

- What does the adolescents' discourse reveal about their attitudes towards and beliefs about sexual health?
- How do they conceptualize and discuss sexual behaviour?

Chapter 6 is concerned with a range of issues relating to reproductive health (such as pregnancy, contraception and sexual relations), while Chapter 7 focuses on young people's discourses regarding sexually transmitted infections, specifically HIV/AIDS.

Chapters 8 and 9 similarly explore adolescents' perspectives in context but focus on the topic of mental health, exploring accounts of and questions relating to psychological distress. Chapter 8 considers the subjects of suicide and self-harm, while Chapter 9 investigates depression. I describe commonalities across these three mental health issues, addressing the specific questions:

- What are the adolescents' experiences and perceptions of psychological distress?
- How do they construct the mental health concerns that most commonly affect them?

Chapter 10 is dedicated to bringing together the main findings revealed by the corpus analysis. In this chapter I outline the potential of the corpus approach for interrogating electronic health discourse, as well as describing some of the limitations of corpus discourse analysis. I also detail the practical implications of the research and its relevance to practitioners working with young people, emphasizing, in particular, the utility of the electronic communication as a means of eliciting problems from adolescents, a client group who are often reluctant to seek health advice from medical practitioners face-to-face (Klein and Wilson 2002).

Taken together, the research questions addressed in this study afford a detailed investigation of young people's online advice-seeking behaviours, including descriptions of patterns and commonalities in their health concerns. The research questions also allow for engagement with subjective presentations of what it is to experience psychological distress (and how such distress is conceptualized), redressing the imbalance in the adolescent health literature, much of which fails to give adequate attention to the discursive routines of adolescent health questioning (McQueen and Henwood 2002).

## 1.5 A note on terminology: 'Email', 'adolescents', 'teenagers' and 'young people'

Throughout this study, the term 'email' is used to apply to the electronic messages submitted to the Teenage Health Freak. It should be noted, however, that these messages do not constitute emails in the traditional sense. They are not sent via the contributors' individual, personal email accounts, but communicated anonymously via a universal posting platform located on the website: the 'Ask Dr Ann' virtual surgery. In this sense, the emails constitute isolated postings which may or may not receive replies from the website doctors (the operators receive a large number of emails each week and, consequently, they can only answer a small number). Despite the unique nature of this electronic mailing facility (and its being distinct from traditional email accounts), I retain the term 'email' since this is the term which appears on the website itself (on the virtual surgery page, Dr Ann speaks of doing her best to answer the large amount of emails she receives).

Another potential source of ambiguity concerns the terms 'adolescent', 'teenager' and 'young people'. Often these expressions are used interchangeably. Occasionally, however, some authors prefer to employ, and persist with, a single term. Williams and Thurlow (2005), for example, solely adopt the label 'young people' in their communication work on 'young people', rejecting 'teenager' for its chronological specificity and 'adolescent' for the negative connotations they believe it conjures. Adolescence, they argue, is, after all, a cultural construct which, according to Coleman (1974: ix), 'can be defined in various ways depending on one's perspective'.

There are advantages and disadvantages to using all these terms – no one label is unfailingly accurate or universally agreed upon. Yet their interchangeability prevents a degree of monotonous repetition. As with many other researchers studying adolescent health, I see no particular benefit of dogmatically limiting oneself to a specific term. Accordingly, as will have been apparent during this introduction, I use all three labels interchangeably, without claiming any significant semantic distinction. This is essentially a matter of style. Cleaving to a specific descriptor is, for me, stylistically restrictive: I prefer the lexical variation that the choice of terms allows.

## 1.6  Who is this book for?

In preparing this text, I have had a broad, interdisciplinary audience in mind. My research, I hope, should be of interest to corpus and applied linguists, as well as to health practitioners and researchers concerned with young people's health. Accordingly I do not presume that every reader will be familiar with corpora and I have therefore endeavoured to provide as accessible explanations as possible of the corpus techniques I use. For corpus linguists, who will already be acquainted with the intricacies of corpora, I hope that this book is further demonstration of the utility of corpus linguistics for analysing discourse from a variety of domains – in this case the analysis of a genre which has received relatively little corpus attention.

# Adolescent Health Communication: Internet Health Provision and the Language of Email

## 2.1 Adolescent health communication: The professional-patient exchange

Research into communication between adolescents and health professionals serves as an important backdrop to this study. As Friedman (1989: 314) comments, a key factor which underlies virtually all issues of adolescent health is the need for effective communication between health workers and young people, especially on sensitive topics such as sexual and mental health.

Although the adolescent health emails featuring in this study constitute only one half of the therapeutic alliance between help-seekers and advisors, they are, for that, still an indubitable (first) part of a professional-patient communicative exchange, a virtual substitute (though by no means a replacement) for the actual, physical GP consultation itself. (The Teenage Health Freak website goes to considerable lengths to simulate the real-life setting of a doctor's surgery, aiming to provide users, as they submit their problems to the online GP, 'Dr Ann', with the virtual experience of face-to-face advice seeking, visually reproducing the format of a doctor's surgery.) With young people reporting that effective communication with health professionals is a major concern for them (Jacobson et al. 1996; Jones et al. 1997), it is necessary to identify some of the key factors that impede the exchange of information between adolescents and providers, factors that may prevent successful health interventions and outcomes.

For all the academic and practitioner interest in adolescent health, there exists only limited research into communication between health professionals and teenagers (Beresford and Sloper 2003; McKay 2003). Unlike the substantial and rapidly expanding research in the field of adult health communication (Sarangi 2004), which attracts a range of interdisciplinary interest, studies of adolescent-professional communication have principally been confined to the behavioural sciences and social policy research – studies which have sought to ascertain the feelings of adolescents about the quality of medical consultation. A number of these studies, moreover, have not focused on communication *per se* but, more generally, on young people's views of health services, with the issue of communication only emerging after it has been identified by the respondents themselves as a significant factor in the quality of health provision (Jacobson et al. 1996).

Furthermore, such research has not been concerned with the actual substance of communication, there being few studies that explore the linguistic and structural encoding of young people's involvement in health care exchanges with practitioners. A small amount of linguistic research exists concerning young people's health communication, but this has focused on the passive involvement of young children (in the presence of parents) in paediatric consultations (e.g. Aronsson and Rundstrom 1988; Tates et al. 2002).

The difficulties that adolescents face when consulting with health professionals are persistent and seemingly ineluctable (McPherson 2005). These communicative difficulties involve both personal and structural barriers (Harvey et al. 2008). With regard to personal impediments to communication, adolescents have been shown to have a poor understanding of confidentiality issues (Churchill et al. 2000; Jacobson et al. 2001), as well as an inadequate ability to precisely and confidently articulate health concerns to doctors (Beresford and Sloper 2003: 176). With regard to the latter issue, adolescents have identified themselves as wanting the communication skills necessary to contribute more fully in face-to-face encounters, especially their not knowing how to formulate questions, a difficulty exacerbated when the sensitivity of the issue at hand is greater (Beresford and Sloper 2003). Adolescents have also reported difficulties putting questions to doctors when they believe that asking a particular question is likely to result in negative consequences, such as revealing potential poor adherence to treatment or the participation in disapproved health behaviours (ibid).

Confidentiality in the practitioner-patient encounter is a particularly important issue for young people (Donovan et al. 1997; Burack 2000; Suzuki and Calzo 2004). For example, in his survey of teenagers' attitudes towards GPs' provision of sexual health care, Burack (2000) found that, despite being aware that they could consult with a GP on their own, the majority of the adolescents still possessed concerns that the doctor would not keep the exchange confidential.

Such a perception, Burack suggests, is likely to negatively influence adolescents' decision to access health services, even if they need to do so (2000: 553). Elsewhere research has similarly shown that, despite wanting to discuss delicate matters with providers, teenagers describe their fear of discussing sex with health professionals owing to any potential disclosure to parents (Donovan et al. 1997) and that parents, owing to this breach in confidence, will discover that they are sexually active (Holland et al. 1996).

In addition to the aforementioned communicative obstacles, another barrier to effective exchanges with practitioners commonly reported by adolescents is the problem of forming therapeutic relationships with and relating to anyone other than peers (Jacobson et al. 1996; Beresford and Sloper 2003). For example, Beresford and Sloper's (2003) study of young people's perceptions of communicating with doctors demonstrated that adolescents reported finding it difficult to talk with a health professional they had not encountered before, and that familiarity with doctors was important if a more fluid exchange of information was to take place. More time spent in clinical consultation would, the adolescent respondents suggested, offer better opportunities to build a rapport with practitioners. Indeed, the short duration of the face-to-face medical consultation has widely been identified as one of the principal structural barriers preventing more open and sustained interaction, a limitation which, by affording teenagers time to think and construct their questions, email exchanges with practitioners might potentially address (as is discussed in § 2.2). Young people have reported that the brevity of exchanges with doctors does not allow for the satisfactory delivery of care (Jacobson et al. 1994; Jacobson et al. 1996; Beresford and Sloper 2003), with studies indicating that GPs are likely to spend less time with adolescents than they are with patients of other age groups.

Jacobson et al. (1994), for instance, found that GPs' consultations with teenagers evinced, on average, a durational shortfall of 2 minutes, regardless of the nature of the consultation in question. They offer three possible explanations for this. First, that adolescents' health complaints are comparatively minor and thus require less attention; second, that doctors keep teenage consultations shorter so as to spend more time with other patients; and, thirdly, and perhaps most significantly, that young people often feel uncomfortable during the consultation (1994: 299). Although the authors are careful not to claim that these reasons unequivocally account for the shorter duration of teenage consultations, evidence from elsewhere in the literature supports the contention that young people experience profound discomfort during the medical interview, a factor which potentially prevents them seeking medical advice face-to-face (Klein and Wilson 2002). The consultation does not always meet the unique health requirements of adolescents (Jones et al. 1997), with, for example, young people consistently reporting that, in such an official setting, they feel that they do not know enough nor have sufficient confidence to sustain the encounter (Beresford and Sloper 2003). Their limited contributions during consultations indicate that adolescent user-involvement tends to be passive, with either practitioners or an attendant parent dominating proceedings (Beresford and Sloper 2003: 173).

Further problems of communicating with doctors have also been attributed to the perceived august status of doctors, against whom adolescents keenly feel their own inferiority (Beresford and Sloper 2003). For example, practitioners' use of a technical register, specifically 'the use of unusual words or medical terminology', is liable to widen the adolescents' perceptions of status difference between themselves and professionals (Beresford and Sloper 2003 175). Moreover, some adolescents perceive doctors as only being primarily interested in attending to their physical conditions rather than to them as individuals, experiences which further contribute to a sense of isolation and disempowerment (Rich et al. 2000).

Although some of the communicative and interpersonal difficulties equally apply to adults (the short duration of the consultation, for instance, is a frequent concern of patients of all ages (Cape 2002)), the level of criticism by young people concerning communication with practitioners would appear to be in excess of those relating to doctor-adult patient communication (Jacobson et al. 1996) – a finding in keeping with the fact that younger patients are liable to report less satisfaction with health services than older patients (ibid.). Given the weight of research evidence describing communicative difficulties in adolescent patient-provider exchanges, there is therefore reason to suggest that, as Jacobson et al. (1994: 298) claim, 'the exceptional potential of the consultation is being under-used by teenagers' and that, consequently, there is need for 'a reappraisal of the interface between teenage patients and primary care to allow for improved communication between the two groups' (1994: 299).

All these aforesaid interactive shortcomings highlight the necessity of increased patient-centred care, including measures such as wider access for adolescents to teenage health specialists outside their local GP surgery, and the development of virtual resources that cater for the unique health needs of young people (Jones et al. 1997). The potential, in particular, of new information sources tailored to the needs of adolescents, specifically the internet, is that, although not a replacement for the face-to-face consultation, they may effectively help young people overcome some of the personal and structural communicative barriers described in this section, as well as empowering them to take greater responsibility for their health (Valaitis 2005). Online health services, such as the Teenage Health Freak website, constitute flexible information tools, increasing young people's access to evidence-based health advice and counselling (Michaud et al. 2004), a theme we pursue in the following section.

## 2.2 The internet, adolescents and health care

The rise of the World Wide Web has led to a substantial increase in the number of websites dedicated to providing health advice and information. Many new fora have been created through which internet users can formulate problems and seek solutions concerning health-related issues. In the United Kingdom alone it is estimated that there are between 15,000 and 100,000 health-related websites (Collste 2002), receiving 22 million hits per month (Ten Have 1995).

Teenagers are acknowledged to be major users and earlier adopters of internet services, having integrated these new electronic resources into their lives (Gray and Klein 2006). In developed countries, it is estimated that more than 80 per cent of young people have access to the World Wide Web and use the internet to seek health advice and information (Gray et al. 2002; Michaud et al. 2004). A significant attraction of internet health provision for young people is that it empowers them to make decisions about their health, offering a convenient and anonymous route to information, services and products which formerly required direct contact with health professionals (Gray and Klein 2006: 519).

Patient use of the internet as a source of health information or 'e-medicine' constitutes 'do-it-yourself-healthcare', establishing a new doctor-patient relationship, a relationship which is likely to affect the standing relation between the patient and their GP (Collste 2002). This virtual relationship has been shown to be particularly appealing for young people (Michaud et al. 2004) who, as described in the previous section, not infrequently experience difficulties accessing and effectively making the most of the primary care system. Unlike traditional health care services, where the emphasis is on service users attending an unfamiliar environment, typically at a time dictated by the professional (Gray et al. 2005a, 2005b), the internet provides convenient unconstrained access to health services.

With regard to communicating with doctors online, electronic communication allows young people to formulate their problems in their own terms, space and time, affording them a platform from which to ask awkward, sensitive or detailed questions without fear of being judged or stigmatized (Cotton and Gupta 2004) – an important factor for adolescents discussing sensitive concerns such as sexual and mental health, both of which, as taboo subjects, are severely constrained as topics of discussion.

### 2.2.1 Internet health care: The variable quality of provision

Despite the large number of high-quality health resources available online and the potential of the internet for effective health interventions with adolescents, Silberg et al. (1997: 1244) characterize electronic medical information as too often resembling a 'cocktail conversation rather than a tool for effective health care communication and decision making'. Indeed many commentators have reported that the electronic landscape is populated by unreliable, misleading and unscrupulous sites purporting to provide accurate medical information (e.g. Ten Have 2002). Moreover, such sites 'often sit byte by byte' with authoritative and reliable health forums (Silberg et al. 1997: 1244), making it a challenging affair for browsers to distinguish between the two in an anarchic and increasingly congested cyberscape (Silberg et al. 1997: 1244; Eysenbach and Diepgen 1998).

In their study of electronic health care, Eysenbach and Diepgen (1998) similarly describe the variable quality of internet sources, calling for greater accountability and stronger regulation of web-based health services. This is particularly important for adolescents, a population of internet users who, although typically adept at accessing information online, 'tend to pay little attention to the source of the information' (Michaud et al. 2004: 201). The internet, in terms of health provision, has been described as a 'double-edged' sword for adolescents (Sun et al. 2005), with the potential to both help and harm young people (Gray and Klein 2006). Eradicating poor quality information thus becomes essential since 'misinformation could be a matter of life or death' (Eysenbach and Diepgen 1998: 1496).

Although it is extremely difficult, if not impossible, to regulate the overall quality of online services targeted at both young people and the general population (Michaud et al. 2004: 201), many of the pitfalls linked to adolescent use of the internet for health provision have led to the recent development of more reputable health forums operated by paediatricians and dedicated teenage health specialists. Websites such as the Teenage Health Freak, for example, are user friendly, interactive and, most importantly, evidenced-based. A distinguishing feature of Teenage Health Freak is that, along with health professionals, adolescents themselves participated in the planning and construction of the site, thereby helping to ensure the reliability and youth-friendliness of its material.

The large number of visits that the Teenage Health Freak website has received since its launch (to date (2012) in excess of 82,800,000 hits), and the fact that it is an electronic resource consistently advocated by practitioners and official health bodies, including the UK Department of Health, is testament to its professional validation and, perhaps more importantly, its immense popularity with young people themselves.

## 2.2.2 Email and the practitioner-patient exchange

So far our consideration of internet health advice and information has focused on electronic resources broadly, without distinguishing the various modes of communication available on the World Wide Web. Email is the most widely known form of computer-mediated communication (Hewings and Coffin 2004) and has significant potential for the delivery of health care (Car and Sheikh 2004a, 2004b). Indeed, as Spielberg (1999: 730) observes, interaction by email format is for many a 'logical extension of communication with an already existing patient-physician relationship'. The asynchronous nature of email presents patients and providers alike with communicative possibilities that other electronic formats do not (Waldren and Kibbe 2004). For example, email, unlike telemedicine (a contemporaneous voice-to-voice service), does not require both patient and practitioner to be simultaneously present and therefore provides continuing access to the health care system (Mandl et al. 1998; Kleiner et al. 2002).

The use of email in a range of health care settings and contexts has been examined, including the physician-patient relationship (Mandl et al. 1998; Car and Sheikh 2004a, 2004b) paediatric triads (doctor, parent, child) (Kleiner et al. 2002), as well as unsolicited requests for physician advice (Eysenbach and Diepgen 1998). Car and Sheikh (2004a) argue that email consultations between doctors and patients have the potential to contribute to the delivery of preventative health care and facilitate self-management of a range of disorders.

Moreover, email is advantageous regarding convenience, access and information sharing and has the potential to meet the widening gap between the need for transmitting information to patients and, as was described in Section 2.1, the relatively limited, and often brief, opportunities for face-to-face exchanges between doctors and patients (Mandl et al. 1998).

The advantages that email can contribute to health interventions, however, have been disputed. Despite the promise of email for health delivery, the medium has still to be realized in routine clinical care. Email is generally considered an effective means of communicating straightforward information and non-urgent requests between patients and practitioners (Car and Sheikh 2004b: 440), allowing patients to maintain continuity with their GPs, facilitate information flow, while contributing to health education and patient responsibility (Mechanic 2001). Yet the disembodied nature of email interaction means that practitioners are unable to examine patients or use touch in the clinical encounter. As with other forms of written communication, the separation in space between writer and reader does not easily provide the 'subtle emotive cues often gleaned from vocal intonation and physical demeanour that aid interpretation' (Car and Sheikh 2004a: 437). During the medical encounter, a substantial part of any verbal message's force and influence derives from the communicative style and clinician's image and appearance as much as the content (437). Without recourse to paralinguistic features participants in email consultations have to rely solely on words, which are alone the conveyors of information, and, consequently, this places extra emphasis on the linguistic ability of practitioner and patient alike. For instance, it is harder for practitioners to check whether patients have understood key parts of the consultation and it is not easy for patients to summarize the main points covered and feedback their understanding (437).

Moreover, the successful use of email relies on a clear and shared understanding by both patient and health professional of the medium's role, advantages and limitations (438). But, as Spielberg (1998: 730) observes, patients might not be able to distinguish between the use of email in informal contexts and more formal contexts such as the medical consultation, potentially leading to misunderstandings about the implications of communicating medical topics. Patients, for example, might not realize that their personal communications to doctors may become part of their medical records which might be seen by others. With regard to the Teenage Health Freak email interface, however, this (and a number of the aforementioned email-related concerns) is inapplicable since the information exchange between adolescents and the online advisors remains confidential. Moreover, on appropriate occasions, such as when the adolescents' health concerns are complex or serious and require immediate attention, the advisors instruct advice-seekers to visit a GP, emphasizing the fact that an online exchange is not a substitute for a face-to-face consultation.

## 2.3 The expressive character of email

As was pointed out in Chapter 1, the term 'email' in this study is used to refer to the adolescent health messages submitted to the Teenage Health Freak website. It should be noted, though, that these electronic messages do not constitute emails in the traditional sense. The messages are delivered through a dedicated posting platform on the website, not via the adolescents' personal email accounts. Nevertheless, in spite of all the various modes of online communication (such as instant messaging, chatrooms, bulletin boards, and so forth), email is the communicative format that most closely resembles the online communiqués posted to the website. Like email, the adolescent health emails are asynchronous (not communicated in real-time), and thus do not require both participants in the exchange to be simultaneously present online. However, unlike traditional email, which typically identifies its users, the health emails are anonymous, a factor that, as is explained below, will inevitably influence the levels of candour displayed by the message writers online.

### 2.3.1 Email and the online disinhibition effect

A characteristic feature of email is that it offers 'a comfortable distance from which to be yourself' (Baron 2000: 234). It is not surprising, therefore, that many users of email display 'remarkable candour in the information they're willing to divulge online' (ibid.). Clinicians, researchers (particularly, but not uniquely, in the field of personality and social psychology), as well as everyday users of the internet themselves, have all similarly noted how people speak and behave differently in cyberspace (Suler 2004: 321). In Suler's words, 'They loosen up, feel less restrained, and express themselves more openly' (ibid.).

The effect of disinhibition is brought about by six factors, namely, anonymity, invisibility, asynchronicity, solipsistic introjection, dissociative imagination and minimization of authority. Although Suler observes that these factors interact with and supplement one another, one or two of them produce the 'lion's share of the disinhibition effect' (322). Accordingly, we will here devote our attention to anonymity, invisibility and asynchronicity – the key disinhibition factors that are most likely to contribute to the expressive nature of the adolescent health emails.

Anonymity is, according to Suler, the principle reason for the online disinhibition effect. Being anonymous involves altering one's identity or effacing it altogether, allowing, in either case, people to dissociate themselves from their own behaviour and activities. Being online anonymously is akin to wearing a protective cloak: people are able to hide their online activities, separating them from their actual (i.e. offline) identities, and hence whatever they do or say online cannot be 'directly linked to the rest of their lives' (2004: 322). This is an important consideration for people seeking health advice online, particularly young and vulnerable individuals. To approach others for help is potentially to validate any sense of failure and weakness experienced by help-seekers, for, in the eyes of other people, seeking assistance 'could be perceived as a shameful act' (Scourfield et al. 2007: 252). However, all information advice-seekers communicate to others online cannot be linked directly to their lives: when obtaining advice over the internet, no one needs know that they have sought professional assistance.

With regard to reducing inhibition online, invisibility works in a similar way to anonymity. In many electronic environments, especially those, such as email, which are text driven, users cannot see one another. Being invisible, Suler notes, 'gives people the courage to go to places and do things that they otherwise wouldn't' (322), as well as producing a reduced sense of public awareness and, with this, a propensity for increased self-disclosure (Joinson 2001). For example, people seeking advice from health professionals over the internet do not have to concern themselves with how they look or sound. Nor do they have to worry about their messages being received with a sigh or frown. In this sense, disclosing problems to health professionals online reflects, according to Suler, the traditional psychoanalytical practice of analysts sitting behind their clients in order to remain distant, physically removed figures. Unable to apprehend neither the body language nor the facial responses of therapists, clients are free to express whatever they wish 'without feeling inhibited by how the analyst is physically reacting' (322). While communicating health problems to professionals online, advisors' gazes remain constantly averted. As Griffiths observes, 'Words that are originated from within ourselves are received by the computer without contest or contempt' and so 'may produce the feelings that tell us we are being accommodated' (2004: 157).

Most professional online health forums (such as the Teenage Health Freak website) are asynchronous, that is, they are not conducted in real time, and hence participants do not receive simultaneous feedback (Crystal 2006: 24). Not having to interact with correspondents in real time, and not having to deal with any immediate reactions from others, further contributes to communicative candour. After sending a message that is personal, emotional or otherwise revealing, advice-seekers may experience asynchronous communication as a kind of 'running away' or escape (Suler 2004: 323). Knowing that they are not involved in real-time, moment-by-moment interaction with others, they are more likely, according to Suler, to feel safe 'putting their messages 'out there' in cyberspace where they can be left behind' (323).

The online disinhibition effect, then, has important consequences for the way in which the adolescents submitting their health concerns to the Teenage Health Freak website reveal personal information about themselves. One of the premises guiding online health forums is that many people tend to make sensitive self-disclosures and share personal difficulties with others in cyberspace (Barak 2007: 972). The anonymity, invisibility and asynchronicity that characterize much online health communication make it an attractive channel for reaching out to populations (such as young people) that otherwise would avoid conventional medical services.

## 2.3.2 The language of email

Email has been linguistically characterized in various ways. As Baron (1998, 2000) notes, one view that predominated in the early days of email, and which still informs popular opinion today, is the view that the medium is either speech written down (letters by phone) or speech by other means. Yet such a dichotomous divide fails to take into account the fact that email is a technology in transition, a communicative modality in flux (Baron 1998).

Arguably the most comprehensive and detailed linguistic assessment of email is provided by Baron (1998, 2000, 2003), who summarizes its various depictions as follows:

- letters by phone (email as form of writing)
- speech by other means (email as a form of speech)
- mix and match (email as a blend of spoken and written forms)
- e-style (email as a distinct language style)
- contact system (email as a still evolving language style)

Such a range of characteristics reveals the difficulty of neatly classifying email. For example, the linguistic attributes of the form correspond, in certain contexts of use, to other communicative domains: for instance, speech and writing, leading Baron to describe email as being 'Janus-faced – at once resembling and not resembling face-to-face speech' (2003: 86).

As with other linguistic commentators on email (e.g. Herring 2001; Carter 2004; Crystal 2006, 2011), Baron describes email not as simply being more speech-like or more like writing, but a contact language, like creolized spoken or written systems, constructed from multiple sources. It is, she suggests, 'schizophrenic' in character, possesses wide stylistic potential, allows individual users 'considerable choice over how to formulate and respond to messages' and so enables them to 'emphasize one contributing strand over another' (1998: 163–64). Email, furthermore, is still in its relative infancy. Consequently it is too young linguistically to warrant a unified grammar of the type long established to account for more mature languages, such as classical Greek and even modern English (1998: 165). Nevertheless Baron does provide a useful summary of the linguistic profile of contemporary email usage, characterizing the medium in terms of four dimensions of human communication:

- *Social dynamics*: **Predominantly like writing**
  - interlocutors are physically separated
  - physical separation fosters personal disclosure and helps level the conversational playing field
- *Format*: **(Mixed) writing and speech**
  - like writing, email is durable
  - like speech, email is typically unedited
- *Grammar*:
  **LEXICON: predominantly like speech**
  - heavy use of first- and second-person pronouns
  **SYNTAX: (mixed) writing and speech**
  - like writing, email has high type/token ratio, high use of adverbial subordinate clauses, high use of disjunctions
  - like speech, email commonly uses present tense, contractions
- *Style*: **Predominantly like speech**
  - low level of formality
  - expression of emotion not always self-monitored (flaming)

(Baron 2000: 251)

Baron essentially characterizes email as a hybrid form of communication, an interface between spoken and written language (Carter 2004). However, the characterization is only an approximation, open to variation, rather than a hard-and-fast, once-and-for-all determination. For instance, the 'heavy use' of pronouns (common to speech) accounts for the interpersonal nature of email; however, in certain contexts, such as the more formal user exchanges, email takes on characteristics typically associated with writing, such as, for example, social distance and objectivity, resulting in fewer pronominal and interpersonal forms.

Another linguistic assessment of email is provided by Crystal (2006, 2011), an assessment which overlaps, in many ways, with Baron's account of the medium. However, unlike Baron, who conceives of email as a communicative hybrid (part speech, part writing), Crystal refers to the uniqueness of the medium. Although acknowledging the various popular characterizations of email as containing mixed elements of communication (part memo, part letter, part speech, part writing, and so on), he considers email to be distinct, affording new communicative opportunities. For Crystal, email has come to inhabit an interactive space not readily occupied by other forms of communication. For example, the convenience and accessibility of the medium, as harnessed by internet health websites, connects clients with busy professionals (Crystal 2006: 126).

Yet, as with Baron, Crystal (2006: 134) argues that the evolution of email is still in its infancy, and that the only certainty with regard to its future is that it will inevitably change. With its spontaneity, speed, privacy and leisure value offering greater scope for informality and emotional expressivity than elsewhere in traditional writing, there is, Crystal observes, a tendency to think of email as being a less formal medium. However, the linguistic forms (the contractions, lower case type, subject ellipsis, colloquial abbreviations and acronyms) that contribute to the informal character of email are not indicative of the variety as a whole – since many messages do not them use them – and, of course, they are found in other forms of communication besides email (ibid.). As the medium matures, it is emerging that email is not exclusively an informal modality. For instance, there is, according to Crystal, growing pressure to produce stylistic consistency regarding composition, a trend which is borne out by the number of style guides devoted to producing effective message copy. Most of these guides are traditional in content, prescriptive in orientation, reproducing, for instance, artificial shibboleths such as side-stepping the passive voice and other so-called grammatical peccadilloes (Crystal 2011: 23).

Prescriptive, netiquette approaches to email construe computer-mediated discourse as linguistically impoverished, a stylistic free-for-all. As Herring (2001: 616) observes, email has been described as 'less correct, complex and coherent than standard written language'. Yet such criticisms are linguistically groundless, since they fail to take into account the communicative context which shapes linguistic production. The so-called errors and non-standard features, or 'structural fragmentation' (Herring 2001), given to email are typically not mistakes (due to inattention or lack of knowledge of standard language forms), but deliberate choices on the part of users to economize on typing, mimic spoken discourse features or express themselves creatively (Herring 2001: 617), or owe to the temporal pressures of message production. Consider, for instance, the following examples, each of which is replete with spelling variation:

- Hav eyou got the tickets yet?
- i ham being bullied at school
- I AM LOSING MY MEMORY. . .!!! pleaaaaaaaaaaaaase tell me what to do

These messages, the first taken from Crystal's personal corpus of emails, the second and third from the AHEC, illustrate two different communicative settings in which misspellings, be they accidental or deliberate, might well occur. However, these unorthodox forms are not by any means ambiguous: reference to the linguistic context in which the messages were produced makes it a straightforward process to recover their meanings and appreciate their stylistic effect. For instance, in the first example, the evidently accidental 'Hav eyou' corresponds to the almost certainly intended 'Have you' (a similar orthographical shuffle provides the semantic solution to example 2), while, in example 3, the writer produces certain stylistic effects, employing capitalization and repeated vowels to mimic the speech sounds of increased and drawn out vocal emphasis, effects which emphasize the urgency of the writer's problem and his/her appeal for advice. Thus, despite the extent of their orthographic irregularity, the semantics of these messages remain undeniably intact.

Therefore the appearance of such non-standard linguistic forms (which commonly occur in online health exchanges) do not necessarily distract from the contents of the messages themselves. Nor, according to Crystal (2006), are readers likely to make social judgements about the writers and question the credibility of their concerns. This is because the recipients of 'error-strewn messages' are commonly aware of the situational circumstances and constraints under which email is composed and, therefore, the concomitant attendance of errors. Respondents are aware of this 'because, several times a day, they know they write under the same constraints themselves' (Crystal 2006: 117).

## 2.4 Conclusion

In this chapter, I began by addressing the subject of communication between young people and health professionals, examining some of the central issues relating to the practitioner-adolescent consultation. Compared to the literature concerned with doctors' communication with older, adult patients, research into adolescent health communication is relatively sparse. What research has been conducted in this minority field, however, has consistently described various difficulties that young people experience when communicating face-to-face with practitioners, particularly when presenting with sensitive health concerns. For example, I showed that adolescents have regularly reported being unable to find the appropriate words to express their problems to health professionals, as well as reporting that they are sometimes reluctant to disclose intimate issues to practitioners for fear that their doctors will not keep the consultation confidential. Young people, moreover, also describe that exchanges with their doctors tend to be short, not allowing them sufficient time to fully communicate their concerns.

These communicative difficulties which arise in face-to-face health care settings, along with the continued burgeoning of the internet, have resulted in an increase in online services dedicated to responding to the health concerns of young people. Electronic modes of communication, such as email, have significant consultative potential, enabling users of the internet to overcome some of the structural and interactional barriers that they encounter in face-to-face exchanges with professionals. However, such modes of online interaction are not without their limitations. For example, as I described in Section 2.2, for all the convenience of access it affords to patients wishing to consult with a practitioner, side-stepping many of the interactional barriers that obtain in face-to-face settings, the disembodied nature of the virtual practitioner-patient exchange means that doctors are unable to physically examine patients. In the virtual context, furthermore, doctors are unable to draw on paralinguistic aspects of interaction which might provide important clues as to patients' conditions.

Nevertheless, the expressive potential of email as a means of encouraging young people to disclose their troubles to professionals is not to be underestimated. As this chapter has shown, the unique linguistic and social psychological dimensions of email make it a particularly effective mode for discussing sensitive medical issues. Email provides a safe distance between parties in any given interaction, facilitating increased personal disclosures from adolescents who might be unwilling to seek advice from their doctors face-to-face.

# 3

# Putting Adolescent Health in Context

Although adolescents are generally a healthy population and seem to take their well-being for granted (McKay 2003), young people make regular choices relating to health: from seeking independent health advice from professionals and using health information sources, to resisting or participating in health-related risky behaviours. There exists a considerable body of research in the field of adolescent health and health communication, predominantly from the areas of medicine and the biological sciences, supplemented by studies from a range of other disciplines. Accordingly the following sections bring together linguistic, sociological, psychological and epidemiological perspectives concerning young people's health, providing a backdrop against which the subsequent corpus analysis is carried out.

## 3.1  Sexual health: Contemporary issues and concerns

Adolescence is a period of transition from childhood to adulthood, marked by 'changes in body, mind and social relationships' (Friedman 1989: 309). The onset of puberty is a universal and defining feature of adolescence, although the timing of this sexual and emotional development shows a wide variability depending on the individual (Friedman 1989: 310). However, recent evidence suggests that both males and females are maturing physically at a faster rate than before, with, for example, the average age of menarche in the United Kingdom now being 13 years (Bradley-Stevenson and Mumford 2007: 474). One of the consequences of this increasing youthful sexual maturation is that young people are becoming able to reproduce at an earlier stage in their lives, although they might not be emotionally or psychological mature enough to manage the responsibilities that a sexual relationship or pregnancy may bring (2007: 474).

The subject of adolescent sexual health has been identified by many researchers and providers of health care as an urgent contemporary concern (e.g. British Medical Association 2003, 2005; Mason 2005; Bradley-Stevenson and Mumford 2007), with the necessity of 'doing something about teenage sexuality and sexual knowledge' pressing on the minds of policymakers (Brown et al. 2006: 169). A British Medical Journal editorial (Stammers 2007) reports how teenage sexual health is in overall decline, noting, for example, the 'increasing rates of terminations and sexually transmitted infections in under 18s' (Stammers 2007: 103). Despite the modest reductions in conception rates in adolescents, teenage pregnancy rates are higher in the United Kingdom than in other western European countries (Family Planning Association 2010a), and young people aged 15–24 continue to be the group most affected by STIs (Family Planning Association 2010b). More generally, research reveals that there has been an increase in teenage sexual experience and decreasing age at sexual debut (Mason 2005), with the consequence that by young adulthood most adolescents have experienced sexual intercourse (Shrier et al. 2007).

### 3.1.1  Adolescents' attitudes towards and knowledge about sexual health

Interest in young people's sexual behaviour has increased in the latter part of the twentieth century (Wellings et al. 2001). During the 1960s and 1970s, research in the United Kingdom and the United States concentrated on conception rates among young people but then, with the advent of the AIDS epidemic in the 1980s, urgently directed its attention to investigating HIV/AIDS, in particular the risk of HIV transmission. At the end of the twentieth century, such were the high rates of teenage pregnancy, as well as the upward trends in sexually transmitted diseases, that the direction of research changed once again, this time centring on 'risk behaviour in the context of both unplanned conception and sexually transmitted infection' (Wellings et al. 2001: 1843).

In order to discover more about how young people perceive risk, greater emphasis was placed on assessing their beliefs about sexual health. Studies consistently reveal that, although often aware of the risks involved in taking part in sexual activity (Widdice et al. 2006), adolescents are liable to have limited and erroneous understandings about reproductive health (Ammerman et al. 1992; Smith et al. 2003; Mason 2005). Such attitudes and beliefs held by young people account for what Moore and Rosenthal (1993: 149) describe as the 'invulnerable adolescent': the young person who believes that they are unlikely to suffer the consequences of taking part in sexual risk taking. The 'invulnerable adolescent' who partakes in risky sexual activity is not only motivated by a limited understanding of reproductive physiology, but also by limited and impaired knowledge about STIs. A wealth of studies has investigated adolescents' knowledge, attitudes and beliefs about STIs (e.g. Lawrence 1993; Moore et al. 1996; Smith et al. 2003). With the advent of the AIDS epidemic much of this research has been devoted to young people's knowledge and perceived risk of HIV/AIDS, often exposing adolescents' misconceptions about the causal transmission of the virus, along with faulty knowledge concerning treatment (DiClemente et al. 1986; Smith et al. 2003; Mason 2005).

A consequence of all this aforesaid research is that it reproduces, whether intentionally or otherwise, discourses that frequently represent young people's sexuality as problematic. As Jackson (2005a: 283) argues, the academic literature is dominated by research that underscores both the failures of young people to be sexually safe and their susceptibility to being 'perpetually "at risk" of being "swept away" at any moment by "unanticipated, unintentional passion"' (Thompson 1990: 342). Tellingly, however, these negative depictions of teenage sexual health are generated by an 'outsider perspective', prompted by what researchers deem to be the issues rather than by what young people themselves conceive of as pertinent. This is, to some extent, reflected in the research methods adopted by the investigators. Much of the aforementioned research has relied on questionnaire or interview methods to ascertain adolescents' attitudes and beliefs about sexual health. Although these are designed to access adolescent perspectives, they are nevertheless restrictive, confining subjects' responses to criteria sets as defined by the researcher. Consequently, complex behaviours reported by participants are liable to be reduced to simple variables, while any variation in meaning and interpretation to such responses is overlooked (Ingham 1993).

A different perspective to that provided by much of the literature emerges when young people are asked to formulate their own accounts, their own 'insider perspectives' (Jackson 2005a). For example, a study by Kirkman et al. (1998), in which teen mothers reported positive stories of personal growth, challenges the prevailing negative constructions of adolescent motherhood (Jackson 2005b: 283). The insider perspective allows researchers to see how young people themselves define and encode sexual health concerns. Studies privileging young people's communication of sexuality issues have principally taken their source data from advice columns in teenage magazines (McRobbie 1996; McCabe 2005). Although teenage magazines afford ready access to the insider perspectives of adolescents' formulation of questions pertaining to sexuality and sexual health, the problems posted to teenage advice columns are subject to the editorial processes of editing and selection (and some may even be fictionalized (Jackson 2005a: 301)) and so are not necessarily representative of the actual concerns contributed by young people.

Unlike the problems submitted to teen magazines, however, the corpus of emails used for analysis in this study is, short of removing identifying information, free of external filtering and thus constitutes a unique resource for achieving robust evidence of how sexual health problems are constituted from the perspective of young people. As Jackson argues, the analysis of material that has not been generated by researchers' questions has the potential to contribute different and new understandings of adolescent sexual and reproductive health – in particular whether teenagers' construction of sexuality-related questions and concerns 'concur with those in the public and academic world' (2005b: 85).

### 3.1.2  Communicating delicacy and taboo: The language of sexual health

Sex is a tabooed topic that extends across cultures (Trinch 2001). Despite an increasing openness towards sexual matters (Moore et al. 1996), sexual health is an issue that is still shrouded in secrecy and mystique, and remains a topic that is severely constrained as a subject of discussion (Allan and Burridge 2006). When people discuss sex and sexual health related matters they are liable to find such subjects difficult to talk about, often employing euphemism to avoid taboo terms that they believe would cause both themselves and their interlocutors undue distress (Trinch 2001: 573).

For example, in a well-known article by Weijts et al. (1993) about discussions of sex in gynaecological consultations, it appeared that speaking about sexual issues by both doctors and patients was often conducted through euphemisms and omissions rather than through explicit references. Patients and professionals collaborated in substituting demonstrative pronouns and adverbs for more direct descriptions, referring to 'it', 'down there', 'that', and so forth, while terms like 'the event itself' and 'afterwards' were used to describe sex, without the nature of the 'event' being specified very precisely.

Although this use of evasive speech may appear, on the surface, to be merely a quaint quirk of interaction, and have little influence on the outcome of the gynaecological consultation, such 'verbal asepsis' (Stewart 2005) does have significant linguistic and ideological repercussions, contributing to the discursive process of 'depersonalisation', a phenomenon whereby, through linguistic evasion, the link between the patient and her most private actions and bodily aspects are loosened (Weijts et al. 1993: 308). In other words, by deliberately avoiding explicit terminology in encounters with patients, professionals help to reinforce the stereotype that female sexuality is something 'dark and mysterious', preventing women from becoming less separated from their bodies and more familiar with the functional elements of their reproductive capacities (1993: 311).

Given the powerful and pervasive influence of sexual taboos, it might be expected that the way in which adolescents communicate concerns related to their reproductive health would, very much like the adults just described, similarly involve circumlocutions, vague language and euphemisms. Yet, despite the extensive research into adolescent sexual health, little is known about the precise nature of young people's use of language, and the discourses they draw upon, when communicating about sex and sexuality. Although surveys and epidemiological work on sexual health have increased, there exists a paucity of data relating to how people communicate sexual issues in naturally-occurring situations (Silverman 1997). Owing to the delicate nature of matters that are sexual and the social sanction of taboo, the right to privacy is, understandably, jealously guarded in this sensitive area of research (Moore et al. 1996: 186).

Much research into adolescent communication about sex and sexuality has been conducted around the topic of parent-adolescent communication (Schouten et al. 2007), with little attention paid to how young people actually discuss sexual matters with health professionals. (As was described in § 2.1, research into adolescent patient-provider communication regarding sensitive topics has predominantly concentrated on young people's perceptions of the consultation, such as their feelings of embarrassment and fears over breaches of confidentiality.) Studies into parent-adolescent communication about sexual issues have repeatedly emphasized the significance of intergenerational talk, showing how it is an important factor in promoting responsible sexual behaviour (Hutchinson and Cooney 1998; Rosenthal and Feldman 2002; Schouten et al. 2007).

Although providing valuable insights into the dimensions that underlie parent-adolescent interaction, not least the positive connection between parental communication and the prevention of sexual risk taking behaviour (Schouten et al. 2007), such research is confined to describing adolescents' attitudes towards talking with their parents about sexuality, assessing, for example, levels of embarrassment and comfort through the use of questionnaires and convenience samples (Ogle et al. 2008). The actual way in which participants discuss their sexual health concerns, that is, the linguistic means by which they encode their beliefs about and perceptions of their problems, are not considered, the research being characterized by quantitative approaches that survey attitudinal patterns of communication.

In the context of professional advice-seeking, the small amount of linguistic research into adolescents' construction and understanding of sexual health issues has demonstrated teenagers' preference for both explicit and informal language. For example, in their study of adolescents' use and understanding of sexually-related terminology, Ammerman et al. (1992) found that young people were much more familiar with, and liable to use, non-technical and slang terms rather than common medical lexis. Moreover, rather than confine themselves to a limited set of genitourinary-related terms, the adolescents were prone to linguistic variety, employing a range of synonyms for communicating sexual and genitourinary matters. One consequence of this lexical diversity was the increased potential for misunderstanding between professionals and their younger patients. Practitioners should therefore not assume, Ammerman et al. (1992) suggest, that adolescents understand what is being said in discussions of sexual health, since standard medical vocabulary common to the professional is unlikely to be familiar to, and so be useful to, the adolescent. However, the same observation could equally apply to older patients, not just adolescents, for research indicates that adults also fail to understand common health terms, and thus possess different understandings from professionals, causing difficulty in effective doctor-patient communication (Hadlow and Pitts 1991).

Contrary to the findings of Ammerman's study, discourse-based research by Harvey et al. (2007) revealed that teenagers commonly adopted a medico-technical register in their (online) requests for sexual health advice from professionals. The adolescents' health messages, moreover, were further characterized by non-euphemistic language, with the young people describing themselves, their anatomy and their sexual identities in meticulous and explicit linguistic detail. As Harvey et al. (2007) observe, their study's findings contrast with the degree of vagueness and apparent difficulty in calling experiences to mind that practitioners and researchers have found elsewhere with adolescents. The authors found that not only did young people describe their sexual health concerns in considerable detail, but their problems were also ethically and morally situated, inasmuch as they were formulated so as to identify that something was wrong with the physical integrity, feeling, size or relational activity surrounding their sexual anatomy.

However, for all the linguistic insight of their study, Harvey et al. have not determined whether the elevated linguistic candour on the part of their teenage subjects is attributable to the independent variable of adolescence (a linguistic characteristic of the age group) and/or the online communicative context in which the health advice-seeking occurred. As we saw in Section 2.3.1, it is well-established that the anonymity and invisibility afforded by the electronic medium allows for more intimate self-disclosure (Walther 1996; McKenna and Bargh 2000; Suler 2004). Thus whether the adolescents would have displayed the same non-euphemistic frankness and meticulous linguistic detail in other communicative contexts, such as in face-to-face encounters, remains yet to be established.

## 3.2 Adolescent mental health

Anna Freud (1958) once famously claimed that 'to be normal during the adolescent period is by itself abnormal'. Freud's observation draws attention to the stereotypical notion of the inherently disturbed teenager and, with it, the widely, if erroneously, held idea that adolescence is a time of inevitable psychological disorder and hyperemotional behaviour (Powers et al. 1989; Hurry et al. 2000). Freud's citation arguably encapsulates one of the most misleading folk beliefs perhaps ever to concern adolescent psychology, a myth that originated in the eighteenth century literary concept of 'Sturm und Drang' (Storm and Stress) but which still unfortunately resonates in the popular imagination today. A term applied to works of German literature noted for their depictions of youthful behaviour and emotion (Arnett 2007: 23), *sturm and drang* was harnessed by psychoanalysts (such as Anna Freud) to characterize adolescence as a 'highly charged and tumultuous stage of development' (Hurry et al. 2000: 1) in which extremes of behaviour and emotion are not only inevitable but essential for subsequent normal personality integration (Powers et al. 1989: 200).

Although still commonly drawn upon as a means for understanding adolescent mental health, the psychoanalytic paradigm of storm and stress, which up to the late 1960s has dominated the adolescent research community (Coleman and Hendry 2000), has since been debunked by research refuting the idea that most adolescents unavoidably experience emotional turmoil (Arnett 2007). For example, research by Offer and Boxer (1991) demonstrates that the majority of teenagers are able to cope effectively during adolescence and generally report feeling good about themselves and their aspirations for the future.

This 'radical revision' (Powers et al. 1989) of the psychological community's conception of adolescent mental health, where the teenage years are no longer deemed to be a period of great psychological upheaval, has had profound consequences for the detection, diagnosis and treatment of mental health problems in young people. For instance, until the 1970s psychiatrists and psychologists previously considered major depressive episodes to be 'rare, even impossible, in children and adolescents' (Mondimore 2002: 1). Depression in young people was commonly believed to be attributed to, and written off, as 'biological, physiological and social changes' (Culp et al. 1995), the 'growing pains' experienced by many teenagers (Weller and Weller 2000). Thus adolescent depression was considered to be 'masked' or expressed in 'depressive equivalents' rather than being a genuine syndrome like that which genuinely afflicted adults (Mondimore 2002: 21). Now, however, psychologists and psychiatrists clinically recognize the syndrome of depression (along with other disorders) in young people, accepting that both adolescents and children exhibit the same depressive symptoms as do adults (Mondimore 2002: 22).

### 3.2.1  Adolescent mental health in context: Suicide, self-harm and depression

Despite the aforementioned enlightened changes in attitudes towards adolescent mental health and development, it is clear that as young people enter the period of adolescence the incidence of mental health problems increases (Hurry et al. 2000: 3). For instance, at any one time in the United Kingdom, one in ten children under the age of sixteen is clinically diagnosed with a mental health disorder (British Medical Association 2006: 2).

A major concern for adolescent mental health has been the rates of suicide, self-harm and depression in western societies. There is international agreement that depression among young people is a significant contributor to the onset of suicide (World Health Organisation 2000). Suicide is one of the leading causes of death of young people aged 15–24, with an average of two young people killing themselves each day in the United Kingdom and the Republic of Ireland (Samaritans 2009).

It is, moreover, almost certain that attempts at suicide and acts of self-harm are under-reported since a number of these will never come to health service attention (Bowen and John 2001: 360). This owes to the fact that such acts are typically conducted secretly and, in the case of self-harm, injuries may well be superficial enough to be straightforwardly treated or hidden by the individual (Gardner and Chowdry 1985). Even with national cohorts, the official statistical estimates are not wholly accurate and not representative of the larger population (Bowen and John 2001). Official youth suicide rates conceal the true scale of the problem since deaths that are recorded as being of undetermined cause are often in fact suicide (Samaritans 1996). The real rate of suicide among youth is, therefore, likely to be up to three times the official recorded level (Madge and Harvey 1999: 145). Such underestimation of both fatal and non-fatal deliberate self-injurious acts only reinforces the necessity of recognizing such behaviours as compelling health and social issues, the reduction of which by any means possible is to be encouraged (Madge and Harvey 1999: 154).

Epidemiological evidence strongly suggests a 'relatively uncomplicated relationship between young people's suicide behaviours and depression' (Bennett et al. 2003). It is not surprising therefore that suicide has been described as the 'mortality of depression' (Eckersley and Dear 2002: 1891). It is estimated, for example, that the disorder occurs within 25 to 75 per cent of all suicides, making it a major risk factor for youth suicide (Apter and Freudenstein 2000). Significantly, adolescents themselves have identified the connection, describing a continuum of depression that ranges from normality through to the extreme of suicide (Bourke 2003).

Suicide is also clinically associated with deliberate non-suicidal acts of self-harm (Abrams and Gordon 2003: 430). Indeed it is estimated that between 30–47 per cent of people who commit suicide have a history of self-harm (Gunnell and Frankel 1994). As with suicide, self-harm in young people is considered to be symptomatic of psychological disorder (British Medical Association 2006), particularly depression (Apter and Freudenstein 2000). Yet estimates of psychiatric disorders in young people who self-harm vary. Hawton and Fagg (1992), for instance, identified comparatively low rates of psychological disorder in self-harming youth, while a more recent study by

Kerfoot et al. (1996) found that up to 75 per cent of adolescents who had taken an overdose were discovered to be experiencing mental illness.

However, intentional self-injury (be it suicide or self-harm) does not necessarily signify an underlying mental health disorder, such as depression. Indeed purely psychiatric explanations of suicidal behaviour have lately lost ground, since only a small percentage of people who injure or kill themselves are mentally ill (Grashoff 2006). Even for those individuals with a proven mental illness, their psychiatric condition may not be the principal factor for their self-destructive acts (Gavin and Rogers 2006: 140), for the risk factors that contribute to suicidal behaviour are complex and multifactorial (Bennett et al. 2003). Among young people, for instance, suicide and self-harming behaviours have been associated with 'severe social and interpersonal difficulties' (Kerfoot et al. 1995: 558), such as, among others, substance abuse, social isolation and family dysfunction (Kerfoot et al. 1996).

To overemphasize the relationship between depression and suicide and self-harm (at the expense of influences other than diagnosis) is to risk overlooking the role that life circumstances play in self-destructive acts. Moreover, as Fullagar (2003: 301) argues, the discourses of mental health and illness actually 'invisiblize the effects of culture' on psychologically distressed youth: in emphasizing 'the diagnosis and treatment of suicidal behaviour, self-harm and depression as mental health problems, psychiatric discourses may contribute to the process of 'subjectification' whereby young people see their own selves as pathological and shameful' (201).

Accordingly, if research is to enhance our current state of knowledge about why it is that young people intentionally injure themselves or take their own lives outside of medicalized explanations (Gavin and Rogers 2006), it is important to focus on the personal and social context of suicide, particularly the specific life circumstances in response to which self-harm and suicide 'might be seen as a viable option' (Smyth and MacLachlan 2004: 85).

### 3.2.2 The neglect of the adolescent perspective

Psychiatric enquiry has dominated the description of mental disorder (Rogers and Pilgrim 2005), including depression, suicide and self-harm (Jack 1992; Bennett et al. 2003; Gavin and Rogers 2006). The relative neglect by non-medical disciplines, such as the social sciences, has resulted in a predominance of the psychiatric perspective with its emphasis on psychopathology and psychiatric epidemiology (Jack 1992: 19).

Psychiatry privileges biological explanations for mental illness (Rogers and Pilgrim 2005). Accordingly a substantial part of the medical literature is taken up by studies that adopt a biological perspective, particularly research that describes the use of different drugs for treating psychopathology (Karp 1996: 11). This predominantly logical-scientific research relies on quantitative assessment and hence privileges the voices of mental health experts in place of distressed people themselves. As Leader (2008: 5–6) puts it, 'Nowhere in the statistics and charts is the actual reported speech of the patients themselves. . . It's as though listening no longer mattered'.

The lack of research that describes the subjective experiences of people suffering psychological disturbance is particularly acute in the context of adolescent mental health. The world of youth psychiatry is largely defined by adults, with emotional disorders in the young being commonly assessed through an adult respondent, such as a parent or guardian (Hurry et al. 2000: 6–8). Thus the perspectives of the young themselves are often obscured or overlooked altogether.

This neglect applies to a wide spectrum of mental health experiences. For example, despite the extensive body of literature in the area of suicide and self-harm, there remains relatively little qualitative research that incorporates young people's experiences of and views on youth self-destructive behaviours (Coggan et al. 1997). Similarly, research into adolescent depression often neglects the voice of the teenager in the development of theory and treatment of this disorder (Dundon 2006). For example, the majority of research examining the contribution of depression to self-destructive behaviour in young people has been conducted from epidemiological and psychiatric paradigms (Bennett et al. 2003). In the sense that such research fails to give detailed attention to the perspectives of the individuals concerned, it is typically decontextualized, 'ignoring the concepts and images within cultures from which individuals make sense of their experiences' (McQueen and Henwood 2002: 1494).

### 3.2.3 Communicating psychological distress: The language of suicide and self-harm

As with matters relating to sexual health, the subject of mental health is also severely sanctioned by taboo and constrained as a topic for discussion (Allan and Burridge 2006). Disclosing, and responding to, concerns about mental health is fraught with interpersonal difficulty. The problem of talking about psychological distress is further exacerbated by the ambiguous and contradictory nature of the mental health terminology itself, particularly the language for discussing suicide and self-harm (Fairbairn 1995). Interaction around the subject of suicide is liable to be tentative and indirect, with practitioners directly avoiding the loaded term 'suicide', using instead implicit and euphemistic formulations – descriptors which potentially impede establishing the likelihood of suicide (Reeves et al. 2004).

Given the powerful social stigma associated with suicide, and the silence that historically attends the issue of this forbidden act or 'last taboo' (Sommer-Rotenberg 1998: 239), it is hardly surprising that communication surrounding suicide should often be characterized by ambiguity and avoidance. So powerfully stifling are the stigma and silence associated with self-destructive behaviour that their effects can be detected in the therapeutic routine, where health professionals, fearful of feeling incompetent, anxious or angry in response to a disclosure of suicidal intent, may well refrain from questioning patients about suicide (Reeves et al. 2004).

Practitioners' views of suicide, specifically whether they are able to morally tolerate the notion of self-destruction, are also likely to affect their intervention with suicidal patients (Lester and Lester 1971), as is the fear that broaching suicide will only intensify patients' suicidal feelings, a factor that helps to account for why some GPs do not make suicidal enquiries of patients who present with depressive symptoms (Feldman et al. 2007). Yet such fears are misguided for, as Fujimura et al. (1985: 613) argue, the reality is that patients are not driven to suicide by being asked about whether they are suicidal or not. On the contrary, patients might be driven to suicide if discussion of their self-destructive impulses is avoided, since what they need is a concerned response from their listeners (Pretzel 1972).

Intriguingly, however, it is not just professionals who are liable to address issues of suicidal ideation and behaviour obliquely. Research indicates that patients also rarely make explicit references to the discursive object of suicide, tending to refer to the notion of suicide using metaphors via more implicit discourse (Reeves et al. 2004: 64). Although adopting a roundabout linguistic strategy does not necessarily evince reluctance on the part of patients to avoid directly communicating suicidal intent, such verbal indirection serves to highlight and re-emphasize the potent influence of suicide's societal stigma, as though to mention the word specifically were too 'difficult or exposing' (Reeves et al. 2004: 64). Naturally, the sidestepping of any explicit mention of suicide by professional and patient alike is liable to lead to difficulties in exploring patients' suicidal intent, particularly with regard to how the subject is negotiated and disclosed during therapeutic exchanges (ibid.).

The stigma surrounding suicide is exacerbated by the 'judgemental connotations' (Sommer-Rotenberg 1998: 240) attached to the formulaic phrase in which, unfortunately, this already loaded term popularly occurs. As Barrington (1969: 153) argues, 'to commit suicide' is a 'tendentious expression . . . calculated to poison the unsuspecting mind with its false semantic overtones, for, apart from the dangerous practice of committing oneself to an opinion, most other things committed are, as suicide once was, criminal offences'. As with a range of words that collocate with the verb 'commit' (e.g. 'murder', 'deception', 'adultery' and so on), 'suicide' forms part of a semantic group that describes heinous and forbidden behaviour. Yet 'suicide' is misplaced in such a set: the expression 'to commit suicide' is, as Sommer-Rotenberg (1998: 239) argues, 'morally imprecise' for it does 'nothing to convey the fact that suicide is the tragic outcome of severe depressive *illness* and thus, like any affliction of body or mind, has in itself no moral weight'. However, since referring to suicide as a 'committed' act is so profoundly graven into our language (Fairbairn 1995: 35), any open and non-judgemental discussion about the subject will prove difficult, with the presence of criminal overtones pulsing in the background. The corrective processes to which some suicidal patients are institutionally subjected do little to lessen the stigmas of illegality and dishonour. Although suicide is not an illegal act (at least in the United Kingdom and a number of other countries), when suicidal patients are identified, they are 'treated in a peculiar way – coercion is applied' (Rogers and Pilgrim 2005: 208).

It is, however, not just the highly emotive and negative criminal connotations attached to 'suicide' that are liable to inhibit the disclosure and exploration of suicidal thoughts: the word itself, along with the terminology associated with suicide and self-harm more extensively, is semantically impoverished and can lead to ambiguity and confusion in communicating about suicide and connected acts (Fairbairn 1995). Indeed, as far back as 1897, Durkheim questioned the communicative suitability of the term 'suicide', commenting that 'not only is the understanding of the word so vaguely defined that it varies from one instance to another according to the demands of the conversation, but it also results in categories of quite different things being brought vaguely together under the same heading' (2006: 15). Specifically, the entire range of self-harming behaviours that can result in death are subsumed under the overarching concept of 'suicide', alongside a few variants limited to tenuous expressions such as a 'cry for help' (Fairbairn 1995: 38).

To illustrate this linguistic inadequacy, Fairbairn cites the 'over-used and degraded' (1995: 39) variant 'attempted suicide', a term that literally implies that death is the actor's intention, but somehow he or she was unable to achieve it. Yet, for many people whose actions are subsequently classified as 'attempted suicide', death was not their intended aim: their acts, as in the taking of a moderate overdose, 'were performed in the belief that they were comparatively safe' (Kessel 1965 cited in Fairbairn 1995). The expression 'attempted suicide' is therefore liable to obscure the true intent of the patient performing the act, for it is used extensively as a blanket term describing all types of self-harming activity that could potentially result in death, even though 'only some acts labelled "attempted suicide" are truly attempts at suicide' (Fairbairn 1995: 44).

The conceptual and terminological inadequacy of language pertaining to suicide appears to be pandemic, emphasizing the universal difficulty of unambiguously discussing suicide and suicidal behaviour while simultaneously reflecting the collective affront that suicide poses to 'our ideas about what living is about' (Fairbairn 1995: 14). As Daube (1972) observes, there is, to his knowledge, no language that has a genuinely separate word set aside specifically for suicide, or more precisely, a word that is neither a compound nor a word that receives its meaning from some additional specification, such as the compound expressions 'self-slaughter', 'self-destruction', 'felo de se', etc. Universal expressions of suicide are typically indirect, reflecting 'the relative normality in human thinking of involuntary dying or of killing someone else as opposed to the abnormality of suicide' (Daube 1972: 391). Suicide is a unique instance of death, 'a dying or a killing with a twist' (Daube 1972: 390), for which correspondingly novel and unavoidably indirect linguistic composites have had to be created. Even 'suicide' itself, a word originating only as far back as the mid-seventeenth century (Noon 1978: 372), is a morphological blend of the distinct Latinate components 'sui' (of oneself) and 'cidium' (to kill), the Latin appearance of the term concealing from us 'that it means simply killing oneself' (Smith 1983: 313). The fact that 'suicide' is a relatively new word reflects the long-held sanction against self-destruction, as though the existence of a word dedicated precisely to the act would in some way condone or justify it, or at the very least make the subject easier to discuss more freely.

### 3.2.4 Communicating psychological distress: Responding to adolescent concerns

The foregoing section has described some of the inadequacies of language for talking about suicidal acts, accounting, in part, for the confusion common in both lay and professional discussions of the nature of suicide and self-harm (Fairbairn 1995). Thus for patients contemplating suicide, the opportunity of freely and unambiguously expressing their suicidal thoughts to an empathetic and non-judgemental listener may never be realized, depriving them of the 'best means of overcoming despair' (Sommer-Rotenberg 1998: 240). The problem is especially acute for adolescents since many young people who experience psychological distress never seek medical assistance from health professionals, nor is their inner turmoil likely to be recognized by others (Jacobson et al. 2001). It is hardly surprising, therefore, that the majority of adolescents who perform some sort of suicidal act do not enter a clinical setting at all (Jan de Wilde 2000).

Yet it is far from the case that most psychologically distressed young people do not wish to communicate their problems to others. For many adolescents who have self-harmed, being able to talk to someone about their distress is perceived as more helpful than specific clinical interventions (Burgess et al. 1998: 217). This helps to account for the fact that some form of communication precedes 80 per cent of attempted and completed adolescent suicides (Handwerk et al. 1998).

Moreover, the acts of suicide and attempted suicide themselves are considered to be acts of communication (Kreitman et al. 1970) or, more specifically, 'cries for help' (Anderson et al. 2005). Acts of deliberate self-harm are viewed in a similar vein: as physical manifestations of an inner, and linguistically inexpressible, 'silent scream' (Pembroke 1994; Strong 1998). Indeed professionals who work with distressed young people perceive their suicidal and self-harming behaviours to be substitutes for conveying mental turmoil via more conventional channels of communication, such as interpersonal exchanges (Anderson et al. 2005). Suicidal and self-harming behaviour is thus intimately bound up with the process of communication, emphasizing the connection that links suicidal ideation, its expression and associated suicide risk in psychologically distressed young people (Handwerk et al. 1998: 408).

Although a substantial amount of the research literature concerning the suicidal behaviour of young people has accumulated over the last twenty years (Anderson et al. 2005), the meaning of adolescent suicide communication is still not very well understood (Handwerk et al. 1998), particularly the meaning of young people's 'lived experiences' of being suicidal (Talseth et al. 2001) or the 'inner world' of the suicidal patient (Talseth et al. 2003). Moreover, there has been, surprisingly, no discursive research investigating suicidal behaviours (Bennett et al. 2003) and only little research exploring the relevant characteristics of suicidal communication in adolescents (Handwerk et al. 1998: 413). As the majority of young people who attempt suicide are likely to express their suicidal ideation beforehand, it is vital to understand more about their patterns of communication, specifically whether there is a relationship between the content of suicidal ideation and communicative patterns (Handwerk et al. 1998: 413). As Anderson et al. (2005: 319) argue, any intervention that is designed to reduce levels of adolescent suicidal behaviour will only work if people develop their understanding of suicidal and self-harming young people.

## 3.3 Conclusion

In this chapter I have provided an overview of research into the present state of adolescent sexual and mental health, paying particular attention to studies that have explored the language and communication of these taboo and sensitive areas. It was clear that sexual and mental health problems are not uncommon in adolescence, and that young people experience numerous difficulties speaking about these concerns. I also examined research that claims that young people's perceptions of sexual/mental health are often based on misconceptions. For example, with regard to sexual health, young people have been shown to lack knowledge of the transmission of sexually transmitted diseases and reproductive physiology – knowledge deficits which supposedly put them at risk of sexually transmitted infection and unwanted pregnancy.

Significantly, however, much of these insights generated by the adolescent health literature originate from researchers' agendas rather than young people's. These outsiders' perspectives do not give full voice to the complexity of the problems personally faced and subjectively experienced by adolescents. An alternative approach to adopt, as I outlined above, is that of the insider perspective. This perspective involves enabling adolescents to define and formulate health concerns themselves, thereby affording researchers a picture of the type of issues which personally matter to young people. However, accessing the insider perspective is not a straightforward endeavour for researchers.

Discourse data, such as advice columns in teenage magazines which are prime sites for collecting insider perspectives, are subject to editorial intervention and thus do not necessarily fully reproduce the problems that young people seek answers for. The advantage of using online health data, I argued, is that it is free from any editorial interference and thus provides less restricted access to unique insider perspectives.

I also described how research into mental health has similarly tended to overlook young people's points of view and personal experiences. Research into adolescent mental research has principally been conducted from a psychiatric perspective (the dominant discipline regarding the study of mental illness), prioritizing quantitative assessment of mental illness and the voices of psychiatric experts over actual suffers and their subjective accounts of emotional turmoil.

Finally, I discussed how communicating mental and sexual health concerns is often constrained by stigma. The language associated with mental and sexual health is ambiguous, vague and euphemistic – characterized by avoidance rather than direct, unflinching engagement. For example, the subject of sexual health is shrouded in secrecy and often broached through omission and circumlocution, particularly in face-to-face settings where participants share the same immediate spatial and temporal proximity. Similarly the terminology used to describe psychological issues such as self-harming behaviours is often perceived to be inadequate, freighted as it is with highly emotional and negative connotations, making it difficult for sufferers to freely and clearly communicate their troubles to others. Some researchers, moreover, have described links between self-harming behaviours and patterns of communication, an association which underscores the importance of examining the discursive resources which young people draw on in order to disclose their psychological despair.

# 4

# Methods and Data: Introducing the Corpus Approach to Health Communication

Although this book is interdisciplinary in focus, drawing on insights and theories from medical sociology, psychology and the health sciences in order to help explicate and interpret the adolescent health emails, my principal analytical approach to managing the data and conducting analysis is corpus-assisted. Such an approach integrates both quantitative and qualitative corpus techniques in order to first provide a broad survey of the adolescent health messages, examining frequency patterns in the messages and identifying salient themes across them (findings which are presented in Chapter 5). This more quantitative analytical approach is then followed up by a qualitative, interpretative discourse-based analysis, examining the messages in greater contextual detail (which I conduct in Chapters 6–9).

Given the primacy of the corpus approach to my analysis, as both a point of entry into the health email data and its subsequent shaping the ensuing contextual analysis, this chapter introduces corpus approaches to discourse analysis and health communication research, describes the research tools and procedures I used to analyse the health email corpus (AHEC), and describes the assembly and constitution of the corpus. I also address some of the criticisms that have been levelled at the corpus linguistic approach to analysing naturally occurring data, anticipating these criticisms, where possible, in light of the present study.

## 4.1  Introducing corpora

Corpus linguists have produced various overlapping definitions of what constitutes a corpus. McEnery and Wilson (2001: 5) provide one such succinct account, summarizing the various points of view:

there is increasing consensus that a corpus is a collection of (1) *machine-readable*
(2) *authentic texts* (including transcripts of spoken data) which is (3) *sampled* to be
(4) *representative* of a particular language or language variety.

Thus a corpus can broadly be defined as a body of naturally occurring language
which has been collected according to the above criteria. Corpora, therefore,
can be distinguished from archives or random collection of texts which are not
necessarily designed to be representative. Machine-readability is a *'de facto'*
aspect of modern corpora (McEnery et al. 2006: 6) and the methodological
advantages of such electronic corpora have been widely articulated (e.g. Sinclair
1991; Butler 1998; Tognini-Bonelli 2001; McEnery and Wilson 2001; McEnery
et al. 2006; Adolphs 2006). Butler (1998), for example, describes the enormous
potential that computers can offer the language researcher, undertaking tasks
which he or she would never be able to perform. The central advantage is the
speed of processing computers afford language study, manipulating (by way of
searching, selecting, sorting and formatting (McEnery et al. 2006)) vast amounts
of textual material so as to describe and explicate textual patterns. Computers
can produce information from texts in a form that reveals patterns that a human
interpreter would never notice (Butler 1998: 213) while avoiding human bias
and therefore making analytical findings more reliable (McEnery et al. 2006).

Thus the data used in corpus studies are more likely to be representative of the
text type under consideration than short fragments of data. Indeed one of the
criticisms of discourse analysis studies, including research into health language, is
that they often use small samples of data (such as a newspaper article, a magazine
advertizement or a single doctor-patient encounter, etc.) and therefore run the
risk of basing claims on small scale data that are not necessarily representative
of that particular sphere of communication. Consequently such findings cannot
convincingly be generalized to wider, typical language use (Stubbs 1997). Using
corpora, however, allows the analyst to account for a wide range of variation
which might be present in the texts and therefore ground generalizations on
more substantial and representative textual evidence.

## 4.2  Corpus linguistics and discourse analysis

I described, in Section 1.3, how discourse can broadly be considered in both
a 'micro' and 'macro' sense. The former construes discourse from a linguistic
perspective: discourse is language in use, a suprasentential entity, and is analysed

and studied with regard to its formal properties. In this line of discourse analysis, the focus is on the structure and organization of a text or texts. The macro notion of discourse is less concerned with the formal structure and organizing properties of language in use. Rather it is concerned with the social and cultural meanings which occur in and are reproduced through texts (or indeed through other semiotic forms such as images, objects, sounds, etc.). In spite of their theoretical differences, it is possible to combine these two broad approaches to discourse, closely examining the linguistic properties of texts in order to uncover and explore discourses. Accordingly, I aim to treat discourse simultaneously as both a means or mode of expression (in this case, computer-mediated communication) and as a way of representing reality – a way of communicating that describes the social and physical world and provides a means of making sense of it. In other words, discourse, in this complementary sense, involves 'patterns of belief and habitual action as well as patterns of language' (Johnstone 2008: 3).

Although the macro formulation of discourse is somewhat abstract in conception, the observable formal properties of language can reveal the existence or traces of a particular discourse or discourses (Baker 2005: 17). For example, a word or phrase or larger unit of language can realize a discourse or part of a discourse. What is important is that some observable instance of language use can alert the researcher to the operation of a particular discourse (even if this discourse is likely to be only partially present in the text). Baker (2010: 123) offers an illustrative example of how traces of discourse(s) are manifest in even seemingly inconsequential pieces of text. For instance, the sentence: 'Falconer was a bachelor but a man in love with life' possesses, according to Baker, traces of a discourse which negatively represent unmarried men (a discourse which, in turn, might be part of a higher ranking discourse that construes marriage as the preferred relationship state). The presence of this negative discourse in the sentence pivots around use of the disjunctive conjunction 'but' which implies that the state of bachelorhood is incommensurate with a love of life (bachelors, the implicature suggests, do not on the whole possess or experience *joie de vivre*). Although this one sentence is considered out of context, detached as it is from the larger text of which it is part, Baker's comments demonstrate how close attention to naturally occurring text potentially reveals the presence of discourse(s) which might otherwise remain unexposed.

One of the main methodological advantages of using corpora in discourse analysis is that such collections of naturally occurring language are substantial enough to reveal subtle patterns and repetitions of language use and therewith expose potential instances of discourse (Baker 2010: 124). Because of this incremental effect of discourse (patterns emerging through extensive collections of texts), the computational nature of corpus linguistics makes it an effective means by which to undertake discourse analysis (Baker 2005: 16). As Hunston (2002: 109) observes, 'patterns of association – how lexical items tend to co-occur – are built up over large amounts of text' and are thus unlikely to be apprehended through conscientious awareness.

Moreover, drawing on corpora can help reveal not only dominant discourses (which may well be present, due to their powerful, commonly established status, in small amounts of linguistic data) but also minority or lower order discourses – views and attitudes that do not reflect received or mainstream beliefs (Baker 2010: 125). Identifying these subordinate discourses alongside hegemonic discourses is important since doing so highlights the fact that discourses do not necessarily sit equally side-by-side but are instead in contest with one another. Not all discourses, as I mentioned in Chapter 1, are equal: some are more powerful than others and are liable to displace or marginalize others. But just because one kind of discourse is less prominent, widespread or authoritative doesn't mean that it isn't worthy of attention. Identifying and explicating minority discourses or attitudes potentially reveals promising avenues of analytical departure, as well as providing a more rounded and comprehensive picture of the theme(s) under investigation.

Although a number of discourse-based studies have begun to turn to corpus approaches as a way of fortifying and developing their analyses, research in this area has still to embrace corpora extensively, and such studies that do are few in comparison with corpus-inspired work relating to other applied linguistic themes, such as lexicographic and lexical studies, grammatical and register variation and genre analysis and so forth. That said, an increasing number of studies have harnessed corpora in order to uncover and explore the operation of discourses in a range of contexts including (to mention just a few) politics (Partington 2003; Orpin 2005; Baker 2006), print media (Mahlberg 2007; Baker et al. 2008), education and academia (Groom 2010; Leone 2010; Sauntson and Morrish 2011), identity and sexuality (Baker 2005), and business and enterprise (McCarthy and Handford 2004; Mautner 2010).

Using both specialized and general reference corpora, such studies have shown how corpus linguistics can provide useful insights into the subtle operation of discourse, and by extension insights into meanings that are 'indicative of the ways in which society creates itself' (Mahlberg 2007: 196). For example, Sauntson and

Morrish (2011) draw on a 13,630 word specialized corpus of university mission statements – by specialized corpus, I here refer to a collection of texts delimited by a particular register, discourse domain, or subject matter (De Beaugrande 2001) – in order to investigate the impact of capitalist, neo-liberal values on British Higher Education. The authors find that, reflecting the encroachment of market forces in society more widely, the universities' mission statements are saturated in neo-liberal discourses which promote the marketization and commodification of education. Through the recurring appearance of a small set of lexical items such as *quality, innovation, excellence, vision* in the documents, Sauntson and Morrish argue that the main purpose of the mission statements is to construct a unique corporate identity for universities, as well as avowing, in the increasing competitive global economy, the values of business and industry.

Mahlberg (2007), similarly drawing on a specialized, purpose-built 150,000 word corpus of newspaper texts, examines the meanings attached to the phrase *sustainable development*, a phrase selected for analysis because of its increasing significance in contemporary society. Mahlberg reveals that *sustainable development* is a pervasive concept, featuring in a range of discourses (not just specialist discourses) and contexts. For example, the phrase is associated with environmental conferences, with education and with organizations. Moreover, in examining recurring instances of the phrase in context, Mahlberg discovers that it is often, in the context of newspaper feature articles, described in sarcastic and ironic terms, presented in terms of large events (such as conferences) rather than being associated with real results and social change.

Larger collections of linguistic data (general reference corpora) have also featured in corpus-conducted discourse analysis. For example, Mautner (2007) offers an insightful analysis of the discourse of aging, investigating the use of the terms *elderly* and *the elderly* in a 57-million-word corpus of media texts. Mautner shows how the terms are typically negatively freighted, modified by words such as *infirm, frail, handicapped, mentally* and *blind*. The situating of the elderly in such a negative discourse, Mautner shows, is further emphasized by descriptions in the corpus of what actions *the elderly* perform. Rarely are the elderly presented as active agents in charge of their own destinies. Rather they are represented as passive entities, reinforcing the negative social stereotype which construes them as being dependent on others. Interestingly, Mautner's findings are echoed by that of Baker (2006) who also subjected the term *elderly* to a corpus analysis using the 110 word British National Corpus (BNC). Baker similarly describes how the term is associated with negative words such as *dementing, frail, housebound, disabled, sick* and *infirm,* all of which provide recurring evidence of 'deterioration discourses' (2006: 118) which construct the elderly as weak and vulnerable, defined in terms of illness or disability rather than independence and empowerment.

The social meanings attached to, and the underlying discourses associated with, certain culturally significant terms are also explored by Teubert and Cermakova (2004) who examine the use of the word *globalisation* in the 450 million word Bank of English corpus. Despite the familiarity and seemingly established use of the word, Teubert finds that it is a contested term, its uses often contradictory, revealing different assumptions and attitudes towards it. On the one hand, globalization is situated in a positive discourse of enterprise and opportunity. On the other, it is part of a destructive discourse construing it as a harmful, unstoppable force – in no way a route to social and economic benefit. Teubert and Cermakova argue that these meanings found in naturally occurring texts – real instances of language use – contradict those of traditional lexicography. Corpora, therefore, offer the discourse analyst authentic insights into language as a social phenomenon and the meanings of culturally significant words.

This brief overview of corpus-assisted discourse research does not exhaust, by any means, all the work that has been done in this area, but hopefully provides the reader with an idea of some of the themes that have been investigated, and thereby demonstrates some of the potential of corpus linguistics for contributing to the study of discourse. With regard to the specific procedures through which corpus-assisted discourse studies are commonly executed (frequency, keywords collocation and concordance), I discuss these methods in more detail in Section 4.4.

## 4.3  Discourse and corpus studies of health communication

Health care has attracted attention from a wide range of disciplines such as health services, ethics, psychology, social sciences, anthropology, media studies and linguistics – to mention but a few. In particular, research on communication in health care settings has, over the last 30 years, contributed significantly to the study of health practitioners and patients (Sarangi 2004: 2). Although, as many commentators have pointed out, the analytical focus of a substantial amount of this research has exclusively been on doctor-patient interaction

(Candlin 2000; Heritage and Maynard 2006), there exists a diverse and ever-increasing body of enquiry into medical discourse. Such diversification, for example, has considered the verbal routines of a variety of non-physician personnel including nurses (Jones 2007), physiotherapists (Parry 2004) and pharmacists (Pilnick 1999) – as well as exploring written medical discourse in various communicative contexts such as medical note taking (Van Naerssen 1985), case histories (Francis and Kramer-Dahl 2004), and patient information leaflets (Clerehan and Buchbinder 2006). Though diverse and wide-ranging, what these studies have in common is their close focus on language in use and the consequent pointing up of the role of discourse in the delivery of health care (Harvey and Koteyko 2012).

Methodologically, much of the aforementioned research has taken a sociolinguistic and discourse analytic perspective (including conversation analysis, text/genre analysis and critical discourse analysis). These perspectives have provided rich points of entry into the interrogation of medical practice. Moreover, many health care language studies have combined perspectives, utilizing theoretical eclecticism in order to better understand complex human communication (Jeffries 2000). There has been, for example, as McHoul and Rapley (2001) observe, a recent tendency for conversational analysis and interactional sociolinguistic methodologies to be supplemented by a strain of critical discourse analysis, with the research impetus being as much to criticize and change practices in health care settings as to describe and understand them (e.g. Lobley 2001; McCarthy and Rapley 2001; Francis and Kramer-Dahl 2004).

Such studies, as Adolphs et al. (2004) observe, are purely qualitative in their approach to analysis, based on relatively small databases and without originating in large collections of data (the present study, which interrogates a substantial amount of linguistic material, is an exception to this). This has led to another recent development in health language research which has seen a number of researchers calling for studies to make greater use of more substantial datasets, while, at the same time, recognizing that principally quantitatively-focused studies alone, which deprive linguistic data of context, are unlikely to be sufficient for providing an understanding of communication (Skelton and Hobbs 1999a, 1999b). Consequently there has been an increase in health discourse studies that integrate both qualitative and quantitative approaches to data analysis, employing, in the first instance, corpus tools as their primary methodology, supplementing these approaches with a range of theoretical and methodological perspectives (Thomas and Wilson 1996; Skelton and Hobbs 1999a, 1999b; Skelton et al. 1999;

Skelton et al. 2002a, 2002b; Adolphs et al. 2004), among whom Adolphs et al. provide the most comprehensive and detailed illustration of how a combined quantitative and qualitative methodology can enhance our understanding of a particular health care setting.

The corpus approach to health communication, however, is still in its relative infancy and it is therefore difficult to know how to assess it (Crawford and Brown 2010: 19). Broadly, corpus studies of health communication have all sought to combine quantitative and qualitative methods, allowing a complementary and novel approach to linguistic analysis (Skelton and Hobbs 1999b). For instance, Thomas and Wilson (1996), in a comparatively early corpus interrogation of health language, make use of a 1.25 million word corpus of practitioner-patient exchanges, methodologically setting out to demonstrate that computer content analysis can overcome the 'shortcomings of straight quantitative analysis' and has 'the potential to provide results which are in some respects comparable to manual discourse analysis' (1996: 92). Although this study thoroughly and systematically details patterns of language, the question arises whether the use of corpus tools actually contributes anything new to the understanding of health communication, whether the use of the computer contributes anything that might be otherwise achieved by manual discourse analytic procedures. Though the use of corpus techniques enabled the researchers to quickly and accurately identify significant aspects of the health practitioners' language use, the study gives little emphasis to actual samples of extended stretches of discourse – specifically how linguistic components actually function in the dialogic context of the practitioner-patient exchanges so considered.

More recent corpus approaches to health communication have focused on a range of doctor-patient consultations (e.g. Skelton and Hobbs 1999a, 1999b; Skelton et al. 1999; Skelton et al. 2002a, 2002b). Skelton and colleagues demonstrate the methodological advantages of integrating quantitative with qualitative approaches, while challenging the presumption made by quantitative studies (the standard analytical measure of clinical communication) that interaction can be reduced to the counting of behaviours (Skelton and Hobbs 1999a, 1999b). For example, Skelton and Hobbs (1999a, 1999b) argue that, since meaning cannot be completely quantified (for words are unlike numbers), any quantitative linguistic analysis must take place in qualitative context. As a starting point for their analysis, they use frequency counts of words and phrases, complementing such quantitative findings with qualitative assessments of how such phrases operate in context. The principle means by which this is achieved is through the use of concordancing outputs. The authors contend that it is only through qualitative methods, such as concordance lines with subsequent recourse to extended stretches of text, that general patterns in health language can be fully explicated. Quantitative methods can identify general patterns, 'but these patterns exist in a complex context that can only partly be described quantitatively' (1999: 111).

Skelton and colleagues' research utilizes corpus tools to examine assorted themes in health communication, including metaphor, pronominal usage and linguistic imprecision, demonstrating a range of uses to which the corpus approach can be effectively put. Rather than providing a broad linguistic characterization of the particular communicative practices in question, the authors confine their analyses to investigating specific linguistic phenomena. For this reason, their studies are not concerned with harnessing comparative data, contrasting, for example, their various datasets with general reference corpora.

Such a methodological approach is adopted by Adolphs et al. (2004) in their corpus analysis of NHS-Direct exchanges between professionals and patient callers. As with Skelton and colleagues' research, Adolphs et al. study avoids the limitations of decontextualized quantitative analyses, adopting a mixed-method approach. Adolphs et al. compare a corpus of health professionals' language with a corpus of general spoken English, identifying a set of keywords that appear with greater frequency in the NHS-Direct consultations. Having isolated a number of linguistic features quantitatively, the researchers examine these key items in their original discourse environment using concordance lines and conversation analysis techniques in order to provide close textual descriptions of interactional processes. These methodological stages of the analysis afford the authors a means of understanding the uniqueness of these professional-patient exchanges, enabling them to characterize the nature of NHS-Direct consultations where they identify an overarching tendency for professionals to use politeness strategies and the language of convergence in their interactions with callers.

## 4.4  Corpus tools for discourse analysis: Wordlists, keywords, collocation and concordance

Sauntson and Morrish (2011: 77) observe that a characteristic feature of many corpus-conducted discourse studies is that they often commence with an analysis of word frequencies in order to reveal information themes across a corpus. Such a procedure provides a basis for further analysis from which the researcher can conduct more qualitative-based examination, such as investigating the semantic environment in which lexical items of interest and significance occur. This, broadly speaking, is an approach that I adopt in my analysis of the AHEC, using a set of research tools (word frequencies, keywords, collocations and concordances) which can be productively combined to rigorously and systematically identify discourse patterns in a corpus. In the following sections, I describe what these processes and techniques involve.

In order to analyse the AHEC, I use the software programme *WordSmith Tools* (Version 5). The programme allows users to generate and sort frequency and keyword lists, compute and sort concordances, as well as producing collocates using a range of statistical measures. Although there are a number of user-friendly corpus analysis packages available which feature these tools, *WordSmith Tools* has been used by a number of researchers conducting discourse-based analysis (e.g. Baker 2005, 2006, 2010; Harvey et al. 2007, 2008; Harvey 2012; O'Halloran 2009; Pearce 2005; Seale and Charteris-Black 2010).

### 4.4.1 Wordlist/frequencies

A wordlist is a quantitative measure that provides a frequency count of all the words or phrases that appear in a corpus. Word frequency information is extremely useful for identifying characteristics of a text or language variety (Scott 2001: 47). For the analyst interested in examining discoursal patterns and commonalities, the value of a wordlist reside in its ability to provide evidence of the 'markedness' of particular discourses or attitudes (Baker 2005, 2006, 2010). The recurring use of certain words or phrases (over other lexical items) can reveal, on the part of language users, a preference for a particular stance or attitude, a way of representing and/or making sense of the world.

In examining how frequency can reveal preferences for particular biases, Baker (2010: 125–6) gives the example of the words *man* and *woman* as used in general English. The words appear in the (BNC) 58,860 and 22,008 times, respectively. This significant preference for the use of *man* over *woman* betrays, on the face of it, a male bias in general language use, with the interests of men seemingly over-riding those of women. This lexical preference, Baker explains, can be accounted for by examining specific occurrences of *man* in the BNC. The word is commonly used as a generic expression to refer to both men and women and is also used as a verb (as in 'man the lifeboats'). In contrast the term *women* is used to refer to women only and is never used as a verb. Such usages, Baker suggests, provide evidence of sexist discourse.

Mautner (2009: 38–42) provides another useful illustration of how, in discourse-based research, frequency can indicate preferences for particular perspectives and beliefs, thus providing an effective point of analytical entry into a corpus. In examining a collection of email exchanges between the former British Prime Minister, Tony Blair, and the journalist, Henry Porter, regarding the topic of anti-terrorism legislation, Mautner found that the word *law* appeared in both Blair's and Porter's emails, but occurred significantly more frequently (0.74 times per 100 words) in Porter's writing than Blair's (0.27 per 100). This marked preference for *law* in Porter's texts reflects his argument that Blair's government had undermined the rule of law. Blair's relative lack of use of the word *law*, Mautner argues, reveals his reluctance to engage directly with Porter's arguments, to side-step his accusations. Blair's infrequent use of certain lexis, in other words, could be interpreted as an avoidance strategy (2009: 40).

Mautner's insight into frequency reveals an important consideration about the quantitative measure in any corpus analysis: frequency, although a *prima facie* indicator of markedness, does not always serve as a marker of dominant discourses or preferences of opinion: considering relatively low frequencies, too, can reveal preferences and default values or other attitudes worthy of investigation. Baker (2010: 126) offers the case of the words *homosexual* and *heterosexual* which occur 821 and 377 times respectively in the BNC. The higher frequency of the former term, Baker suggests, is due to society's problematizing homosexuality vis-à-vis heterosexuality, with the latter being considered to be the 'normal' state of affairs. Hence *homosexuality* is the more frequent term – is marked – since society deems it unusual (2010: 126). Thus, Baker argues, it is important for corpus analysts not to take frequency rates at face value: a close examination of context is essential, as is relating 'the frequency of words to other types of (non-corpus) evidence' (ibid.).

## 4.4.2 Keywords

Wordlists, although an important first step in corpus analysis, in that they provide an immediate snapshot of the characteristics of a particular language variety, may only provide statistical information that helps confirm expectations surrounding the genre of a text (Baker 2006: 124). Keywords, on the other hand, that is, word forms that occur in one particular corpus with a greater significant frequency than in another dataset, provide a measure of saliency, as opposed to pure frequency, and thus are a more sensitive measure of quantitative analysis than frequency lists (McCarthy and Handford 2004: 174). Importantly, moreover, keywords, according to Scott (2001), are often likely to be words that human beings would identify as being thematically central to a text and are thus indicators of the 'aboutness' of a particular corpus. Consequently, in order to identify the key health themes distributed across the AHEC, and especially the various concerns that constitute both sexual and mental health, I supplement the findings derived from the raw frequency lists with a keyword analysis.

In their ability to indicate the propositional content of a text (Stubbs 2010: 24), keywords are an important tool for conducting discourse analysis. Indeed, since they are also an important indicator of expression and style as well as content (Seale et al. 2007), keywords have been used by a number of researchers as a useful means of identifying writers' and speakers' positions in texts, revealing insightful and sometimes unexpected information about the values and beliefs expressed by language users in a range of communicative contexts.

Fairclough (2000), for example, uses keywords in order to conduct political discourse analysis, namely his examining a corpus of New Labour texts. In identifying a series of keywords that characterize the language of New Labour (a number of which relate to the theme of change), Fairclough was able to show that the nature of the change promoted in New Labour discourse was rather ambiguous: despite the recurring rhetorical emphasis on political renewal and new deals, the proposed changes to British political and economical systems were expressed in rather nebulous terms such that it was difficult to apprehend the precise nature and extent of these intended reforms.

In a more recent study, Baker (2006, 2010) uses keywords to examine how rhetorical arguments were characteristically constructed in the British Houses of Commons during the anti-blood sports legislation debates that took place during 2002–2003. Interrogating a 130,000 word corpus of Commons' debates, Baker compares the arguments presented by those both for and against the proposed changes to the law. Both sets of speakers, Baker found, used distinct keywords in order to convey their specific stances on the issue, with the anti-hunt politicians framing their argument, through use of words such as *cruel, bloodthirsty, obscene,* 'in terms of moral repugnance' (2010: 137), and the pro-hunters describing the anti-fox hunting law as impinging on civil liberties and freedoms (through the use of the keywords: *freedom, offence, sanctions, criminal*).

Regarding keywords and the analysis of electronic health communication, researchers have increasingly utilized keywords in order to conduct discourse and thematic analyses of computer-mediated texts (e.g. Seale et al. 2006; Seale 2006; Seale and Charteris-Black 2010; Harvey 2012). The work of Clive Seale and colleagues is particularly illuminating in this regard. The authors' research focuses on online discussion groups that provide support for breast and prostate cancer sufferers. Using keywords to identify interesting areas of text worthy of further investigation in a corpus of 2,145,337 words, the authors compare keywords appearing in these two types of cancer support groups. They found that personal pronouns (*I, she, her, me*) and words referring to people (*mum, women*) predominated in the breast cancer forums, whereas in the prostate forums there were no personal pronouns as keywords but a number of keywords relating to more medical-technical phenomena and personnel (*urologist, PSA, brachytherapy, prostatectomy*). These respective keyword patterns demonstrate, according to the researchers, how women on the breast cancer supports groups were more likely to discuss feelings, people and relationships, while the men with prostate cancer tended to focus on technical and research-related aspects of their conditions. In the context of conducting both quantitative and qualitative health research, the promise of using keywords rests, Seale and Charteris-Black (2010: 55) assert, in their ability to reveal things that are difficult to see in a conventional reading of texts, as well as challenging and extending analysts' pre-existing ideas.

### 4.4.2.1 Generating keywords

Keywords are derived empirically from mechanical criteria: they are words which occur statistically more frequently in one text or corpus compared to another text or corpus (Baker 2010: 134). Accordingly they should not be confused with words deemed to be of significant social and cultural import, words that are intuitively identified by the analyst, such as those selected and interrogated by Raymond Williams (in his landmark publication *Keywords* (1983)). The advantage of using statistical keywords is that, since they are generated by purely computational measures, they remove the *a priori* biases of the analyst from the identification of themes of significance and interest (Baker 2004; Seale et al. 2006). Thus keywords present the analyst with evidence that a conventional thematic qualitative analysis might obscure from view (Seale 2006).

In terms of calculating keyness, a word is considered to be statistically key if it occurs with unusual frequency (either positive or negative frequency) in a text, or corpus of texts, compared to another text. *WordSmith Tools* provides a robust means for identifying statistically prominent words (Tribble 2000). For WordSmith, a word is considered key if it:

- occurs in the target corpus [i.e. AHEC] at least as many times as the user has specified as a Minimum Frequency;
- its frequency in the corpus when compared with its frequency in a reference corpus is such that the statistical probability as computed by an appropriate procedure is smaller than or equal to a p value specified by the user.

(Scott 2008: online)

The 'appropriate procedure' used in calculating the keywords in the AHEC is the log-likelihood analysis. As Scott (2008) observes, the log-likelihood procedure works by comparing actual observed frequencies between two sets of words with their expected frequencies. If the difference between the actual and expected frequencies is substantial, then it is likely that the relationship between the two items is statistically significant in that it is not down to chance. Thus the procedure is reliably able to generate words which are both characteristic and uncharacteristic of the target corpus.

The p (probability) value signals the amount of confidence that a word is key owing to chance: the smaller the value, the more likely that the word's appearance isn't due to coincidence (Baker 2006: 125) but is present (in the case of the AHEC) as a result of the teenagers' intention to use that word consistently in their requests for health advice. For the calculation of keywords in the AHEC, I used a probability value of $<0.000001$. According to convention, the general practice is that, in disciplines such as the social sciences, a p value of $<0.05$, which indicates a confidence of 95 per cent that the result has not arisen by chance, is the base mark of acceptability and thus worth reporting (Baker 2006; McEnery et al. 2006). The p value threshold 0.000001 is comparatively lower, meaning there is a one in a million chance that the keyness result is down to error. Although this threshold means that fewer keywords will be obtained, Scott (2008) argues that the notion of risk is less important than selectivity: such a low value will produce a more manageable total of keywords, as well as a total amount which is far less likely to have resulted due to chance. The keywords that I draw on in this study, and the significance of these words, are discussed in Section 5.3.

### 4.4.3 Collocation

Despite the many methodological and analytical advantages that keywords offer the discourse analyst, the procedure of identifying keywords does not in itself 'constitute an analysis or interpretation of a corpus' (Bondi 2010: 3). Keywords reveal promising points of entry into a text or texts – but an interpretation of a corpus is derived through an examination of how keywords appear in context and of their patterns of co-occurrence with other words (Baker 2005: 27). In order to obtain a more contextualized picture of some of the dominant ways in which adolescents communicate health concerns, I follow up a keyword analysis with a series of collocational analyses, focusing on a range of sexual and mental health related keywords. An examination of these collocates allows for a 'drilling down' into the AHEC to address progressively more detailed and contextualized levels of enquiry (Harvey et al. 2007).

The essence of collocation is co-occurrence, the phenomenon whereby a word commonly appears with (or near to) another word. Collocation is thus, as Baker (2006: 96) puts it, 'a way of understanding meanings and associations between words which are otherwise difficult to ascertain from a small-scale analysis of a single text'. Examining collocations can help reveal the attitude of language users and the 'semantic prosody' (Sinclair 1991) associated with a particular term. For example, Stubbs (1996: 173–4), in a now well-known illustration, demonstrates how the word 'cause' has a marked negative semantic prosody. Drawing on a general corpus of 120,000 words, Stubbs shows how the typical collocates of the term are 'overwhelmingly unpleasant', the most characteristic including words such as *accident, concern, damage, death, trouble*. Given this negative semantic prosody, 'cause' is unlikely to appear with collocates that have positive associations: *cause for concern* is much more common than *cause for confidence* (1996: 174). There is, of course, nothing intrinsically negative about the word *cause*. Rather, as Baker states, the word in social usage, is typically associated with negative events and hence has become imbued with negative associations (2010: 133).

Similarly, in an examination of the words *spinster* and *bachelor* as they appear in the BNC, Baker (2005, 2006) illustrates how collocates can indicate speakers' and writers' attitudes and underlying discourses. Both *spinster* and *bachelor* share one semantic attribute (the state of being unmarried), but the two words convey, Baker (2005: 29) observes, very different associational meanings. *Bachelor,* for instance, is more likely to collocate with words that have more positive connotations (*eligible, party, flat*) than *spinster* (*widows, sisters, rape*) (although further investigations of these collocates in their particular contexts of use would be necessary to identify their precise meanings). The value of collocational analysis is that it provides researchers with the 'most salient and obvious lexical patterns surrounding a subject, from which a number of discourses can be obtained' (Baker 2006: 114).

Collocation can be measured in various ways. It can be informally assessed (e.g. by observing that, say, 'blond' is much more likely to collocate with 'hair' than it is with 'paint') or, more reliably, by using a frequency count or statistical measure, such as a mutual information (MI), a statistical measure which calculates the strength of collocation or the extent to which words appear together compared with chance (Hunston 2002). In this study, however, I have decided to calculate collocation using the log-likelihood measure. According to Baker (2006: 102), using the log-likelihood measure is an effective means of identifying both a mixture of grammatical and lexical words, where other measures, such as MI, can privilege relatively low frequency words, giving them statistically significant high scores (Baker 2005: 31). Indeed some of the strongest, most salient collocates of the keywords I analyse, generated using the MI calculation, are unusual and irregular constructions, misspelt words. For example, strong collocates of the keyword *sex* include 'words' as *anol* (7.31), *anel* (6.99), *penatrive* (6.99) *hade* (6.92), each of which appears no more than seven times in total throughout the AHEC. Moreover, since MI calculation of collocation can favour very low frequency words (as the above examples attest), it tends to favour lexical words at the expense of functional items, a set of words which occur with high frequency in all forms of language. Although functional words in themselves are not indicative of content and therefore of the expression of adolescent attitudes towards and beliefs about health and illness, they nevertheless can be useful in identifying broader patterns of which they are part and can be indicative of themes and discourses (Baker 2006: 123).

Using WordSmith Tools's log-likelihood algorithm, the collocates I derived were obtained from a span within five places to the left and right of the keyword. As Baker (2005) observes, this range was not so wide as to produce collocates that might only have a tenuous connection to the node word (i.e. are so distant that they cannot be said to be true collocates) nor so narrow as to exclude potential collocates. Such a span size, moreover, is likely to yield noun phrases or multi-word fixed expressions of which the search term is part.

## 4.4.4 Concordances

Although examining collocates affords an immediate overview of the themes and topics surrounding a given keyword and an emerging picture of situational occurrence, collocational analysis alone provides only restricted information concerning how words function in context. Accordingly, in order to appreciate greater subtleties of meaning, a concordance analysis is necessary – an analytical procedure I conduct in order to examine sexual and mental health-related keywords later in subsequent chapters.

Unlike the purely quantitative focus of frequency and keyword lists, which separate words from their textual origin, a concordance analysis combines both quantitative and qualitative approaches, constituting an effective means of exploring the way that words are actually used *in situ* (Baker 2006: 71). Concordance lines consist of all the occurrences of a particular term surrounded by a few words of co-text (what we might call contextual detail). The lines below provide an example of how concordances typically appear in a concordance analysis. These concordance lines, generated by *WordSmith Tools*, feature the word *pregnant*, a keyword that appears 5,575 times in the AHEC. In presenting words in their original context of use, concordances allow the analyst to uncover subtleties of meaning which might otherwise be impossible to apprehend, particularly when there are many occurrences of the node word (the word of interest) in question.

| N | Concordance |
|---|---|
| 169 | for 5 mounth iv had sex inprotectaswell but i'm not pregnant well thats what the test says i'm scerd to go |
| 170 | with some one last week and i dont no if i could be pregnant or not he said hes nt sure if he comed inside |
| 171 | with all types of birth control. Is this true? Could I be pregnant? Please Help Is sex dangerous at our age? |
| 172 | is just beginning to get heaveier, does this mean i am pregnant? PLEASE help,im going out of my mind |
| 173 | bloated for any reason. Im thinking that i might be pregnant but took a test earlier this month and it came |
| 174 | line in the square window is not unusual when you are pregnant"and the last test i took had a faint blue line in |
| 175 | went inside me without a condom. I don't think I'm pregnant but I won't know for sure as my period isnt |
| 176 | of things-what should i do? I am Worried i may be Pregnant, I Cant Remember if i had a period in july or |
| 177 | it, like virtually on top and now i am 20 days late am i pregnant?Please Help!! iv got ejaculation sleeping. |
| 178 | What could be some reasons for this??? im 16 and pregnant nearly 7months but im worried how i am |

Although here is not the place to conduct an in-depth analysis, it is possible to see from examining the above concordances that the word *pregnant* (which in other contexts would carry extremely positive associations) carries a negative semantic prosody, constituting as it does a source of concern for the writers of these emails. The contributors express 'worry' at the prospect of being pregnant, are uncertain about whether they are pregnant and are 'scared' of the results of pregnancy tests. This is not, by any means, the whole picture; but, from examining these relatively few concordance lines, it is possible to see interesting patterns forming – emerging commonalities which provide insights into the writers' attitudes and emotional reactions to the content of their messages.

As Hunston and Thompson (2000: 39) observe, a large number of occurrences of a particular word are needed to appreciate the evidence for its positive or negative evaluation, and concordance lines provide convenient access to such samples. However, a multi-million word corpus (and the AHEC is no exception) is likely to contain many words that appear exceptionally frequently – words worthy of further exploration via a concordance analysis. Such large quantities of concordance lines makes it impossible, or at the very least infinitely time-consuming, to look closely at each individual concordance line, even those narrowed down by prior collocational analysis. Accordingly, I adopt Sinclair's (1999) procedure of first randomly selecting 30 concordance lines, observing their patterns, then proceeding to another randomly chosen 30 lines, then another, until a saturation point is reached (i.e. where no new patterns are apparent). However, since it can be hard to identify overall trends in large quantities of concordance lines (Scott 2008), I supplement Sinclair's proposal with Scott's recommendation of sorting concordance lines alphabetically. This entails organizing the concordances so that words immediately before and after the node appear in alphabetical order. As Baker (2006) points out, concordances thus sorted can more readily assist researchers in uncovering patterns of language use, enabling them to pinpoint discoursal commonalities which are far harder to apprehend in concordance lines as they would originally appear in a corpus. This sorting procedure was also useful in terms of confirming (or otherwise) intuitions first derived from reading the randomly selected concordance lines.

One of the potential methodological setbacks of using concordances is that although they allow for an examination of words in their original context of use, the contextual information they do provide is confined to the small extent of the few words appearing either side of the node. For example, the concordance lines above offer only so much contextual information about how the word *pregnant* appears in the full body of the original emails: not all of the message text is reproduced in the span of these concordances. This is a particular problem for corpora which are compact of large texts such that short concordance lines are only able to reproduce minute fragments of these original texts. However, as I explain in the following section, the small size of the health emails (an average of ten words) allows for an examination of each message in its entirety. Using *WordSmith Tools* it is only a matter of clicking on a particular keyword in context to view the complete, original message. Accordingly, after reading concordance lines, I have then been able to examine the original emails, confirming or otherwise updating my original interpretations. The short length of the emails, moreover, allows me to fully reproduce the messages that I present as illustrative examples in my analysis, thereby providing readers with the complete messages themselves rather than the truncated lines which characteristically make up concordances.

## 4.5  Limitations of the corpus approach

In the foregoing sections I have given an overview of some of the theoretical underpinnings of corpus linguistics, along with its key methodological procedures for analysing large quantities of language in use. Corpus linguistics, as with any methodology and analytical approach, has its limitations. The most sustained criticism levelled against corpus approaches derive from Widdowson (1991, 1996, 2000). In his 1991 paper, Widdowson questions the representativeness of corpora, arguing that corpus linguists 'do not present language beyond the corpus' (1991: 14).

Widdowson's criticism here is primarily concerned with the size and plurality of language use: no corpus or series of corpora can ever represent the sheer infinite variety and size of English in actual use. Consequently, he questions the validity of corpus materials used for pedagogical purposes since such materials only provide 'a partial account of real language' (2000: 7). Though his comments apply to the context of English language teaching, the criticism here articulated equally applies to other uses of corpora in discourse analysis. For instance, Widdowson criticizes discourse analysis that uses large datasets, arguing, quite rightly, that it is not practically possible to scrutinize every feature of a text for its functional significance (2000: 11). (In fact, for Widdowson, it is not even possible to exhaust the linguistic properties of small texts, let alone extensive data sets typically examined by corpus analysts.) As consequence analysts are compelled to select certain features and neglect the rest, producing, as a result of this selectivity, a necessarily restricted and partial analysis which neglects the communicative plurality and possibilities of texts.

Though accepting the general thrust of Widdowson's contention, I would argue that his beef here is principally concerned with the suitability of multi-million word corpora to represent language use, as opposed to specialized corpora, which represent a specific communicative domain or linguistic variety. In relation to the present study, the corpus analysis of the two million word AHEC, I submit that it will be obviously impossible to provide a detailed description of every feature of the corpus and, consequently, my analysis will necessarily be selective, an initial point of entry being determined by frequency and keyword lists and word clusters that aim to identify and describe characteristic linguistic features which can then be subjected to closer scrutiny. It is not my research aim to generalize findings from the AHEC to the language as whole, or to adolescent health communication more broadly (in all its various linguistic incarnations). In any case doing so would be impossible since the findings based on a particular corpus (such as the AHEC) can only textually uncover what is true in that corpus (McEnery et al. 2006). Accordingly, my research findings are limited to providing insights into the nature of adolescent health emails, specifically the communicative context of advice-seeking online. Thus my findings will not necessarily be representative of electronic health discourse in general but only the kind sent to the Teenage Health Freak website.

Widdowson's related claim of not being able to analytically exhaust all the features of even the smallest text is valid but, in my opinion, surely defeatist. Of course, no linguistic analysis can ever be exhaustive, and it would surely be misguided for any study to claim that its analysis and findings were determined once and for all, and not open to interpretation, to alternate readings. Yet one of the advantages of corpus linguistics is that, given the public availability of corpora and corpus tools, the findings that it generates are open to scrutiny and so can be verified. For example, in order to address a particular research question, a substantial amount of corpus-based studies utilize publicly available corpora such as the Bank of English corpus or the BNC (Kreyer 2003; McEnery 2005), making it possible for other researchers to see whether they might reproduce (or not) the findings and insights generated by these original studies.

Another of Widdowson's (1996: 73–74; 2000: 7) criticisms is that corpus linguistics reveals facts about language use that are not accessible to introspection or elicitation. The word frequencies, collocations, patterns and so forth detailed by corpus studies are provided by the analyst-observer, not the introspection of the insider, the individual language producer who gave rise to the communication in the first place. Widdowson observes that how words appear in a corpus does not necessarily correspond with the intuitions that their producers have about language use, providing the following example. If speakers of English are asked to provide examples of a sentence, they are likely to provide instances of the simple subject-verb-object (SVO) construction ('The girl (S) kicked (V) the ball (O)'; 'He (S) eats (V) his lunch (O)', etc.) – sentences which he considers prototypical. However, such constructions are unlikely to appear frequently in corpora of real language (Widdowson 1996: 74). Accordingly, these types of construction will not be accorded the same reality as observed data, even though they may have a significant 'psychological reality' for individual language users themselves (74). Corpus linguistics does not consider this kind of data or evidence of linguistic competence. Although, he concedes, this does not invalidate the insights that corpora contribute to linguistic analysis, it means that the validity of observed or attested data is 'not absolute but relative: one kind of data is no more "real" than another' (75).

Broadly speaking, then, Widdowson questions the ability of corpus linguistics to reveal a complete linguistic reality. Corpora can only provide a 'restricted account of experienced language' (2000: 5). However, it is important to note that corpus linguistics does not make such a claim. As Stubbs (2001: 151), in a response to Widdowson, argues, corpus linguistics gives priority to describing 'the commonest uses of the commonest words' and so is concerned with what frequently and typically occurs in texts: the relevant opposition being between what is typical and what is probable in language use. Corpus-based studies, therefore, aim to articulate a theory of the typical, and it is against such a background that irregular and unusual instances of language will stand out and hence can be identified and described.

Another noteworthy critique of corpus data is provided by Mishan (2004). Section 4.1 outlined the nature of the data used in corpus studies, describing how corpora, in using naturally occurring language (language that has not been collected under experimental conditions) are authentic. Yet Mishan critiques the authenticity of corpora, claiming that, owing to the form a corpus takes, authentic source texts that comprise it 'forfeit a crucial criterion for authenticity, namely context, in the transition from their original source to electronic data', thereby obscuring other authentic attributes such as communicative intent and sociocultural purpose (2004: 219). Source texts are denuded of their distinguishing features and, collected in a corpus, become part of one indistinguishable, homogenized whole.

> What was a blaring 72-point font newspaper headline appears in the same size and typeface as a medicine instructions leaflet; a memo that was originally typed, and advertisement copy that was designed to appear in arty, colourful font, are now indistinguishable . . . Appearance, to coin a phrase, really does matter. (Mishan 2004: 220)

Consequently samples of language collected in a corpus have only a 'reflected reality' (Widdowson 2000: 7). Corpus data possess merely textual traces of the original communicative event: once in a corpus they become part of the larger whole and, owing to the sheer amount and variety of language reproduced in that corpus, lose the original context on which their authenticity and meaning depended (Mishan 2004: 220).

Even fervent advocates and established practitioners of corpus linguistics recognize such methodological challenges. For instance, Sinclair (1991) concedes that samples making up a corpus do not easily detach from their context of production and therefore are not representative of the text type being analysed, thus generating 'the problem of finding and identifying typical examples' (Sinclair 1991: 5). While Tognini-Bonelli (2001: 2) observes that corpora (unlike an individual text that exists in a unique communicative context as a single, unified language event) bring together many different texts and so cannot be identified with a unique and coherent communicative event, with citations in corpora remaining fragments of texts.

However, the aforementioned criticisms, though relevant to all kinds of corpora, principally apply to large general corpora which comprise texts from a wide representative range of communicative contexts in order to represent the language as a whole. These texts, owing to their original (substantial) size, are not fully reproduced in their original form and thus end up as fragments. The AHEC, however, is compact of texts (emails) that relate to the same communicative domain, retaining their original textual format. Not only are these compositional factors, I suggest, important regarding representativeness but, in bringing together complete texts which can be resolved into and analysed as single, unified communicative events, they also provide the corpus with a coherence not afforded to more eclectic corpora.

In terms of the context of situation, a further methodological advantage of the AHEC is that the corpus compiler-cum-analyst, who has some degree of familiarity with the sociocultural and textual environment in which the discourse was first produced, can act as a kind of mediating informant and shed light on the corpus data (Flowerdew 2004: 16). For example, it is, as Aston (2002: 11) observes, far easier to interpret concordance lines if the analyst knows precisely what texts comprise a corpus since this 'allows a greater degree of top-down processing'. The point can be illustrated by considering the following two short concordance outputs of the noun *depression* taken from the AHEC:

> im 2 scared 2 go 2 the doctors or nurse because my **depression** is gettin worse I am anorexic and bulimic and suffer from severe **depression**

Though appearing in the concordance fragments, the nodes above are easily traceable to the emails in which they originally appeared and the text of these messages can then be reproduced and thus singled out for analysis:

> i dnt know if u can help, but i am overweight!! i am constantly depressed all the time iv tried all kind sof things 2 cut down on what i eat, more exercises, tried makin mysel sick, not eating, just nothing seems 2work, im 2 scared 2 go 2 the doctors or nurse because my **depression** is gettin worse as all i can do is cry these days, i really dnt know what 2 do anymore, iv also been self harming. Thanks C
>
> Dear Doctor Ann. I am anorexic and bulimic and suffer from severe **depression**. I cant help having these weight problems because Im very overweight, 20 kilograms above my high average at a height of 1. 72. I cant help feeling depressed because of my weight and my life. I need help

Once isolated, the analyst has access to the complete, original email and the message can be interrogated not only in terms of its individual lexical items but also in terms of discourse significance where lexical items are examined within different sections of a text (Flowerdew 2004: 15). In the above instances, for example, the analyst is able to chart how the various lemmatizations, along with lexis relating to mental illness, are distributed and function throughout the emails. Furthermore, contextual information surrounding the original production of the messages is also recoverable. The corpus provides details of the date of message submission, its sequence number (as received by the website) and, where they have been supplied, the age and gender of senders.

Mishan, along with Hutchinson and Waters (cited in Mishan 2004), observe that texts can only be truly authentic in the context for which they were originally written. Although agreeing with this claim and conceding that the AHEC (like any corpus) does not, after the transition from data source to storage, fully recontextualize the emails which comprise it, I would argue that it does preserve, to a not insubstantial degree, the authentic quality of the original discourse. In particular, access to the entire original texts, coupled with related contextual information, help retain the communicative integrity of the email, a factor which also has beneficial significance for corpus representativeness, which I discuss in Section 4.7.1.

## 4.6  Introducing the Teenage Health Freak website

The data for this study are health emails from Teenage Health Freak website (www.teenagehealthfreak.org), a UK internet-based database dedicated to adolescent health. The inception of the Teenage Health Freak site coincides with the expansion of the internet and the proliferation of Web-based services which provide advice and information in the field of physical and mental health (Michaud et al. 2004). With the burgeoning of general electronic health provision, there has been a concomitant increase in websites developed with the aim of making available information for young people on health in general or specific areas of health.

Set up and operated by adolescent health specialists, Dr Ann McPherson and Dr Aidan Macfarlane, the Teenage Health Freak website has been running and continuously updated on a weekly basis since its launch in the summer of 2000. The site is designed to be user-friendly, interactive, confidential and evidence-based, employing non-technical, accessible language and arresting, colourful graphics. In order to incorporate their views on what kind of services and facilities would be beneficial to them young people themselves were actively involved in the design of the website. Figure 4.1 below reproduces the website's homepage.

The homepage presents users with a range of information options and services. For instance, an A–Z feature allows users to locate information on a specific health theme by letter: 'Abortion, Abstinence, Abuse, Accidents, Acid, Acne' and so forth. The information contained in these links are what Michaud et al. (2004: 201) characterize as 'cringe-free' and evidence-based. In addition to these A–Z health themes, users can look up topics under the headings: Alcohol, Body, Drugs, Feelings, Illnesses, Relationships, Sex, Smoking, Weight and

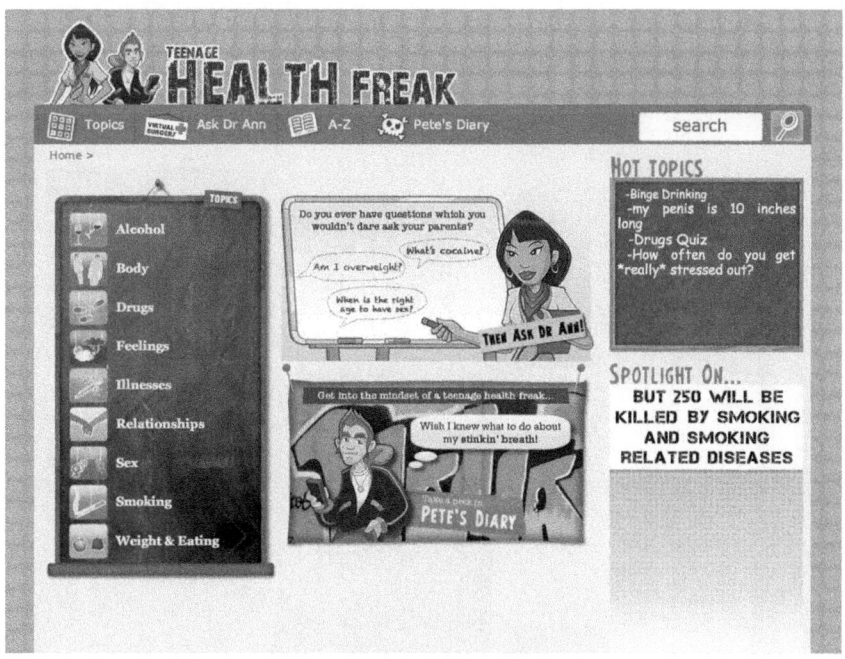

**Figure 4.1** Teenage Health Freak website (www.teenagehealthfreak.org).

Eating. All the information contained in these sections is regularly updated and any modifications are signalled on the site.

### 4.6.1 The interactive, virtual surgery: 'Ask Dr Ann'

A central feature of the Teenage Health Freak site is the 'Ask Dr Ann' webpage (Figure 4.2). This interactive facility allows teenagers, anonymously and in confidence, to email their requests for health advice and information to the virtual GP, 'Dr Ann'. The virtual persona of the website's resident doctor is a face for the real advisors, a group of health professionals, who respond to the young advice-seekers' emails. Given the large amount of emails received, the doctors are unable to answer all the questions submitted to the site. However, all users, straight after having posted their concern, are automatically referred to a section on the site that provides advice and information relating to the subject of their enquiry. Questions that are answered are routinely posted on the virtual surgery. The site daily updates new key questions and answers that appear on its Web pages. The aim and importance of this facility is summarized by Michaud et al. (2004: 200):

**Figure 4.2** Interactive 'Ask Dr Ann' webpage (www.teenagehealthfreak.org/askdrann).

> In reviewing questions posed and answers provided young people are able to see that they are not alone in doubts, confusion and the challenges that puberty and adolescence present. For health professionals, the exchanges provide a unique view of the issues and troubles adolescents face in their everyday life and as such represent an invaluable training tool.

When users submit a health concern via the 'Ask Dr Ann' webpage (Figure 4.2), they are asked to select their 'sex' and 'age' through two drop down menus (this can be done prior to or after the completion of their submission). Although users are invited to register this personal information, doing so is not a prerequisite for submitting an email and not every user provides this information. It is not therefore possible to identify the age and gender of every user contributing information to the site (nor is it possible to make precise demographic claims about contributors since, although the website is accessed by a range of young people, predominantly from Anglophone countries, the emails cannot be traced back to specific service providers).

Advice-seekers type their messages into a narrow text box situated towards the bottom of the screen. Though providing the impression of presenting limited word space, the text box in fact does not possess a character limit and so users can submit very extensive messages. However, the appearance of a text box kept to a minimal size is designed to ensure that the character count of messages is limited so that they can be processed and managed more easily by the website. The seemingly limited scope of the text box may well account for the relatively small word count of the average question (ten words) submitted by the adolescent help-seekers. Table 4.1 provides a breakdown of the average message length by gender.

As can be seen from Table 4.1, female advice-seekers typically submit longer emails (13 words) than their male counterparts (eight words). Female contributors, moreover, submit more questions (53 per cent) to the website than young men (37 per cent). However, these figures are not wholly representative of the complete gender distribution since 10 per cent of the total messages (11,766) are unspecified (i.e the senders of these messages have not supplied any demographic information).

Each email submitted to the site, whether responded to by 'Dr Ann' or not, is automatically logged and securely stored on the Teenage Health Freak's sitemanager webpages, access to which is restricted to the Web designers who maintain the site and the doctors who supply content. All the archived messages retain their linguistic form so that their original word choice, syntax and orthography (all the textual nuances of individual expression) are thus preserved and available for analysis. The sitemanager also stores contextual information relating to the submission of messages, logging the date on which each email is sent (day/month/year), whether it has been answered or not by Dr Ann, and, where contributed, the sex and age of contributors.

**Table 4.1** Summary of the AHEC by message length

|                        | All       | Male    | Female    | Unspecified |
|------------------------|-----------|---------|-----------|-------------|
| Total messages         | 113,480   | 41,830  | 59,884    | 11,766      |
|                        |           | (37%)   | (53%)     | (10%)       |
| Total words            | 2,217,919 | 667,277 | 1,442,784 | 107,858     |
|                        |           | (30%)   | (65%)     | (5%)        |
| Average message length | 10        | 8       | 13        | 6           |

## 4.7 The adolescent health email corpus (AHEC): Data collection and design

This study is based on a corpus analysis of 113,480 messages, a collection of messages which amount to a total of just over two million words. This collection comprises all the emails submitted to Teenage Health Freak during the period 2004–2009, the data made available for the study by the website operators. Compared with general or what Kennedy (1998: 45) refers to as 'second generation mega-corpora' (such as the 450 million word Bank of English corpus or the 100 million word BNC), a collection of two million words is comparatively small. Yet, for a specialized corpus, two million words is, by no means, a small amount (according to Flowerdew (2004: 19) a corpus is generally considered small if it contains no more than 250,000 words).

Moreover, many corpus linguists advise that the appropriate size of a corpus depends upon what language variety the corpus is meant to represent and, naturally, what research question(s) are to be asked of it (Sinclair 1991; McEnery and Wilson 2001; McEnery et al. 2006). For the purpose of beginning to identify and describe patterns and commonalities in young people's accounts of health and illness, I argue that two million words is a sufficient amount of data. My aim is not to validate a hypothesis concerning a specific lexical item: for example, the frequency of the distribution of a particular word, for which there needs to be a large corpus so that such an item can be modelled as contrasting with all others of the same category (McEnery et al. 2006: 72). Since my general research aim is to investigate the more common, recurring features of adolescent health language, the corpus need not be as large as one used solely to investigate infrequently occurring features (Flowerdew 2004: 26).

Another consideration concerning corpus size is that the larger a corpus built to represent a specific genre, the more difficult it is to undertake rich, accurate descriptions of language in use. As McEnery et al. (2006) observe, many corpus tools impose a limit on the amount of concordances that can be produced, making it difficult for a frequently occurring linguistic feature to be extracted and studied closely. The sheer amount of data contained in a very large corpus defies manual analysis by a sole researcher by virtue of the sheer volume of examples likely to be discovered (2006: 72). On this basis, McEnery et al. do not suggest that corpora assembled for a specific purpose must be small, for a corpus that can only provide a limited number of linguistic features in concordance will not serve as a reliable basis for quantification, but observe that specialized corpora can act as a spur to qualitative research.

As mentioned above, the methodological advantage of using specialized corpora is that their smaller size lends them to more detailed examination. It is not the function of specialized corpora to represent the language as a whole, and so to comprise a wide range of text types. For such a purpose general corpora have been compiled, corpora with which, owing to their extensive size, broad generalizations about language structure and use can be made. Yet, as Flowerdew (2004) argues, the drawback of using general corpora is that, owing to their size, they are prone to being mainly used for quantitative analyses and so are less conducive for analysing language use in specific situations (Connor and Upton 2004: 2). Specialized corpora, on the other hand, given their size and composition, their essential manageability, are often subjected to qualitative-based analyses. The close examination of concordance lines with recourse to the linguistic co-text afforded by qualitative approaches, for example, provides a rich source of data to complement more quantitative-based studies (Flowerdew 2004). Indeed, a characteristic feature of many specialized corpora studies (including the health communication studies considered in § 4.3) is their use of both quantitative and qualitative data (McCarthy and Handford 2004).

### 4.7.1 Representativeness and issues of corpus integrity

Allied to issues of corpus size is the concept of representativeness, an essential feature of corpus design (McEnery et al. 2006; Adolphs 2006). As was mentioned in Section 4.1, corpora are made up of principled collections of text in order to represent a language or particular text type. For Biber (1993: 243) representativeness is 'the extent to which a sample includes the full range of variability in a population'. The representativeness of a corpus, a sample of language or language variety, is determined by the range of text types included in it and how the chunks of the various text types are selected (McEnery et al. 2006: 13). Yet selecting types and sizes of text chunks in order to ensure that a corpus is representative is not straightforward and raises many procedural questions. Leech (1992) regards representativeness as a leap of faith, while Tognini-Bonelli (2001) claims that there is no way of objectively ensuring, or evaluating, the representativeness of a corpus. It is not surprising, therefore, that she should characterize the question of representativeness as a 'vexed' one (2001: 57).

Corpus designers have to make important decisions about the size of samples contained in a corpus – whether, for example, a sample is representative of the text as a whole from which it was taken and how long should individual texts that inform the corpus be? Although this is also an important issue for creators of specialized corpora, the size and range of texts is particularly crucial for the construction of general corpora since their aim is to be maximally representative of the language they are supposed to represent (McEnery et al. 2006). One strategy, be it for compilers of general or specialized corpora, is to ensure that each document in a corpus is of equal size, containing the same amount of words. However, such an approach runs the risk of including parts of individual texts that do not necessarily reflect the entire text (Sinclair 1991). Accordingly, Adolphs (2006: 20) recommends that corpus creators should aim to keep all individual texts in a corpus intact, including them as complete documents. However, given the overall finite size of any corpus, its inclusion of complete texts might not make it as balanced as a corpus containing a wider range of segments of a constant size (McEnery et al. 2006: 20). This is particularly the case for general corpora which, in order to be representative, aim to include a wide a range of texts as possible. Sampling, therefore, is inevitable if a corpus is to be balanced and representative (ibid.).

To some extent, the textual nature of the data comprising the AHEC circumvents many of the methodological difficulties corpus builders have in achieving representativeness. This is not to claim, by any means, that the corpus is infallibly and wholly representative, but simply that the unique form of its data makes balance and sampling somewhat easier concerns to respond to. One of the major advantages and practicalities of assembling the AHEC in terms of sample size is that every email sent to the Teenage Health Freak website (during the period 2004–9) is reproduced in the corpus in its original form, and, as mentioned previously, the average size of each message, each text, is relatively small (ten words) – exceptionally small when considered against the 4,000 and upwards word segments that comprise some general corpora (such as the written components of the BNC). This avoids the problem that corpus creators face of predetermining the sample size of texts contributed to the corpus. Given their manageable size, it has not been necessary to put a cap on the size of each email. Doing so would, of course, interfere with the integrity of each message, removing specific terms or concepts in an email that may be relevant for the full meaning of a particular problem communicated to the website. Consequently each email, regardless of its individual proportions, appears complete in itself. Moreover, since each email is wholly reproduced, this further sidesteps the potentially knotty issue of deciding which parts (initial, middle or end?) of text chunks that contributed to a corpus should be sampled. Does, for example, a general corpus which includes a selection of fictional texts in its make up only include (if not reproduced in their entirety) the beginning of novels? The email texts comprising the AHEC relate to the same communicative domain (i.e. an online health advice-seeking interface). Thus the question of deciding which varieties of texts to be included – a question which always faces compilers of general corpora which are made representative by dint of their balancing texts from a wide range of categories – does not apply so pressingly to the AHEC. Thus in terms of the distribution of only one category of text (health email), I would argue that the corpus is sufficiently balanced to fulfil the research aims of the study. Of course, the variety of topics that potentially fall under the category of health is broad, and one could strive for a corpus that contains – if there are sufficient of each in the first place – an equal distribution of health issues. Yet doing so would be to skew the corpus by design (McEnery et al. 2006) since the frequency and distribution of problems would have already been predetermined by the researcher, not the adolescents themselves who have communicated their concerns to the website, and thus would fail to represent the naturally occurring rates of health issues and account for the most common types of problems submitted. Consequently, I have made no attempt to balance the corpus by means of including a set number of emails relating to the various medical concerns which teenagers express – ensuring, for example, that there are an equal number of problems concerning sexual health, mental health, drugs and alcohol, pharmacy and so forth. Rather I have preferred to let the adolescents, as it were, represent and balance their concerns for themselves.

## 4.7.2  A note on corpus preparation and (mis)spellings in the corpus

Although receiving the email data from the website operators was a straightforward process, the corpus had to be structured through a number of processes for it to be fully usable for analysis. The data were supplied in MS Access and then transferred into an MS Excel spreadsheet. Catherine Smith, a computational linguist, developed a Python script to turn the MS Excel spread sheet into XML. Further clean-up was achieved by using a Python script to address any character encoding problems and remove duplicate messages sent on the same date (occasionally, as a result of help-seekers repeatedly submitting the same message, duplicate messages appeared in the dataset).

Another issue regarding the textual integrity of the corpus concerns unconventional and non-standard word forms – the misspellings, rebuses and abbreviations that occasionally appear in the adolescents' communiques. It could be argued that, given the unique linguistic make up of the health emails, the AHEC is not an ideally suitable dataset for conventional corpus interrogation. As was described in Section 2.3.2, the situational pressures of online message production, along with language use that mimics spoken discourse, not infrequently result in misspellings and other linguistic irregularities that are less common outside electronic modes of communication. Moreover, owing to the inevitable presence of morphologically complex medical and technical terms in the emails, further misspellings are likely to accrue, potentially skewing frequency and keyword counts, statistical measures which provide important quantitative insights into characteristics of the corpus.

To illustrate the problem, let us consider the term 'chlamydia', the spelling of which, as Dr Ann comments in one of her virtual surgery postings, can cause problems even for health professionals. The are 129 occurrences of the word in the corpus, of which 92 are spelt correctly and 37 incorrectly. Examples of the various (9 in total) misspellings include: chlamida, chlamidia, chlymadia, chylmidia, chlymedia and so forth. Therefore the analyst reading frequency and keyword lists cannot take such quantitative information at face value, that is, relying on the conventional spelling of a word to accurately reflect its true frequency. For instance, since it is the most common incarnation, 'chlamydia' appears first in the frequency list, but is separated from its misspelt counterparts which appear, in various positions, further down the list. Unless the analyst is prepared, somewhat laboriously, to scour the list manually, such variations will, of course, be overlooked and an inaccurate frequency reading obtained.

Despite being impossible to do this for every frequency token in the corpus, manually surveying frequency and keyword lists is the procedure I have adopted as a way of deriving more reliable frequency information, particularly with complex words (such as 'chlamydia') that are more likely to be misspelt. Although such a strategy does not guarantee freedom from oversight, it at least ensures a further degree of quantitative validity, accounting for any irregular orthographic forms which the computer does not process as one type.

### 4.7.3 Permissions and privacy policy

The Teenage Health Freak website possesses a privacy policy which informs users of the website what happens to any information that they supply to the website. The policy informs potential contributors that in submitting their questions they are not required to provide their names, email addresses or other information that could possibly identify them and that, in the event of their inadvertently supplying any personal information, measures will be taken to ensure that it is automatically removed. Users are also informed that the information they have provided will be used to answer specific questions and 'to keep up to date with teenagers' health concerns'. It is also pointed out that the information they supply may be used for research purposes and that, in using the website, they consent to the collection and use of the information they so contribute.

Despite these measures to ensure confidentiality, there are rare times when health concerns contributed by adolescents do in fact contain personal information – details that have not been automatically removed by the website. For example, users, on occasions, complete their messages citing their first name and, on what appear to be very rare occasions, sign off using their full name. Sometimes users also refer to other people in their messages. Accordingly, I have deleted this information (full names or otherwise) from emails when I have encountered it, replacing proper nouns with the tag [name]. My intention in doing so is both to preserve the textual integrity of the original message (accounting for the fact that a writer wished to communicate a personal reference) and to help ensure that contributors remain anonymous.

## 4.8  Conclusion

In this chapter, I have outlined some of the key methodological and analytical principals and procedures of corpus linguistics. In addition, I described the operation of the Teenage Health Freak website and the composition of the AHEC, detailing the makeup of the corpus, the data collection process that informed it and describing how it differs from other specialized corpora. At the outset, I outlined how collections of naturally occurring texts have been utilized in discourse analysis studies and what, broadly speaking, corpus approaches can contribute to discourse and health communication research. The value of the corpus approach, I argued, is that using corpora allows researchers to identify discoursal patterns that might not emerge (or emerge much less clearly, less firmly) in smaller collections of linguistic data – a consideration that applies especially to the genre of health communication, studies into which have tended to be qualitative in operation, focusing on relatively small datasets.

I also described the methodological techniques which I use to analyse the AHEC, namely, wordlists, keywords, collocation and concordance. Taken together these staple procedures constitute a powerful repertoire for conducting quantitative and qualitative discourse analysis, and I detailed some of the ways in which these techniques can be used to interrogate discourses inhering in large collections of texts. However, despite the undoubted effectiveness of these procedures (particularly when used together), it should be realized that corpus tools are not ends in themselves. These staple techniques are not a failsafe method of linguistic analysis, since real and apparent meanings of words and phrases are unstable. For instance, the sequence 'it's hot' could potentially be a comment on temperature or a request to open a window (Skelton and Hobbs 1999a, 1999b: 109). This is in line with McEnery's (2005) more general contention that corpora, though able to yield and describe significant linguistic findings, cannot provide explanations for what is observed. Consequently it is important to supplement the more quantitative tools (such as wordlists and keywords) with qualitative, contextual analysis.

To some extent, the unique composition of the AHEC allows me to overcome a number of problems concerning decontextualization. All corpora are decontextualized, incorporating collections of texts which have been removed from their original context of production and (typically) reduced in size in order to be assimilated into a corpus. The AHEC, however, is made up of a large number of small texts (health emails) which can be analysed as whole messages rather than as fragments. This allows, I argued, for a closer, more thorough analysis of keywords in context than that afforded by normal concordance procedures, allowing the emails to be examined in terms of discourse significance where words and phrases are examined within different sections of the entirety of each message.

With regard to the composition of the AHEC, I detailed the procedures by which the corpus was assembled and provided a break down of the average message in terms of message length and the age and gender of the author. I also drew attention to the issues of spelling variation and how the presence of irregular words could potentially skew frequency counts and the procedures I have adopted in order to derive reliable frequency information.

Finally, I explained the ethos and operation of the *Teenage Health Freak* website, paying particular attention to the 'virtual surgery', the interactive feature of the site which allows users to submit their health questions to the virtual GP, Dr Ann.

# Surveying the Adolescent Health Email Corpus: Frequency and Keyword Information

## 5.1 Introduction

The Teenage Health Freak (THF) website receives on average 400 requests for health information each week. The health forum solicits input across a range of issues, reflecting the variety of questions which young people have about their physical and emotional well-being. The purpose of this introductory analysis chapter is to quantitatively survey the key health concerns communicated by the adolescents, while describing some of the general textual properties of the emails in advance of the more qualitative contextual analysis of sexual and mental health messages conducted in the subsequent chapters. Using the quantitative measures of frequency and, in particular, keywords, the analysis seeks to categorize the content of the adolescents' health concerns, with particular emphasis on the keywords that constitute the emerging salient themes of sexual and mental health.

One way of approaching the aims above is to consider the extent to which the AHEC is similar or dissimilar to other varieties of English. For example, are there lexical overlaps between the adolescent health emails and the language of general spoken and written English? As McCarthy and Handford (2004: 172–3) observe, such comparative questions originate in the tradition of identifying language varieties in terms of their similarities with, and differences from, casual conversation, where conversation is the benchmark, the standard against which other linguistic varieties are measured.

Consequently, since electronic communication, in terms of its textual composition, shares close similarities with spoken language varieties (Yates 1996; Gains 1999; Crystal 2006), I first compare the adolescent health corpus with a collection of general spoken English from the BNC. Yet, as was discussed in Section 2.3.2, electronic communication has been described as a hybrid form, what Baron (2000: 248) refers to as a 'language centaur', a linguistic variety compact of both speech and writing. Accordingly, I also supplement the comparison with spoken English with a corpus of general written English.

## 5.2 Frequency

Word frequency information is extremely useful for identifying characteristics of a text or language variety (Scott 2001: 47). Accordingly, I generated a frequency list for the AHEC, comparing it against both spoken and written word lists of general English from the BNC. Table 5.1 below provides a comparison of the top 50 most frequently occurring words in the AHEC with the BNC spoken and written samples. As can be seen, all three corpora are dominated by grammatical or functional items, which is hardly surprising given that nearly all varieties of language constitute a high number of grammatical words (McEnery et al. 2002, 2006: 53). Perhaps the most striking difference across the three corpora concerns the quantity and distribution of personal pronouns. Although the AHEC and BNC spoken corpora possess high levels of pronominal forms, the AHEC abounds in first-person singular variants, including both subjective and objective pronouns (e.g. *I* and *me*, which occupy the first and eleventh slots, respectively) and possessive pronouns (*my* [3]), while the second person pronoun *you* ranks at 14. Corresponding high-ranking slots in the BNC spoken corpus are occupied by the first and second pronouns (*I* and *you* [3 and 5, respectively]).

Conversely, personal pronouns in the written corpus occupy comparatively lower frequency positions. Here the dominant pronouns tend to be third-person forms (e.g. *he* [16], *his* [25], *they* [31], *she* [33], *her* [34], *their* [38]), pronominal forms which do not reflect the personal and interpersonal orientations associated with Biber et al. (1998) first dimension of English, the emphasis of which is on relationship building rather than on the production of factual information (Tribble 2000). The AHEC and BNC spoken corpus, on the other hand, are imbued with pronominal references that reflect the interactive and interpersonal nature of these two modes of communication. As with other asynchronous varieties of computer-mediated communication, the AHEC makes considerably less use of third-person reference than writing. Thus the frequencies in Table 5.1 appear to support Yates' (1996) contention that, at least in terms of personal reference, computer-mediated communication bears resemblance to spoken language.

**Table 5.1** Comparison of top 50 most frequently occurring words in the adolescent health email corpus (AHEC) and BNC spoken and written English corpora

| | AHEC | Frequency | % | BNC spoken | Frequency | % | BNC written | Frequency | % |
|---|---|---|---|---|---|---|---|---|---|
| 1 | I | 153,222 | 6.93 | THE | 413,014 | 4.13 | THE | 5,631518 | 5.63 |
| 2 | AND | 66,274 | 3.00 | AND | 265,797 | 2.66 | OF | 2,867825 | 2.87 |
| 3 | MY | 59,681 | 2.70 | I | 246,286 | 2.46 | TO | 2,360013 | 2.36 |
| 4 | TO | 51,093 | 2.31 | TO | 236,051 | 2.36 | AND | 2,355329 | 2.36 |
| 5 | A | 50,766 | 2.30 | YOU | 207,095 | 2.07 | A | 1,957476 | 1.96 |
| 6 | IS | 40,501 | 1.83 | A | 207,095 | 2.07 | IN | 1,794141 | 1.79 |
| 7 | HAVE | 38,258 | 1.73 | IT | 180,450 | 1.80 | THAT | 891,911 | 0.89 |
| 8 | DO | 35,025 | 1.59 | THAT | 180,332 | 1.80 | IS | 885,149 | 0.89 |
| 9 | THE | 34,524 | 1.56 | OF | 177,363 | 1.77 | FOR | 811,643 | 0.81 |
| 10 | IT | 33,790 | 1.53 | IN | 142,856 | 1.43 | IT | 800,414 | 0.80 |
| 11 | ME | 28,386 | 1.28 | IS | 98,086 | 0.98 | WAS | 797,721 | 0.80 |
| 12 | WHAT | 27,549 | 1.25 | ER | 88,187 | 0.88 | ON | 648,418 | 0.65 |
| 13 | BUT | 24,147 | 1.09 | ON | 82,256 | 0.82 | WITH | 611,542 | 0.61 |
| 14 | YOU | 21,795 | 0.99 | YEAH | 81,550 | 0.82 | AS | 610,530 | 0.61 |
| 15 | OF | 20,842 | 0.94 | WE | 79,368 | 0.79 | BE | 590,129 | 0.59 |
| 16 | AM | 20,774 | 0.94 | WAS | 78,599 | 0.79 | HE | 564,053 | 0.56 |
| 17 | SEX | 17,335 | 0.78 | THEY | 71,135 | 0.71 | I | 559,033 | 0.56 |
| 18 | CAN | 16,557 | 0.75 | FOR | 70,946 | 0.71 | BY | 494,697 | 0.49 |
| 19 | IM | 15,193 | 0.69 | HAVE | 69,615 | 0.70 | AT | 474,061 | 0.47 |
| 20 | ON | 14,879 | 0.67 | IT'S | 68,567 | 0.69 | ARE | 416,170 | 0.42 |

*(Continued)*

**Table 5.1** (Continued)

| | AHEC | Frequency | % | BNC spoken | Frequency | % | BNC written | Frequency | % |
|---|---|---|---|---|---|---|---|---|---|
| 21 | IN | 14,640 | 0.66 | WHAT | 67,338 | 0.67 | NOT | 402,600 | 0.40 |
| 22 | HOW | 14,534 | 0.66 | BUT | 65,996 | 0.66 | FROM | 400,852 | 0.40 |
| 23 | WITH | 14,483 | 0.66 | ERM | 62,128 | 0.62 | YOU | 398,900 | 0.40 |
| 24 | GET | 14,410 | 0.65 | WELL | 61,827 | 0.62 | THIS | 395,310 | 0.40 |
| 25 | THAT | 14,375 | 0.65 | SO | 60,918 | 0.61 | HIS | 394,915 | 0.39 |
| 26 | THIS | 13,817 | 0.63 | BE | 60,889 | 0.61 | HAD | 390,904 | 0.39 |
| 27 | IF | 12,751 | 0.58 | THIS | 59,156 | 0.59 | HAVE | 383,355 | 0.38 |
| 28 | FOR | 12,496 | 0.57 | NO | 58,341 | 0.58 | BUT | 379,743 | 0.38 |
| 29 | HELP | 11,756 | 0.53 | ONE | 57,672 | 0.58 | WHICH | 342,667 | 0.34 |
| 30 | WHEN | 11,394 | 0.52 | HE | 57,325 | 0.57 | OR | 332,070 | 0.33 |
| 31 | REALLY | 11,137 | 0.50 | KNOW | 57,318 | 0.57 | THEY | 323,000 | 0.32 |
| 32 | ABOUT | 10,909 | 0.49 | DO | 57,315 | 0.57 | AN | 316,971 | 0.32 |
| 33 | BE | 10,233 | 0.46 | THERE | 55,224 | 0.55 | SHE | 308,706 | 0.31 |
| 34 | ARE | 10,207 | 0.46 | OH | 52,167 | 0.52 | HER | 287,690 | 0.29 |
| 35 | HE | 10,071 | 0.46 | AT | 49,351 | 0.49 | WERE | 284,234 | 0.28 |
| 36 | HAD | 10,051 | 0.45 | NOT | 49,125 | 0.49 | THERE | 246,251 | 0.25 |
| 37 | LIKE | 10,027 | 0.45 | GOT | 48,464 | 0.48 | WE | 242,090 | 0.24 |
| 38 | NOT | 9,868 | 0.45 | IF | 48,280 | 0.48 | THEIR | 240,834 | 0.24 |
| 39 | WAS | 9,269 | 0.42 | WITH | 47,431 | 0.47 | HAS | 239,984 | 0.24 |
| 40 | SHOULD | 8,696 | 0.39 | ALL | 45,662 | 0.46 | BEEN | 238,266 | 0.24 |

| | | | | | | | | | |
|---|---|---|---|---|---|---|---|---|---|
| 41 | KNOW | 8,657 | 0.39 | THAT'S | 45,065 | 0.45 | ONE | 236,350 | 0.24 |
| 42 | WANT | 8,423 | 0.38 | ARE | 45,022 | 0.45 | ALL | 233,030 | 0.23 |
| 43 | PENIS | 8,240 | 0.37 | AS | 43,317 | 0.43 | WILL | 231,167 | 0.23 |
| 44 | THINK | 8,229 | 0.37 | DON'T | 42,195 | 0.42 | WOULD | 211,445 | 0.21 |
| 45 | OUT | 8,171 | 0.37 | THINK | 41,103 | 0.41 | IF | 204,863 | 0.20 |
| 46 | SO | 8,121 | 0.37 | JUST | 40,082 | 0.40 | CAN | 195,203 | 0.20 |
| 47 | OR | 8,088 | 0.37 | YES | 39,613 | 0.40 | MORE | 192,505 | 0.19 |
| 48 | SHE | 7,990 | 0.36 | LIKE | 38,188 | 0.38 | N'T | 189,912 | 0.19 |
| 49 | DON'T | 7,701 | 0.35 | ABOUT | 36,842 | 0.37 | WHO | 182,202 | 0.18 |
| 50 | PLEASE | 7,505 | 0.34 | CAN | 36,232 | 0.36 | WHEN | 180,579 | 0.18 |

An expected, but no less striking, observation is the difference between the AHEC and spoken corpora in terms of their interpersonal orientation. The dyadic and multi-party nature of conversation, with its emphasis on both speakers and listeners, is reflected in the very high frequency positions of the pronouns *I* (3) and *you* (5) in the spoken corpus, with both pronouns sharing a similar percentage coverage: 2.46 per cent and 2.07 per cent. Interestingly, although the AHEC is overwhelmingly self-oriented, it is not simply monologic in terms of address. Although the young people in the AHEC are writing about themselves and their personal problems, and we would, naturally, expect the individual, linguistically realized through first-person pronominal forms, to be the principal focus and reference of the messages, the frequent appearance of *you* in the corpus suggests a significant interpersonal element, with the authors regularly appealing to a second person directly (typically Dr Ann) ('I would REALLY appreciate it if *you* can answer my questions!') or referring to a hypothetical, general second party, reference to whom, although ostensibly implicating another, may also potentially include the personal predicament of the writer (e.g. 'Can *you* get an abortion without seeing a doctor', 'Do you have to wear a condom?').

Thus, on first inspection, the health concerns presented by adolescents, despite their overwhelmingly personal orientation, also appear to share central interactive properties which characterize conversation. Yet, given the nature of writing to another, such a finding is perhaps not so surprising for, as Morrison and Love (1996: 45) observe, the genre of the letter is, by definition, interpersonal in that 'its form purports to be one side of an exchange between one individual [i.e. the adolescent writer] and another [the website doctor]'.

The high frequency of the auxiliaries *have, am* and *is* indicate that the AHEC is characterized by present tense verb forms. Choice of tense indicates how the writer views objects and facts (Werlich cited in Wodak 1981: 197) and in the context of the adolescent health problems, the present tense describes states that purportedly exist at the present time (Biber and Conrad 2004), marking their currency and relevance at the moment of articulation (Harvey et al. 2007). It is, then, to be expected that the present tense should appear so commonly in the AHEC and that, given the self-focus of the requests for health advice, it should also commonly co-occur with pronominal forms relating to the first-person singular.

However, use of the first-person pronoun is potentially not the only way in which teenagers are able to communicate personal information and concerns relating to themselves. As Table 5.1 above shows, the third-person singular forms *he* and *she* also appear in the adolescent health messages. As with other third person terms (such as 'friend' and 'mate'), *he* and *she* can be replacement subjects for the first-person reference 'I'. Indeed it is not uncommon for people when communicating acutely sensitive information to others to disguise their disclosures (Holmes et al. 1997), substituting references to a second-person or third party for the first-person: 'If *you* have unprotected sex are *you* at risk of getting HIV?', 'My *friend* is self harming how can i help her?').

In avoiding the first person, use of which personalizes the writer's perspective (Wodak 1981: 198), the teenage contributors are potentially able to fictionalize their real and very personal predicaments, distancing themselves from their concerns by transferring them to a third-party or 'friend' who becomes the subject of the complaint (although, of course, such accounts of the predicaments of a third-party may also be genuine advice-seeking attempts on behalf a friend). The indexical distance that such second and third person terms afford thus provides a means of preserving the self-image of contributors, as well as ensuring them a sense of anonymity while discussing sensitive subjects such as sexual and mental health. This is particularly the case with disclosures concerning suicide and self-harm – forbidden acts which have been described as the 'last taboo' (Sommer-Rotenberg 1998: 239) and as such possess incredibly powerful social stigmas. The issue of how the adolescents might be indexically disguising their disclosures, particularly in relation to the concern of self-destructive behaviour, is further discussed in Section 8.2.

Although the AHEC shares similarities with general spoken and written English, the frequency patterns described so far begin to disclose an emerging unique linguistic repertoire, the character of which becomes more pronounced if we set aside the grammatical words and consider lexical or content words. Focussing on lexical words allows us to get more at the 'aboutness' of a text or texts (Scott 2001): lexical items provide informational content and thus insights into the thematic focus of corpora. They are, accordingly, better able to reveal the most important and prevalent concepts that are at the heart of the adolescent health complaints.

The emerging distinctness of the adolescent health corpus is made apparent by the frequent appearance of the lexemes *sex* and *penis* in Table 5.1, both of which, on the face of it, relate to the theme of sexual health. This emerging, dominant topic-picture of sexual health and sexually related concerns is brought into fuller focus if we consider a more extensive range of common category-forming words in the AHEC. Accordingly, Table 5.2 lists the 50 most frequent lexical items in the corpus.

**Table 5.2** Top 50 content words in the adolescent health corpus

| Word | Frequency | % | Word | Frequency | % |
|------|-----------|---|------|-----------|---|
| 1. SEX | 17,335 | 0.78 | 26. GIRL | 3,832 | 0.17 |
| 2. GET | 14,410 | 0.65 | 27. FRIENDS | 3,683 | 0.17 |
| 3. HELP | 11,756 | 0.53 | 28. GAY | 3,572 | 0.16 |
| 4. REALLY | 11,137 | 0.50 | 29. STOP | 3,562 | 0.16 |
| 5. LIKE | 10,027 | 0.45 | 30. BOY | 3,545 | 0.16 |
| 6. KNOW | 8,657 | 0.39 | 31. PEOPLE | 3,526 | 0.16 |
| 7. WANT | 8,423 | 0.39 | 32. YEAR | 3,265 | 0.15 |
| 8. PENIS | 8,240 | 0.37 | 33. MUM | 3,061 | 0.14 |
| 9. THINK | 8,229 | 0.37 | 34. GETTING | 2,909 | 0.13 |
| 10. PLEASE | 7,505 | 0.34 | 35. WEIGHT | 2,899 | 0.13 |
| 11. ANN | 6,098 | 0.28 | 36. GOING | 2,864 | 0.13 |
| 12. FEEL | 6,067 | 0.28 | 37. DAY | 2,859 | 0.13 |
| 13. PREGNANT | 5,575 | 0.25 | 38. DOCTOR | 2,745 | 0.12 |
| 14. PERIOD | 5,075 | 0.23 | 39. LOVE | 2,706 | 0.12 |
| 15. GO | 4,982 | 0.23 | 40. MAKE | 2,688 | 0.12 |
| 16. GOT | 4,830 | 0.22 | 41. NEED | 2,687 | 0.12 |
| 17. BOYFRIEND | 4,507 | 0.20 | 42. BAD | 2,686 | 0.12 |
| 18. TIME | 4,465 | 0.20 | 43. BIG | 2,641 | 0.12 |
| 19. NORMAL | 4,383 | 0.20 | 44. YEARS | 2,601 | 0.12 |
| 20. WORRIED | 4,336 | 0.20 | 45. WRONG | 2,598 | 0.12 |
| 21. DR | 4,290 | 0.19 | 46. AGE | 2,571 | 0.12 |
| 22. FRIEND | 4,106 | 0.19 | 47. SCHOOL | 2,561 | 0.12 |
| 23. TELL | 4,053 | 0.18 | 48. GOOD | 2,506 | 0.11 |
| 24. OLD | 3,900 | 0.18 | 49. SCARED | 2,484 | 0.11 |
| 25. STARTED | 3,885 | 0.18 | 50. YEARS | 2,467 | 0.11 |

In addition to *sex* and *penis* further common context-specific lexical words can be identified. These items, which constitute a category of mainly nouns, verbs and adjectives further reflect some of the common concerns of the adolescents. For example, the words *Dr, doctor, help, worried* identify the medical context of advice-seeking, while *weight* relates to the theme of body size and appearance. Again, however, the most dominant cluster of words to emerge refers to the domain of sexual health, namely, *pregnant, period, boyfriend, girl, boy, gay.* Although the terms *boyfriend, girl, boy, started* do not themselves intrinsically relate to the topic, further contextual analysis as conducted in the following chapter reveals that such words are commonly associated with matters relating to sexual health and behaviour. For instance, the terms *boyfriend, boy, girl* are all collocates of the word *sex*, and regularly appear in the context of problems concerning sexual relationships, particularly the difficulty of deciding whether to engage in sexual activity or not. As analysis will show, adolescents describe dilemmas surrounding sexual activity, positioning themselves in a 'male-sex drive discourse' (Hollway 1984) in which they are construed as the object of the male-sex drive, that is, the sexual demands of men.

Thus far, then, our investigation of frequency patterns has revealed an adolescent preoccupation with seeking advice concerning matters of sexual health. Yet is this really such a remarkable finding? Given the physical, emotional and psychological changes that take place during adolescence (Suzuki and Calzo 2004), specifically sexual maturation and the accompanying sexual drive and interest in sex (Subrahmanyam et al. 2004), it is to be expected that problems concerning such matters would be the central focus of teenagers' questions. To some extent, therefore, the frequency lists we have examined so far have perhaps only helped to confirm our expectation surrounding the genre of the text (Baker 2006).

Further, such raw frequency information does not help us to identify other potential health themes that, although not appearing as regularly as sexual health, are nevertheless key concerns to the adolescents. Scrutinizing the entire frequency list for further context-specific lexical items would be impractical – the list extends to 45,509 distinct words (types) – far too many to be practically and closely surveyed. Keyword lists, on the other hand, yield more manageable thematic data, and so at this point we turn to the quantitative aid of keyword measures in order to further survey the AHEC.

## 5.3  Keywords and key concerns in the AHEC

Although the frequency lists examined above are a useful means for beginning to understand the overall stylistic orientation of the corpus, they do not, according to Tribble (2000: 79), identify words which 'matter', that is words which, in our case, best define and characterize (McCarthy and Handford 2004: 174) the teenage health messages. For instance, the raw frequency counts identified words that were common to all three corpora (spoken, written, computer-mediated), particularly functional items, revealing a significant degree of overlap among the corpora. In particular, we noted the high occurrence of personal pronouns across the corpora ('I', for instance, is the most common item in the AHEC and third most common in BNC spoken corpora), but did not establish whether these interpersonal items (and other context-specific words relating to sexual health) are alone responsible for the distinctness of the AHEC. Thus the most frequent words that appear in a corpus are not necessarily the words that best define it.

Keywords, however, constitute a 'more sensitive' measure of quantitative investigation (McCarthy and Handford 2004) and a more useful point of entry into a corpus. Identifying, categorizing and making connections between keywords constitutes an important analytical step in this study, allowing me to identify words worthy of further investigation – words that are potentially indicative of patterns and commonalities across the sexual and mental health questions posed by young people. Respecting the operation of keywords, Bondi (2010: 4) draws our attention to the underlying metaphor of the notion of a key, a tool that affords access to somewhere or something, a metaphor which suggests the power of opening and revealing what is unknown. In harnessing keywords (and cleaving to the aforementioned trope), I aim, as it were, to open the door to the AHEC, using these salient lexical items to gain access to aspects and features of the corpus that are liable to be hidden or not obvious (Bondi 2010: 5).

As discussed in Section 4.4.2.1 keywords are generated by comparing one corpus to a reference corpus. In order to generate keyword lists, I compared the AHEC with the 100 million word BNC (a general reference corpus consisting of 90 per cent written and 10 per cent spoken language components). The size of the comparative corpus one uses to generate a list of keywords is liable to determine the amount of keywords produced. As Berber-Sardinha (2000) observes, using a reference corpus which is five times as large as the target corpus is likely to yield more keywords than a smaller reference corpus would. Accordingly, I used both the 10 million word spoken and 90 million word written components of the BNC as a reference corpus with which to compare my one-million word email corpus. The BNC is designed to be representative of general English usage: both its spoken and written components contain a variety of genres, including newspapers, journals, periodicals, academic books and popular fiction (written), and casual conversation, discussions, lectures, debates, meetings and classroom interactions (spoken).

Although the keywords generated for the purpose of this study are appropriately derived from both general spoken and written English (reflecting the hybrid nature – part written, part spoken – of electronic communication), it should be realized that comparing the adolescent emails with different corpora, say, for example, a corpus of adult health email concerns, would likely yield a number of different keywords and, potentially therefore new departures of enquiry. This raises the perennial question of the suitability of reference corpora. The principle behind generating keywords is that, ideally, the researcher should aim to compare like with like, that is, comparing one's target corpus with a similar set of texts. For example, comparing a collection of spoken medical interviews with a corpus of romantic novels' texts will not produce a list of keywords that truly reflects what is salient in the clinical corpus. As Scott (2008: online) puts it, choose your comparison corpus in a principled way: 'compare apples with pears, or, better still, Coxes with Granny Smiths'.

However, recent research into keywords indicates that the empirical, statistical keywords procedure (à la Scott) is actually more robust than has been previously recognized. For example, Scott (2009) conducted a number of intriguing keyword processing experiments in which he used seemingly inappropriate reference corpora to evaluate the usefulness of the keywords generated by these peculiar datasets. In one study he, rather deliciously, compared a short (615 word) doctor-patient interview with a reference corpus containing all the plays of William Shakespeare (approximately 70,0000 words), thereby pitting contemporary naturally occurring clinical discourse against late sixteenth and early seventeenth century poetic drama. Despite the yawning quantitative and stylistic disparity between the two corpora, Scott found that the process produced a manageable amount of keywords – keywords, moreover, which were not absurd but could be expected to repay further contextual study (2009: 80). Scott concludes that, based on his experiments with three different types of datasets, there appears to be no such thing as a really bad reference corpus: even a manifestly absurd reference corpus can be a reliable indicator of propositional content.

So much for eccentric reference corpora. What about an irregular target corpus? As we have seen, the AHEC, with its misspellings, rebuses and other typographical inconsistencies, is not an orthographically conventional corpus. Given the appearance of a number of these so-called non-standard forms, there is the possibility that such irregular items (unlikely to be similarly prominent in a reference corpus of general English) might potentially skew keyword counts and thus be an undue influence on the results of the analysis (Biber et al. 1998: 249). Yet here again Scott's keyword procedure proves itself to be reassuringly robust. For instance, Smith et al. (forthcoming) examine the effect of spelling variation in the AHEC. Using the BNC as a reference corpus in both cases, the authors compare the keywords generated using the original version of the corpus (replete with all its orthographical quirks) with a 'cleaned up' version devoid of misspellings. Although the volume of keywords produced was greater (3,608 against 1,900) with the unexpurgated AHEC, the differences made in the ranks of shared words was very small. The keywords that were only designated key in the original corpus also tend to occur towards the bottom of the keyword list (making it less of an issue for research focusing on words towards the top of the list). Smith et al. conclude that, in using the original version of the corpus, the overall effect on the keywords generated is small. Consequently, for born-digital data such as the health emails the correction of spelling is not necessarily a key task.

In the event the two keyword lists yielded by WordSmith produced a total of 4,197 keywords: AHEC with BNC spoken 3,025 and AHEC with BNC written 4,172. Although this is a substantial amount of keywords – too many to examine individually in any contextual detail – the keywords so generated afford a convenient means of revealing lexical elements in the AHEC which are unusually frequent and from which it is possible to identify meaningful clusters of content items indicative of the various health concerns and issues communicated by the adolescents. Table 5.3 provides an overview of the keywords (the keywords are presented not in order of keyness or frequency, but according to specific semantic themes).

To some extent the grouping of keywords according to semantic domains reflects the conventional qualitative procedure of thematic coding (Seale and Charteris-Black 2010: 541). The keywords in Table 5.3 immediately direct us to lexical elements in the AHEC from which it is possible to identify meaningful clusters of content items indicative of the various health concerns and issues communicated by the contributors to the Teenage Health Freak website. Although (for the sake of space and economy) not all the keywords are reproduced, the keywords in the table provide an overview of a number of the themes which are salient in the corpus. Beside keyword categorizations of health concerns, other categories include the themes of school, relationships, family and help-seeking.

The principal decision for resolving the keywords into the semantic groupings in Table 5.3 is that the themes they indicate broadly correspond to the health categories that are signposted on the Teenage Health Freak website itself. Categories such as 'Moods', 'Drugs and Alcohol', 'Weight and Eating', 'Not Feeling Well', 'Relationships', etc. are all topics which the website provides information on for its users. Yet it should be noted that, although informed by clearly defined

**Table 5.3** Keyword categorization of themes in adolescent emails

| Theme | Examples of keywords |
| --- | --- |
| Sexual health | Sex, sexual, penis, abortion, pregnant, period, orgasm, infertile, HIV, AIDS, STD, STI, sperm, contraception, clitoris, vagina, vulva, PMS, erection, condom, masturbate, gay, abortion, foreplay, intercourse, virgin, unprotected, lesbian, oral, pill, ovulation, herpes, thrush, chlamydia, pregnancy, tampon, testicles, genitalia, viagra, scrotum, labia, glans, ovaries, foreskin, balls, fanny, bisexual, miscarriage |
| Mental health | Depression, depressed, suicide, suicidal, die, kill, overdose, slit, slitting, wrists, ECT, cutting, anxiety, panic, selfharm [self] harming, [self] harmer, sad, unhappy, upset, cry, crying, compulsive, OCD, hyper, afraid, fear, cope, esteem, stress, stressed, ADHD, paranoid, mental, batty, mad, mood, moods, moody, psychiatrist, depressants |
| Body weight | Anorexia, anorexic, weight, size, heavy, overweight, fat, obese, chubby, curvy, underweight, skinny, thin, bulimia, BMI, exercise, diet, kilograms, KG, KGS, bulimia, calories, food |
| Drugs/alcohol | Drugs, cannabis, cocaine, heroin, pills, addicted, craving, alcohol, drunk, drinking, poppers, mushrooms, marijuana, crack, ecstasy, addict, stoned, LSD, cigarettes, dope |
| Serious conditions | Cancer, cancerous, epilepsy, diabetes, diabetic, polycystic, anthrax |
| Medication Medicine | Medication, medications, drugs, prescribed, antibiotics, tablets, pill, pills, paracetamol |
| Pain and injury | Ache, aches, attack, bleed, blood, blister, bruise, bruises, burns, cramps, headache, headaches, migraine, migraines, hurt, hurting, pain, painful, soreness |
| Appearance | Ugly, cellulite, implants, clothes, face, freckles, bald, hair, hairy, zits, spots, acne, wart, warts dandruff, height, manboobs |

*(Continued)*

**Table 5.3** (Continued)

| Theme | Examples of keywords |
|---|---|
| Help-seeking | Advice, answer, reply, email, emails, emailed, hotmail, Dr, doctor, doctors, doc, docs, emergency, NHS, information, info |
| Relationships | Dating, date, crush, fancy, fancied, flirt, dump, dumped, boyfriends, relationship, boyfriend, girlfriend, girlfriends, friend, friends, jealous, kiss, kissed, snog, snogging, love, loves, mate, mates, partner |
| Family | Family, parents, brother, sister, sisters, cousin, granddad, mum, mums, mom, moms |
| School | Education, school, exams, GCSE, class, classmates, teacher, bully, bullied, bullying |

semantic areas, the categories in the Table 5.3 are, to some extent, arbitrary and overlap. For instance, the keywords *HIV* and *AIDS* could also fall under the rubric of 'Serious conditions' and *depressants* and *prozac* under 'Medication'. Moreover, as we will see in Chapters 8 and 9, issues concerning body image are intimately connected with mental health, with, for instance, bodily appearance occasionally being cited by the adolescents as a reason for depressive episodes and suicidal impulses. Similarly, the medical literature concerning dual diagnosis has described links between alcohol/drug-taking and mental health concerns (e.g. Davies 1998) and so there is a case for grouping the themes of drug and alcohol abuse under the rubric of mental health. For all that, Table 5.3 provides us with a clear and reliable summary of the health themes that most commonly concern the adolescents and the various key elements that constitute these themes.

Significantly, the lexical patterns clustering around the topic of sexual health that were identified in the prior frequency analysis are further replicated and expanded. Terms relating to reproductive health again predominate in the keyword lists, and the keywords reproduced in Table 5.3 provide a more accessible and lexically comprehensive picture than the raw frequency measures, revealing a range of topics and problem areas that can be subsumed under the broad theme of sexual health, for instance: *pregnant, pregnancy, period, PMS, abortion, miscarriage* (reproductive physiology), *condom, condoms, pill* (contraception), *HIV/AIDS, chlamydia, thrush, herpes* (sexually transmitted infections), *bisexual, gay, lesbian* (sexuality). In Chapters 6 and 7, a number of these sexual health concerns and the communicative patterns in which they are embedded are closely examined, with, specifically, analysis focusing on the keyword *sex* and its common collocates in order to interrogate adolescent understandings of and attitudes towards contraception, STIs and conceptualizations of sexual activity.

Another impression derived from the keywords is the explicit nature of sexual terminology used by the teenage contributors. A survey of these terms in Table 5.3, for instance, reveals the recurring presence of 'orthophemisms' (Allan and Burridge 2006), that is, language that is direct and neutral (i.e. non-euphemistic), e.g. *sex, penis, vagina, masturbate, erection*, as well as terms that denote precise anatomical detail, such as: *glans, scrotum, labia, vulva, clitoris*. As was described in Chapter 3, research into sexual health communication in face-to-face settings has described the defining presence of euphemism and circumlocution (e.g. Weijts et al. 1993; Stewart 2005; Bergstrom et al. 1992).

Although this is not to claim that the adolescents never employ euphemistic or child-like language when describing the sensitive topic of sexual health (terms, for example, such as *willy, privates, downstairs* appear in the corpus, *although* these are non-key and hence comparatively rare), the spread of keywords in Table 5.3 above reveal a preference for direct sexual terminology, as opposed to vague and circumlocutory expressions. As with other internet health forums, where intimate details of bodily experience appear to be discussed more freely than they are offline (Seale et al. 2006), the regular occurrence of orthophemistic terms may similarly reflect the preference for direct and open communication on the part of the adolescents, although, of course, a qualitative analysis of the keywords and their contexts of use is first required to substantiate such a claim. (The interface of linguistic candour and online communication, along with the implications of email for soliciting health concerns from young people, are developed in the concluding chapter of this book.)

In addition to sexual health, Table 5.3 lists a wide range of keywords relating to the theme of mental health. Although a number of topics can be identified under the general theme of mental health, what clearly emerges in the table is a preoccupation with depressive disorders and self-destructive behaviours, with, for instance, the presence of a range of keywords relating to the subject of depression (*depression, depressed, sad, unhappy, prozac*), suicide (*suicide, suicidal, overdose, wrists*) and self-harm (*self-harm, self, harm, harmer, cutting*) such that these areas of focus can be seen as being central to, or forming a signal component of, the adolescents' emotional health concerns. Although other keywords relating to mental health are also in evidence (e.g. *anxiety, panic, moody, stress, mad, batty*, etc.), these do not concentrate so persistently around distinct mental health phenomena (such as self-injury and depression).

The adolescents' emphasis on depression, suicide and self-harm is particularly telling, corresponding as it does with the increasing prominence of mental health problems experienced by young people in contemporary society (Hurry, Aggleton and Warwick 2000). As was pointed out earlier in the discussion of adolescent mental health, rates of self-destructive behaviour and depression among teenagers have increased in recent years and are a current cause of concern for health professionals and policymakers (British Medical Association 2006), not, of course, to mention the young people themselves and their families and friends.

Yet despite the increasing prevalence of these mental health phenomena, research indicates that they may be poorly understood, even among professionals, particularly the issue of self-harm (Mental Health Foundation 2006). Although the mental health literature has repeatedly demonstrated insightful links between depression and self-destructive behaviours, professional emphasis has been on the actual behaviour itself, rather than its underlying causes and the perceptions of sufferers themselves, often leading to inappropriate treatment (Mental Health Foundation 2006). The constellation of keywords relating to depressive disorder, suicide and self-harm, along with an interrogation of their contexts of use potentially provide a valuable linguistic resource for exploring the adolescent perspective, not least the identification and description of discourses which influence young people's conceptualization and expression of psychological problems: it may be, for instance, that the links between depression, suicide and self-harm identified in the mental health literature do not apply to the adolescents or that other situational factors are equally significant. This specific issue, along with a broader contextual examination of the adolescent mental health concerns, is taken up in Chapters 8 and 9.

The remaining health-related keywords in Table 5.3 reveal the topics of body weight/image, drugs and alcohol, serious and minor conditions and medication, all of which are testament to the variety of health issues that concern the Teenage Health Freak contributors. However, since this study is confined to an analysis of adolescent sexual and mental health, we will not here elaborate on these themes, suffice it to say that adolescent health communication extends beyond that of sexual and mental health (no matter how prominent these two themes appear in the AHEC), with corpus research having recently begun to address some of these other health areas, specifically adolescents' concerns over medicine (Gray et al. 2008a) and body image (Gray et al. 2008b).

To sum up then, this short introductory analytical chapter has prepared the ground for the contextual corpus analyses to come. Although space and the sheer amount of corpus data prevent a completely comprehensive survey of the AHEC (as Baker (2006) observes, no corpus analysis can ever be exhaustive), the use of quantitative measures have nevertheless provided statistical and stylistic insights into the central themes and textual characteristics of the adolescents' health messages.

Although the frequency analysis only marginally identified and described the content of the AHEC, the complementary keyword analysis provides a more widespread picture of the health concerns appearing across the adolescents' health emails, pointing up, in particular, an overwhelming preoccupation with the theme of sexual health. Given the biological changes that take place during the teenage years, it is to be expected that adolescents should have an interest in matters of sexual health. What, however, makes these quantitative thematic findings interesting is that, as Suzuki and Calzo (2004) observe, while young people are often reluctant to seek face-to-face advice concerning sexual health issues from others (Ackard and Neumark-Sztainer 2001), these were nevertheless the dominant concerns contributed to the Teenage Health Freak website. These initial thematic insights, then, provide support for the fact that specialist online health forums such as Teenage Health Freak may circumvent the awkwardness connected to asking questions about sensitive problems such as sexual and mental health (Suzuki and Calzo 2004).

## 5.4 Conclusion

In this the first of five analytical chapters, I have provided an initial survey of the AHEC, using frequency and keyword techniques. The purpose of this quantitative-based starting point was to reveal characteristic information about, and themes within, the AHEC, thus affording an 'access route' (Scott 2010: 44) to a more in-depth qualitative analysis of the corpus. The frequency analysis revealed a number of significant textual characteristics. The most common words in the corpus, which was to be expected, were grammatical words. Personal pronouns, in particular first-person pronouns, were especially prominent (in comparison with general spoken and written English), which reflect both the self-oriented and interactive nature of the email messages. I also observed that the high frequency of third-person terms such as *he* and *she* (and *friend* and *mate*) potentially indicated another stylistic strategy through which the email writers may refer to themselves. Using a third-person reference (in place of a first-person pronoun) allows the adolescents to disguise themselves and attribute their personal health concerns to others, a not uncommon strategy when people seek advice about sensitive, face-threatening problems.

The frequency analysis also revealed the prominence of certain lexical words. For instance, terms relating to sexual health loomed large as did lexis relating to the medical context of advice-seeking. Although the appearance of these high frequency words began to reveal some of the characteristic semantic themes in the AHEC, the wordlist analysis only took us so far in accounting for the distinctness of the corpus, its 'aboutness'. The keyword analysis, however, yielded a number of lexical words which were indicative of themes which could be effectively grouped into semantic domains. Although, given the sheer quantity of keywords, it was not possible to reproduce every keyword relevant to each domain, the keyword categorization provided a useful overview of the themes and issues characteristic of the health emails.

The keyword groupings were particularly useful with regard to making connections within and across semantic domains, thus enabling the pinpointing of certain keywords for contextual examination in the ensuing chapters. For example, with regard to sexual health, a number of keywords were indicative of reproductive concerns (words, e.g. such as *sex, pregnant, period condom, pill*, etc.) and issues regarding STIs (*STI, AIDS, HIV, chlamydia, STD*, and so forth). The examination of such words offers promising departures for discovering more about the discourses surrounding sexual health.

Keyword patterns similarly emerged around the theme of mental health. As with sexual health, mental health is a broad topic but the presence of a number of related keywords suggested that a particular network of psychological issues were prominent. For example, terms such as *depression, depressed, cutting, harming, suicide, suicidal* highlight the occurrence of affective disorder and self-injurious behaviours in the adolescents' health messages, reflecting, or at least offering evidence for, the connection among depression, self-harm and suicidal ideation established by psychiatric research (Bennett et al. 2003). Of course these specific mental (and sexual) health associated keywords do not reflect all the issues and concerns that relate to these areas of health, but they are, notwithstanding, lexical elements that promise to profitably repay closer examination.

# Communicating Delicacy:
# Reproductive Health Concerns

In the previous chapter, I undertook a number of staple computational procedures which yielded initial insights into the AHEC, presenting an emerging picture of the nature of adolescent health communication. This initial characterization of the corpus was principally quantitative and exploratory in approach, utilizing raw frequency counts and, more extensively, keyword categorization as a starting point for the subsequent contextual analysis of items at the level of concordance (Adolphs 2006: 40). Although a range of salient health themes and topics were identified, the most central concern communicated by teenagers was, overwhelmingly, sexual health. Having identified some of the main features of the terrain through quantitative means, I now move on to adopt a qualitative approach to the analysis of the data, exploring the theme of sexuality and reproductive health in context.

## 6.1 Sex in context

The principal focus of this chapter concerns the central expression *sex*. The word *sex* features prominently in both the frequency and keyword counts described in Chapter 5, appearing as the highest ranking lexical item in both statistical measures, the sheer weight of corpus evidence, its saliency in the data, justifying the word's receiving closer contextual scrutiny. The word also collocates with a number of sexual health-related keywords identified in Table 5.3, terms including *pregnant*, *condom*, *condoms*, *HIV*, *AIDS* which I also examine in greater contextual detail. Furthermore, given the reluctance of teenagers to talk freely about sex and delicate health problems with others, particularly their parents and doctors (Ackard and Neumark-Sztainer 2001; British Medical Association 2005), examining how adolescents apply and evaluate the concept of *sex* in their health messages should help advance understandings of how young people request advice on sensitive matters surrounding reproductive health, as well as providing insights into the discourses surrounding sexual health and, with this, their attitudes and beliefs about this area of concern.

In order to obtain a more contextualized picture of some of the dominant ways in which adolescents communicate issues surrounding reproductive health, it was first decided to generate a list of collocates that commonly surround the keyword *sex*. Examination of a selection of these collocates provides a snapshot of the most common contexts in which this central term is used. Although my analysis here is necessarily selective (it is not possible to pursue all the collocates and their contexts of use), it provides an emerging picture of the way in which adolescents discursively construct questions about sexual health.

## 6.2  Identifying sexual health related themes from collocates

Table 6.1 shows, in order of collocational strength, the left and right collocates for the keyword *sex* (for the sake of space only the top 50 words – from a total of 1,369 – are reproduced here). As can be seen, the most regularly occurring collocates are functional words, consisting of auxiliary verbs, pronouns, prepositions and conjunctions. According to Baker (2005: 67) the high concentration of such words is 'not surprising' for, as Scott (2000: 111) observes, the 'most frequent collocates of almost any node item in English will generally be *the, of, was*, etc.'. Note also the high frequency of interrogatives, for example, *what, how, when, can* – functional items that, although in themselves are not indicative of any specific content or theme, more broadly betray a preoccupation with questions specifically involving matters of sex and sexual health, which might, in turn, be symptomatic of beliefs and conceptions on the part of adolescents.

The lexical collocates provide a semantic profile of the word *sex*, and thus an emerging picture of the various, and most common, contexts in which it is used. For example, the collocates *unprotected, pregnant* and *condom* relate to the topics of contraception, conception and sexually transmitted infection; *age, first* and *time* potentially refer to issues surrounding the legality and timing of sexual activity; while the appearance of the terms *want(s), gay* (in the sense of same-sex relationships) *oral* and *anal* (which describe certain sexual activities) invoke what McRobbie refers to as 'new sexualities' – namely, 'the production of ever more free sexual practices' (1996: 185). Interestingly what relates all these themes thrown up by the collocates is that they broadly overlap with the concerns signalled by policymakers and researchers who identify a contemporary

**Table 6.1** Functional and lexical collocates (calculated by log-likelihood) of 'sex' shown in order of collocational strength. The frequencies in brackets indicate how many times each collocate appears within five spaces to both the left and right of the search term

| Left-hand collocates (functional) | | Right-handed functional collocates (functional) |
| --- | --- | --- |
| have (7,257), I (6,933), had (4,463), with (210), to (3,447), having (1,771), and (1,815), my (1,272), you (1,573), you is (1,476), a (961), do (1,289), but (371), we (756), what (762), the (739), how (733), when (733), can (691), for (447), if (683), me (831), am (520), it (649), about (548), after (377), does (291), he (249), are (331), of (503), without (83), not (314), during (190) | sex | have (1,105), I (5,214), had (5,214), with (3,356), to (796), having (65), and (2,681), my (2,644), you (845), is (1,382), a (2,118), do (1,218), but (1,748), we (424), what (1,256), the (1,384), how (677), when (431), can (691), for (655), if (420), me (667), am (742), if (891), about (295), after (146), does (263), he (441), are (320), of (367), without (205), not (290), during (38) |
| **Lexical** | | **Lexical** |
| want (1,247), boyfriend (487), unprotected (619), oral (545), first (203), time (287), anal (278), wants (362), age (211), condom (71), girlfriend (160), get (395), pregnant (291), boy (152), hurt (104), gay (226) | sex | want (289), boyfriend (688), unprotected (28), oral (53), first (708), time (394), anal (24), wants (36), age (239), condom (295), girlfriend (195), get (372), pregnant (184), boy (248), hurt (179), gay (125) |

decline in adolescent sexual health, in particular, concerns about the increasing rates of terminations and sexually transmitted infections, and the increase in teenage sexual experience and decreased age at sexual debut (cf. § 3.1). Thus the subsequent analysis will concentrate on these overlapping areas, while drawing on other collocates that, although not as salient as those in Figure 8, nevertheless reveal important complementary insights into adolescent knowledge and understanding of sexual health.

## 6.2.1 HAVE 'sex' – the primary construct and concern

If we include all its various realizations (e.g. *have, hav, has, had, having, haveing,* etc.) by far the most common collocate of *sex* is the lemma HAVE (15,626 occurrences).

Although functioning as both a left and right collocate, the most regular position occupied by this auxiliary is immediately prior to the node word, thus giving rise to the construction *have sex*. The pattern of *have* (or one of its lemmatizations) + *sex* appears 14,021 times, accounting for 80 per cent of the total number of instances of the word *sex* (17,335) in the corpus. Therefore the adolescents regularly communicate and situate concerns around sexual health through the verb phrase 'HAVE sex'. Although both perfective and progressive aspects also occur (*had sex* (4,463), *having sex* (1,771), *havin sex* (90), *haveing sex* (77)), the most common instantiation involves the base form of the verb, although the themes and concerns articulated by the various aspects broadly appear to overlap.

The adolescents use the underlying structure *have sex* in their emails to ask questions about the timing of having sex (messages 1, 3, 4, 8, 9, 10 in the following examples), to discuss the consequences of taking part in sexual activity (1, 2, 4, 7, 9) and whether it is appropriate to have sex (1, 4, 5, 6, 8, 9, 10, 11). Accordingly the adolescents appear to draw on discourses of personal responsibility which show a moral awareness of sexual behaviour, as the following emails illustrate:

(1)
I am still a virgin but feel ready to **have sex** with my boyfriend- will it be ok even with these white spots?

(2)
Hey Dr Ann i been thinkingg aboutt sex since i was 10 and im like boy crazy and now i think im bcoming sex crazy! i mean i just recently broke up with my boyfriend becuz i didnt have feelings about him anymore. But next time im hoping to get a better boyfriend better than my ex and if we get to know each other well i wanna have sex with him but im scared i might get pregnant or get sexually transmitted diseases i dont want to wait til im 16 (the legal age to have sex) i feel like im some kind of sexually rebel! so next time i get a new boyfriend and we get to know each other well is it ok to **have sex** (a safe sex)

(3)
should i wait till after 13 to **have sex**

(4)
my bf wants to **hav sex** wiv me an i wanna but he wants to do it at my house when my parents are in and i dont want to as i am underage and don't want them knowing.

(5)
i am 14 and have been with my boffriend for a year i am considering haveing sex with him but i have not yet started my periods is it ok for me **to have sex** even

though my periods havent started will it effect wen my periods start an if i didnt use protection could i get pregnant

(6)

i think my boy friend wants **hav hav sex** but i dont want to but i do so can u help me (i am embarased in front of him

(7)

i have a girlfriend and she is really good looking i want to **have sex** with her but i am not sure how to ask or wether i should i know about all of the risks and i have got a condom what should do?

(8)

I am 16 and havent **had sex** with my boyfriend yet-im still a virgin. should i **have sex** with him now that its legal? we are both very happy with the way things are but all my mates say that me and my bf are crazy that we're still virgins and have been together since we were 12! however, we are both christian and think it is better to **have sex** after marriage. what do you think? is it better to follow our faith and if we do what do i tell

(9)

i just wondered if you allowed to **have sex** while on the pill taking stage before the 7 day break thnxxxxxxxxx

(10)

I was wondering what i should do if im 15 and my boyfriend is pressuring me into **haveing sex** with him he says he loves me but im just to scared what should i do a

(11)

if you **have sex** under 16 and the other person was over 16 can you get the other person done if it happend along time

Riley (2004: 27) maintains that the expression 'have/having sex' is utilitarian, occupying a default position or descriptive middle ground between two extremes: on the one hand, the 'graphic viscosity' of bold formulations such as 'fucking' and, on the other, 'honeyed, even hypocritical' euphemisms such as 'making love' (2004: 28). Similarly, Manning (1997), drawing upon evidence from the then 211 million word Bank of English Corpus, a general reference corpus possessing a wide variety of both spoken and written English genres, observes that, as a verb phrase, 'have sex with' is a more neutral term to encode sexual activity. Moreover, as a reciprocal verb, that is a verb that describes the actions and processes 'in which two or more people, groups, or things do the same thing to each other' (Manning 1997: 444), its use by speakers and writers has ideological consequences concerning the representations of actors and the events in which they partake. In the extended concordances above, for instance, despite the apparent reciprocity involving proposed sexual activity, the adolescents mainly use a singular subject (either a first or third person reference) rather than a plural subject in the form of the personal pronoun 'we' or noun group + noun group such as 'my boyfriend/girlfriend and I'. As Manning argues, the use of a plural subject entails the speaker or writer representing both participants as being equally involved in the activity – 'the action or activity is construed as unambiguously reciprocal' (1997: 47). For example, 'We want to have sex' implies an equal role for both participants in that they are equally desirous, whereas the alternate formulation, 'I want to have sex with her/him' serves to highlight the goal of the subject, while the intention on the part of the second participant is obscured altogether.

Rather than both mentioned participants mutually communicating a reciprocal interest in potential sexual activity, the emphasis appears to be on the wants and needs of a specific individual. As the examples above reveal, this appears to translate into the pattern of 'boyfriends' seeking 'sex' with a partner (it is also potentially revealing that the terms 'boyfriend' (4,507 occurrences) and 'girlfriend' (1,689) are much more typically used in the emails than the term 'partner' (203), one of whose regular meanings is to indicate 'an egalitarian' (Jackson 2005b: 293) or same-sex relationship). Thus these encodings of participant relations can perhaps be seen as reflecting what Hollway (1984) identifies as the 'male-sex drive discourse', a discourse which constructs men as pursuers of women who, in turn, are perceived as 'the object of the male-sex drive' (Gilfoyle et al. 1992: 210). Such a discourse legitimates the notion that 'sex is something that men do to women' (Jackson 1982: 23). If we consider, for example, the most common lexical item through which sexual desire is directly communicated, WANT (see Table 6.1 above), it becomes clearer that young men are the subjects who predominantly seek to engage in sexual activity. Of the 362 occurrences of *wants* (the form inflected for third-person singular forms), 181 involve male subjects in *wants* + *sex* clauses, compared to 77 involving female subjects. The following emails are typical illustrations of the male sex drive discourse:

(12)

my **boyfriend wants** sex with me and i said i do to but im scared incase it hurts or it doesnt go right

(13)

i think my **boyfriend wants** hav hav sex but i dont want to but i do so can u help me (i am embarrassed in front of him)

(14)

ive been asked out by 3 boys and i only like one but all **he wants** is sex sex sex

(15)

my boyfriend is not a virgin but i am he said **he wants** me to have sex with him but i am scared should i do it anyway?

(16)

hey ann my **boyfriend wants** sex but i dont want to yet im scared help me

(17)

my **boyfriend wants** to have sex with me and im ready to but im not confident of my body and im worried about what he would say.

(18)

i'm going out with an older guy, we've been going out for quite a while. Anyway recently things have gotten more serious and now **he wants** sex. i'm only twelve but i really love him and i don't want to split up. What shall i do???

(19)

I'm going out with a boy thats 16 and far more experienced than me, and hes said **he wants** sex but he won't push me into anything. But I don't want to humiliate or upset him by saying no. . . Help! What do I say to him that won't hurt him?

(20)

im 14 and my **boyfriend** is 17. **he wants** sex but i dont feel he respects me enough. i dont want ot say no to him either. i am a virgin and he isnt . i feel stupid having sex with him because of this. what shall i do?

(21)

My **boyfriend wants** us to have sex. but im not sure. i don't know how to? but i don't want to tell him that coz ill sound silly

These examples serve to highlight the dilemmas that adolescents, particularly young women, experience surrounding the commencement of sexual activity. For instance in the above messages, where men are positioned as active sexual subjects, the young women often define themselves as interpreters and victims of male power in a system where they are expected to submit (van Roosmalen 2000: 221). Moreover, as Cook (1984: 9) observes, although young women's emerging sexuality offers excitement for a promising future, it is also, as the examples would appear to attest, a source of vulnerability when they are not free to decide when and if to make themselves sexually available. Such 'vulnerability' is manifest in the adolescents' postings in which the writers seem to ethically and morally situate their anxieties, for instance overtly recognizing an imbalance or injustice in a relationship, but without being certain of how best to respond to these demands to partake in sexuality activity. For example, the contributors express the belief that not having sex might lead to their being rejected by their partners: 'i really love him and i don't want to split up. What shall i do???' (18); 'But I don't want to humiliate or upset him by saying no' (19). Additionally, the contributors convey the difficulty of finding the right words with which to say no to their partners' demands for sex: 'What do I say to him that won't hurt him?' (19), 'i don't want to tell him that coz ill sound silly' (21).

Thus, for these help-seekers, recourse appears to rest in appeals to an outside authority for advice on subsequent courses of action (i.e. in requests to the online health advisor). Yet, equally, the young women's emails can be read as confronting male norms of sexual behaviour. In questioning the demands that young men place upon them, the authors appear to disrupt the male cultural expectation of leadership in sexual actions (Hyde et al. 2005) and so present resistance to, or at least question, the skewed power dynamic underscoring heterosexual relationships (Holland et al. 2000; van Roosmalen 2000).

### 6.2.2  What is 'sex'? Conceptions of sexual behaviour

Our interrogation of a number of the instantiations of the verb phrase HAVE *sex* has, so far, focused on how the construction is used by adolescents to communicate a desire for sexual activity, as well as to formulate questions about readiness for 'sex'. However, as many researchers in sex research and sexual health promotion have argued (e.g. Richters and Song 1999; Randall and Byers 2003), it is important that studies and surveys of reproductive health are clear in their sexual behaviour terminology since '"sex" is a term that is frequently used, and yet poorly defined' (Randall and Byers 2003). This, as Cameron and Kulick (2003: ix) observe, is a linguistic concern: knowledge and understanding about sex is 'bound up with the language we use to define and talk about it' and so it is no easy matter deciding 'what is or what isn't considered to be "sex"' (ibid.). Questions concerning the conceptualization of sexual activity are particularly important in the context of adolescent health, for research has shown that young people frequently differ in their understanding of what sexual behaviours constitute having sex (Richters and Song 1999). One important consequence of this is that ambiguity over terminology (with its potentially idiosyncratic application) is liable to contribute to concerns about the validity of self-reported sexual behaviour (Randall and Byers 2003) and therefore potentially undermine research into sexual health based on young people's perspectives. Thus, in order to assess their knowledge and beliefs about sex and sexual health, this section aims to investigate how the adolescent contributors to Teenage Health Freak conceptualize 'sex' and 'sex'-related behaviours.

As was noted at the beginning of Section 6.2.1 both Riley (2004) and Manning (1997) considered the construction 'to have sex' a comparatively neutral formula with which to describe sexual activity. Riley, however, also provides a more critical evaluation of the expression, arguing that its descriptive ability is 'grossly inadequate', in that it 'suggests a kind of casual feeding' (2004: 27). From the examples we have considered so far, it would appear that the phrase is used in a commonsensical way by the adolescents such that the exact nature of the event remains unspecified or is taken for granted. However, despite this apparent absence of reflexivity and overt interrogation of the term, it was noted earlier (Table 6.1) that a number of interrogatives collocated with *sex*, the most common by far being *what* (occurring 1,008 times), followed by *how* (672) then *when* (616). Given this range of question forms, then, the adolescents do in fact devote a number of their emails to interrogating and situating queries around sexual behaviours, particularly via interrogative structures headed by *what*, a pronoun which is 'used to request specific information from a general or open-ended possible range' (Carter and McCarthy 2006: 388).

In terms of its position, *what* appears as both a left-side and right-side collocate of the word *sex*. The most dominant positions (566 and 311 instances of *what*, respectively) are at the R1 and L2 positions (one place to right and two places to the left of *sex*). In all the R1 constructions, the interrogative *what* is not part of a phrase or clause containing the word *sex* but fronts questions immediately following the term, as in: 'we had unprotected sex what should i do?'. However, at L2, the position of *what* forms part of a more predictable pattern, featuring as it does in the recurring definition-related question: 'What is sex?' (306 occurrences). Similar definition-probing uses of left-sided *what* are further apparent, with the interrogative being used to pose fundamental questions concerning conceptualizations of sexual activity, such as 'What is oral sex?' (60), 'What is anal sex?' (35), 'What is bum sex?' (5), 'What is gay sex'? (3), 'What is safe sex?' (2), 'What is penetrative sex'? (1), 'What is cyber sex?' (1), 'What is lesbian sex?' (1).

This recurring concern with terminological definitions provokes the questions: what exactly do the users of the Teenage Health Freak website understand by and how are they applying the term in their questions? Since it is not possible to elicit responses from the contributors about their conceptualizations, these inter-related questions are impossible to answer with complete certainty. However, evidence from the corpus provides some indication that the adolescents construe 'sex' as heterosexual penetrative intercourse, echoing the claims commonly made elsewhere in the research literature that, for young people, penile-vaginal intercourse is almost universally included as behaviour that constitutes 'having sex' (Abrams et al. 1990). For example, consideration of the 404 occurrences of *penis* and 119 of *vagina* that collocate with *sex*, reveals that a number of them (51 and 122, respectively) are part of questions in which 'sex' is explicitly defined in terms of heterosexual coital activity, as the following examples typically illustrate:

(22)

Hi Dr. Ann I really need help. . . I almost had sex but it didn't get that far because I wasn't ready. . . but his penis touched the outter part of my vagina like no where near the opening part. . . on top where your hair is. . . . what I'd like to know is can I still get pregnant by that????????We NEVER HAD SEX!!!! His penis never went in me!!! So am I still at risk????

(23)

Worried about not being able to get my boyfriend's penis inside of me during sex

(24)

I thought the vagina was a clear tube. If I push along the bottom my finger can get through – is this where a penis would go during sex? I'm scared my vagina is deformed and i may need an operation to remove the flesh. Please help.

(25)

Please help!! I am worried that my vagina is to tight for sex. I know that they say that when you are truly ready for sex there is no penis in the world that will fit your vagina but mines is very tight! How big should the opening of your vagina be. HELP!!!!

(26)

its my first time haveing sex how do i put my penis inside her vagina sex posessions

(27)

I am worried, EVERY TIME I TRY TO HAVE SEX WITH MY GIRLFRIEND MY PENIS SLIPS OUT!! I HATE IT BUT IM NOT SURE WHETHER IT'S MY PENIS

BEING SMALL OR MY GIRLFRIEND BEING WIDE? WE NEVER USED TO
HAVE THIS PROBLEM BEFORE. PLEASE HELP!

(28)
We came very close to having sex- his penis touched my vagina but didnt penetrate.
A couple of days later my period started but my period had just finished less than
a week earlier. I know your periods can be irregular but I started my periods a long
time ago and they have been regular for years now. Can you explain why they have
started?

Although the term 'sex' potentially includes a multitude of acts (Abrams et al.
1990), here (as examples 22–28 suggest) the concept is purely restricted to
vaginal penetration, with activity outside of this considered to be 'very close to'
or 'almost' having 'sex'. Such descriptions reflect what Jackson (1984) refers to as
the 'coital imperative' – a discourse that constructs coitus – or penetration of the
vagina by the penis – as the quintessence and most natural form of heterosexual
sex, thus prioritizing it over and above other sexual practices (McPhillips
et al. 2001). Although other sexual activities are mentioned that fall short of
penetrative intercourse, these appear to be 'optional extras' (Jackson 1984: 44) –
constructed as marginal or preliminary activities *en route* to sex but not a
substitute for 'real sex' itself.

Further evidence confirming this coital imperative, taking for granted that
intercourse is an essential element of heterosex, can be found in the emails
that describe same-sex and non-coital sexual activities. The term *sex* occurs
17,335 times in total in the corpus. As we noted above a significant proportion
(14,021 or 80 per cent) of these instances appear in *have + sex* constructions.
Consequently, when *sex* appears in the corpus it is typically without qualification
and is therefore unmarked – unmarked in the sense that *oral sex* (503), *anal
sex* (252), *bum sex* (59), *cyber sex* (8) all consist of modifying elements that
expressly mark them as distinct and separate types of sexual behaviours. In the
same way, *gay sex* (88), *lesbian sex* (49), *homo sex* (4) and *gay/lesbian sex* (2)
are used to distinguish them from so-called 'real' heterosexual intercourse. Not
surprisingly, therefore, expressions such as *straight sex* or *heterosexual sex* do not
appear in any of the emails. This supports Baker's (2005: 66) observation that
heterosexual activity is unlikely to be explicitly described since it is 'assumed
to be present anyway'. Conversely, when same-sex sexual activity is referred to,
as the previous forms of modification make evident, it is much more likely to
be explicitly qualified as such than are descriptions of heterosexual penetrative
intercourse. Thus the adolescents' express signalling of gay and lesbian sexual

activities as exceptional and minority cases appear to be part of a cultural imperative that places heterosexual coital sex beyond choice (McPhillips et al. 2001).

Apart from sidelining both non-heterosexual and non-coital sexual activity, a further influence of the coital imperative is its implications for safer sex. For instance, the promotion of condom use as a method of safer sex is liable to reinforce penis-vagina penetration as fundamental to sex (Holland et al. 1992). However, advocating the use of condoms is only one way of promoting safer sex and one that, in excluding and leaving unnamed other ways that young people might be sexually active, 'privileges a risky practice' (Hillier et al. 1998: 16). Thus the promotion of non-coital sex is potentially a viable message for young women and men (McPhillips et al. 2001). Yet as the foregoing corpus analysis has suggested there is evidence that the adolescents are liable to perceive non-intromission practices as being merely peripheral to sex. Consequently, in a context where the prevailing image of sexual activity is 'ineluctably defined by penetration and ejaculation' (Miles 1993: 498), the coital imperative functions as a powerful obstacle to safer sex, since any instruction to practice alternative sexual techniques is likely to be met with incomprehension.

## 6.3  Sex, conception and pregnancy

Table 6.1 revealed that a number of collocates of the keyword *sex* relate to the theme of conception and sexually transmitted infection, for example; *unprotected* (647), *pregnant* (495), *condom* (366). Further collocates, though not appearing in Figure 8, include: *pill* (112), *STI* (64), *protected* (61) and *STD* (15). What is immediately striking about the frequencies of these collocates is the difference between the number of occurrences of *pregnant* and the synonymous terms *STI* and *STD* – a disparity which is reflected throughout the corpus as a whole, with *pregnant* occurring 5,575 times in total and *STI* 604 and *STD* 213 times. Thus in relation to sexual and reproductive health, the adolescents would appear to display significantly greater concern regarding issues relating to conception than sexually transmitted infections.

Issues relating to the theme of pregnancy are a central concern in the emails of the adolescents. The adjective *pregnant* is a keyword compared with both spoken and written general English, as well as being the thirteenth most common lexical item in the AHEC and the most frequent word expressly relating to the subject of conception. Of the 5,575 occurrences of *pregnant,* a significant proportion (65 per cent) appear in constructions in which the term complements copular verbs, of which the most frequent are BE (1847) and GET (1730). Their most regular linguistic contexts of use are shown in Table 6.2 below. The clusters appearing in the table were generated by examining all the concordances which featured BE and GET *pregnant.*

Many of the structures involving either BE or GET convey modal meanings. Modality is realized through the high number of modal verbs, particularly

**Table 6.2** Most common contexts of use in which BE, GET and pregnant figure. Only structures that occur at least 20 times are given

|  | Word | Frequency |
|---|---|---|
| 1 | can you *get* pregnant | 475 |
| 2 | I *am* pregnant | 414 |
| 3 | could I *be* pregnant | 249 |
| 4 | I could *be* pregnant | 199 |
| 5 | I might *be* pregnant | 197 |
| 6 | can I *get* pregnant | 194 |
| 7 | *am* I pregnant | 192 |
| 8 | I may *be* pregnant | 87 |
| 9 | think I *am* pregnant | 65 |
| 10 | if I *am* pregnant | 62 |
| 11 | she *is* pregnant | 56 |
| 12 | can I *be* pregnant | 55 |
| 13 | could I still *be* pregnant | 43 |
| 14 | me *being* pregnant | 34 |
| 15 | possible to *get* pregnant | 30 |
| 16 | if you *are* pregnant | 29 |
| 17 | can I still *get* pregnant | 28 |
| 18 | me *getting* pregnant | 24 |
| 19 | she might *be* pregnant | 21 |
| 20 | chance of getting pregnant | 21 |
| 21 | will I *get* pregnant | 20 |
| 22 | can she *get* pregnant | 20 |

epistemic modals – forms through which the adolescents communicate questions about the probability or possibility of conception, for example, 'Can I get pregnant', 'Could I be pregnant', 'I might be pregnant', etc. Apart from through these core modal verbs, modal meanings are further expressed by other discursive means, which again communicate possibility and mitigate certainty: 'possible to get pregnant', 'if you are pregnant', 'think I am pregnant'. Preference for these particular linguistic forms, therefore, places emphasis on the semantic notions of either 'getting' *pregnant* or on the possibility or likelihood of actually 'being' *pregnant*. Although BE and GET both most commonly occur at the L1 position (i.e. immediately prior to the node word *pregnant*), there is a preference for the lemmatized form *get* (1,424 occurrences as opposed to 1,159 occurrences of *be*). Of the 1,424 occurrences of *get* + *pregnant*, a significant proportion (777) are followed by the description of a circumstance, activity or condition, introduced by a preposition, conjunction or adverb, for example:

| | |
|---|---|
| *get pregnant if* | 261 |
| *get pregnant from* | 196 |
| *get pregnant by* | 113 |
| *get pregnant when* | 38 |
| *get pregnant without* | 33 |
| *get pregnant after* | 30 |
| *get pregnant and* | 23 |
| *get pregnant with* | 23 |
| *get pregnant even* | 18 |
| *get pregnant on* | 17 |
| *get pregnant at* | 13 |
| *get pregnant or* | 12 |

Through these structures the adolescents present a range of questions relating to issues of contraception and pregnancy, which in turn provide insights into their knowledge, attitudes and beliefs about reproductive and sexual health, as the following typical examples illustrate:

(29)
can i get **pregnant if** i have sex just before I start my period or when im on it?

(30)
is it true you are less likely to **get pregnant when** taking the combined contraceptive pill on days 8–14 of taking it?

(31)

i had sex about 3 days ago, my boyfriend used a condom, i was a virgin, people say you **can't get pregnant when** you loose it because u release some blood after you had sex so i would believe that the blood flow would have carried away the semen im confused!!!

(32)

is it possible for me to **get pregnant by** having sex after period finishes?

(33)

my ex bf fingered me about 2 months ago. I havent had a period since and im so scared. I know that you **can get pregnant from** being fingered if the boy has sperm on his hands but i know the sperm has to be quite young. i am rly scared though and dont know what to do.

(34)

Need some help with something that has being confusing me. Can you or can't **you get pregnant when** on the pill, i know you can get STD's and STI's, but i have no idea what the chances are of getting pregnant. Help me please!!!

(35)

Can you still **get pregnant if** the condom bust inside you but your partner didn't cum inside you? Can you get pregnant from precum?

(36)

can you get **pregnant with a** condom on?????????????????

(37)

can you still **get pregnant even if** you are on the morning after pill?

(38)

I am on the pill and i just wanted to know could i still **get pregnant if** i have a period in my 7 day break or if i am bleeding am i definately not?

(39)

I heard you could **get pregnant** by being fingered. is that true?

The concerns here about the risk of 'getting pregnant' broadly fall into three recurring discursive themes: questions about various sexual activities and their relation to pregnancy (32, 33, 39), physiological and biological concerns (29, 31) and issues relating to methods and reliability of contraception (30, 34, 36, 37, 38). On the face of it, these emails would appear to betray a fundamental lack of knowledge regarding reproductive physiology and contraceptive methods.

The breadth of questions posed by the adolescents seemingly attests the extent of their ignorance as well as potential misconceptions of the mechanics of fertility, particularly the timing of the fertile period within the menstrual cycle and the risks and consequences involved in practicing various sexual behaviours. Thus these emails could be interpreted as resonating with much of the literature in the field of adolescent health that has consistently discovered that young people possess sketchy, and erroneous, knowledge about sexual and reproductive health (Kraft 1993; Peremans et al. 2000; Mason 2005).

However, evidence from the corpus permits alternative readings of these teenagers' questions. It is possible to interpret the emails as being provoked by popular myths – the pervasive circulation of folk beliefs and misinformation about reproductive health that regularly attend adolescence. As Peremans et al. (2000: 139) argue, the influence of peers concerning myths about contraception is considerable. Thus the questions can be seen as a means of challenging potential false beliefs and misconceptions circulated by peers that, in some cases, may cause young people unnecessary anxiety or, worse still, encourage them to partake in risky sexual activity. This can be seen explicitly in a number of the emails above in which questions are prefaced by the clause *is it true* or a related expression such as *people say* or *I heard*. The words *true*, *say* and *heard* are all collocates of *pregnant*, occurring 31, 18 and 15 times, respectively, and co-occur with questions relating to the subject of reproduction.

The expressions of which these words are part perform a hedging function, indicating a tentative alignment with the proposition in the question. They serve as 'disclaimers' (Hewitt and Stokes 1975) which, by indicating a 'willingness to receive discrepant information, change opinion . . . or be better informed' (Hewitt and Stokes 1975: 4), legitimate enquiries to the online doctor, warding off, in advance, perceptions of ignorance. These disclaimers therefore signal that the popular beliefs and attributions so interrogated are clearly imputed to others (to some external source), are perceived as questionable, and so are not necessarily shared by the advice-seekers themselves. The nature of these questions suggest, then, that the adolescent enquirers are alert to popular misconceptions and folkways regarding the reproductive process, qualifying the supposed lack of knowledge and ignorance that their questions about the subject might first superficially betray.

Yet even if, biomedically speaking, the adolescents present their knowledge of human sexuality as partial and potentially ill-founded, their submissions can nevertheless be seen as positioning them as concerned and responsible subjects (Harden and Willig 1998) who are eager to identify and avoid partaking in sexual activities liable to put them at risk of pregnancy. Unlike the 'invulnerable' teenagers described elsewhere in the literature of adolescent sexual health (see § 3.1.1), that is, individuals who believe they are unlikely to suffer the negative consequences of their actions, the concerns in the emails above, and those which they more broadly represent, attest an adolescent population who appear to have given some consideration to whether they, or their partners, might conceive as a consequence of sexual activity. Their concern is manifest not only in the topic and frequency of questions relating to contraceptive behaviour but also through linguistic representation: 'to get pregnant' is constructed as a negative state of affairs and therefore an outcome to be avoided. This attitude is communicated directly through the use of loaded and emotive terms which commonly attend emails about the likelihood of conception. For instance, the words *pregnant* and *pregnancy* possess a range of collocates that are freighted with negative meanings and associations such as: *worried* (266), *help* (168), *scared* (128), *risk* (38), *fear* (8), *terrified* (8). Just as patients, when first visiting their GP, commonly present their problems using extreme case formulations and upgrades in order to justify their case (Ruusuvuori 2005: 127), so the adolescents similarly employ loaded terms to signal the extent of their concern and thus present their problems as severe enough to warrant professional help. For example:

(40)

IM **SCARED** MY GIRLFRIEND MITE BE PREGNANT I KNOW THE CONDOM WASNT SPLIT BUT SHE KEEPS BEING SIK SINCE WE HAD SEX SHE WONT TAKE A TEST WAT CAN I DO?

(41)

Hi Dr. Ann, I'm on a birth control pill and am faithful about taking it. However, I was on antibiotics for a UTI for 10 days recently. My boyfriend and I used condoms during those 10 days and are continuing to use them afterwards (for this pill cycle). We have not had any broken/slipped condoms and I think we use them correctly, but I still have this nagging **fear** that I could be pregnant because of what I've heard about antibiotics decreasing the pill's effectiveness. Help!

(42)

hi there my friend had sex and the condom ripped now shes **scared** because she might be pregnant she wont try the pregnant shes toooooo **scared** what shall she do help me please im getting **worried**

(43)

this is a question about pregnancy. I had sex with my boyfriend on october 31 [today is november 15]. We used a condom with spermicide, and he pulled out before he cummed . Is there a high **risk** of pregnancy? Im really **worried**. Please answer!

(44)

I am **worried** about pregnancy, I think I am pregnant because I have missed 2 periods and I am worried. I have talked to my boyfriend but he didn't want to know and then he dumped me. I don't know what to do, I really don't wanna tell my parents as they will flip. Please help me.

(45)

Please can u help me. . . im on the contriceptive pill, but i was 14 hours late taking it. I had sexual contact with my boyfriend during the day i forgot to take it, but have followed the instructions on the package on what to do if you forget. however is there any **risk** of being pregnant?

(46)

a few months agow i was realy stresst out and before i new it i had an unprotecdid sex.but it helpt me calm down.now im **scared** incase im pregnant.

(47)

i **fear** i may be pregnant i am not quite sure who the father is, how can i find out for certain about both my problems??

(48)

I had sex with my boyfriend at the end of March. We used a condom, and it didn't split or slip off, but I am **terrified** of being pregnant. My period was 3 weeks late, so we bought a pregnancy test, and it was negative. I came on my period, and it was normal, but i was still **scared** i was pregnant. My next period was really light, and only 3 days long, and now my next period is late. I'm gettin really bad stomach pains. I've done 5 pregnancy test!!I'm just **scared**! It was my 1st and only time I had sex. Please put my mind at rest!

In many of the above, worries and fears about pregnancy surround the misapplication and/or potential failure of contraceptives, particularly condoms (messages 40, 41, 42, 43, 48). The condom is the most frequently referred to method of contraception in the adolescent health corpus: the words *condom* and *condoms* occur 1,600 and 404, respectively, followed by the *pill* (2,027) and the *morning after pill* (274). Other methods are comparatively rare: for example, *contraceptive injection/implant* occurs only 16 times, *coil* (14), *withdrawal method* (7), *spermicide* (6) and *cap* (5). The condom is unique in that, unlike other forms of birth control, it serves both contraceptive and prophylactic functions. It is widely accepted that, other than abstinence, condom use is the most effective means of preventing sexually transmitted infections, including HIV, and therefore equates with safer sex behaviour (Moore et al. 1996; Moore and Rosenthal 1993; Klein et al. 2001).

The question arises, then, whether the adolescents' lexical preference for the condom over other methods actuates the advice of health educators and service providers that condoms are an essential accessory to sexual intercourse (Moore and Rosenthal 1993). The examples above provide only partial contextual insights into experiences of and attitudes towards the condom; in order to provide a more representative picture, it is necessary to consider use of the term throughout the corpus. Table 6.3 lists the top 20 lexical collocates most commonly associated with the terms *condom* and *condoms* and thus provides an overview of some of the most typical themes and potential discourses relating to condom usage.

What, arguably, is most noticeable about these collocates are the overlapping occurrences of the words *use*, *used* and *using* which are associated with both *condom* and *condoms*. These specific collocates make the lemma USE the most frequent lexical collocate of the lemma CONDOM. The most common underlying structure is USE + *a* + *condom*, as in the phrases *use a condom* (occurring 256 times), *used a condom* (165), *using a condom* (69), while the pattern USE + *condoms* is less frequent: *use condoms* (73), *using condoms* (22), *used condoms* (14).

Examination of the most common realizations (i.e. *use a condom* and *use condoms*) of these two fundamental patterns reveals that the majority (213 or 65 per cent) are part of emails that describe the actual or potential non-use of condoms and concerns about pregnancy. Mention of STIs in relation to condoms makes up 17 per cent (56 occurrences), while the remaining 18 per cent (60 instances) relate to questions concerning why, how and whether to use condoms. The focus on the non-use or absence of condoms in connection with sexual behaviours is also apparent in several other linguistic contexts. For instance, *without a condom* occurs 138 times, *without using a condom* (24), *never used a condom* (4), *didn't wear a condom* (4). Conversely, explicit mention of habitual or consistent condom use is significantly less frequent: *always use a condom* (14), *always used a condom* (8), *use a condom everytime* (2), *usually use condoms* (2), *use condoms all the time* (1). A recurring and central theme of questions about the

**Table 6.3** Collocates, in order of collocational strength (log likelihood), of condom/condoms that appear within five spaces to the left and right of the search terms

| **Condom** | use, sex, used, split, using, boyfriend, wear, splits, pregnant, broke, time, pill, took, pulled, came, wearing, safe, female, fit, times |
|---|---|
| **Condoms** | use, free, get, using, buy, sex, flavoured, pill, used, protest, safe, allergic, different, fit, need, boyfriend, split, female, found, protection |

condom, then, is absence – the actual or hypothetical non-use of condoms during sexual activity. A closer consideration of the structure *use a condom/use condoms* reveals more about the factors that influence condom use and non-use:

(49)

Me and my boyfriend recently had sex and he didnt **use a condom** but i felt really good afterwards, the problem is i dont want to get pregnant but i liked it without a condom. . what do i do?

(50)

if have already started ur periods but ur not on can u still have sex and not **use a condom** and not get pregnant at the same time? plz help thanx

(51)

i'm on the pill so we dont **use condoms** because it feels better is that ok?

(52)

how do u **use a condom**

(53)

i am pregnant! i dotn no how to tell my family or my boyfriend i am scared he will leave me! we did **use a condom** but it obviously split or just didnt work!i dont no how to handle it because i am so young! please help me!

(54)

Is there still a risk of pregnancy if you **use a condom**? Is it safer to use the pill aswell?

(55)

i had sex with my boyfriend for the first time last night, unfortunately, we were so wrapped up in the moment that we didn't **use a condom**. we are not both a little worried that i may be pregnant, and i'm thinking of taking the emergency contraceptive pill. however, i started my period this morning, and one of my friends told me that having sex during your period reduces your chances of getting pregnant due to your body 'shedding' the lining of your uterus. is that even mildly true?

(56)

why should i **use a condom**

As can be seen from even from these examples, the adolescents appear to perceive condoms principally as a means of birth control, not as a means of protection against disease, suggesting that they are more concerned about the risks of unwanted pregnancy than those of acquiring STIs (Kvalem and Traeen 2000). Although there is evidence that condoms are considered a means of prophylaxis, and are sometimes used in this way, concerns over infection consistently appear to be overlooked in light of the overwhelming worry of conception. (Note also how in Table 6.3 *pregnant* and *pill* feature as strong collocates of *condom(s)* while collocates relating to the semantic field of sexually transmitted infection are absent.)

A number of these emails, moreover, demonstrate that condoms are negatively evaluated, constructed variously as an intervention that interferes with sexual pleasure and the spontaneity of intercourse: 'i felt really good afterwards' (49), 'we don't use condoms because it feels better' (51), 'we were so wrapped up in the moment that we didn't use a condom' (55); as a source of ignorance and mystery: 'how do u use a condom?' (52), 'why should i use a condom' (56); and as offering ineffective protection: 'we did use a condom but it obviously split or just didnt work!' (53). These negative attitudes towards condoms perhaps help to explain why these adolescents use them inconsistently or, for some of the young people, not at all. However, as the following further examples of the *use a condom/use condoms* structure highlight, the reasons for failing to use condoms are not always so directly communicated, if provided at all: accounts of risky sexual activity are presented but not the reasons behind it:

(57)
I am 15 years old. And i was in a long term relationship with my boyfriend. We have had sex for a while now but only recently i have found out he **doesn't use condoms**. When he told me this i broke up with him knowing that i might be pregnant. Last week i took a pregnancy test and i am pregnant. . .Please help me?! I dont know who to turn to. I have not even told my friends im realy scared. Shall i abort?

(58)
I had sex with my boyfriend. we **didnt use a condom** but i did take the morning after pill. I did five home pregnancy tests and they all said i was negative and not pregnant but my tummy is growing a bit since we had sex. how reliable are these home pregnancy tests and could i still be pregnant. . i have gotten my period but im still so worried. Please help me im despret

(59)
me and my boyfriend have had sex before but recently i went on top and i bleed after feeling a sharp pain! we **didnt use a condom** and are worried we have got an sti or something

(60)
HI, I HAVE HAD SEX WITH MY BOYFRIENS AND WE USUALL USE CONDOMS AND I AM ON THE PILL BUT I **DIDNT USE A CONDOM** ONCE

AND MY PERIOD WAS A DAY LATE A VERY LIGHT ALSO I FEEL VERY
TIRED AND UNWELL ALL THE TIME, QUEEZY, COULD I BE PREGNANT?

(61)

i had sex and the boy **didnt use a condom** all the clinic's my area are closed so i
can't get the morning after pill what shall i do

(62)

I'm really worried. . . . I had sex for the first time and I'm scared because we used
a condom the first time but he took it off before he came. . . . but he took it out
before he came so he didnt cum inside of me. . . . the second time we **didnt use a
condom at all**. . . . is it possible to get pregnant off of precum? is it possible for guys
to tell when they are about to precum? I'm really scared right now and I dont have
anyone to turn to who wouldnt tell my parents about it. . . . . . . . help me!!

Since mention of the non-application of condoms is framed in terms of both
the potential and actual negative consequences of having sexual intercourse,
these emails imply that the senders are aware that condoms are, and should be,
used for contraception and disease protection. Yet, as has often been described
in adolescent sexual health research, levels of knowledge and information are
not necessarily related to safer sex activity (Kegeles et al. 1988; Moore and
Rosenthal 1993; Turk and Hocking 2005). Knowing the contraceptive and
prophylactic properties of condoms, for example, does not necessarily ensure
a greater intention to use them (Moore and Rosenthal 1993). The notion,
therefore, that there is a rational link between beliefs and sexual behaviour
is a questionable one (Gavey and McPhillips 1999) since this connection
overlooks situational factors that influence sexual activity (Wight 1993a). As
Ingham et al. (1992: 165) observe, a significant impediment that intervenes
between 'what young people "know" and their willingness and/or ability to act
on such "knowledge"' is their perceived invulnerability to sexually transmitted
infections. As the foregoing analysis has shown, foremost in the minds of
adolescents are profound anxieties about the likelihood of conception rather
than concerns about the risk of venereal infection. Consequently, this greater
fear of pregnancy, and preoccupation with avoiding conception, appears to
efface, or at least overshadow, concerns about infection, potentially impeding
safer sex behaviour.

Another important factor regarding safer sex practices is negotiation and
joint decision-making (Hillier et al. 1998). In a number of the emails above (58,
59, 62), the decision to forego using condoms is ostensibly attributed to both

partners. For example, 'we didn't use a condom' (59), 'we didnt use a condom at all' (62). The use of the first-person plural pronoun *we* suggests that agency was jointly shared between both parties. However, there is evidence in the corpus that such outcomes are not quite so unitary, with the decision not to use a condom being made by men, despite the wishes of women for condoms to be worn or at least the possibility of their use to be considered. For instance, the verb phrase *wear a condom* occurs 41 times, of which 6 expressly relate to issues surrounding negotiating condom use. Further concerns about men's reluctance to practice this barrier method include: *he didn't use a condom* (6) *my boyfriend wont use a condom* (2), *he wont use a condom* (2). Tellingly, apart from one instance of *she didn't use a condom*, there are no equivalent formulations communicated from young males' perspectives present in the corpus (i.e. 'My girlfriend/she won't use a condom'), suggesting that, as has been reported elsewhere in the literature, that young men are more likely to believe that responsibility for precautions is not theirs but their partner's (Moore et al. 1996). Although these occurrences are relatively small, if we consider them collectively a vivid picture nevertheless emerges of some of the troubles young women have negotiating condom use:

(63)
hi im a 12 female and wanting sex with my bf he wants to have sex with me bu he says **he wont use a condom** he wants to have a kid with me what shall i do?

(64)
Soon I am going to take the relationship between my boyfriend and I further and we have decided to give each other oral sex. Do I need to ask him to **wear a condom** before I start?

(65)
my boyfriend **wont use a condom**

(66)
am thinking about having sex with my boyfriend who i have being with awhile. i wanted to know if you could just talk me through what happens during sex and would it make a difference if my boyfriend **didn't wear a condom** because i have been told it's much better without?

(67)
I know this sounds silly but how do i give my boyfriend oral sex. I know he should **wear a condom** and i want it all to be safe, but i don't know how to do it. Please help!

(68)

Hia, my bf has just found out ive started my period, im afraid now all he'll want is sex because he can get me knocked up, ive said i would have sex with him but **he wont use a condom** i dont know what to do

(69)

hey i know your busy but i'm really stuck. me and my boyfriend want to have oral sex but i'm confused as to whether he should **wear a condom**? we're both virgins and have had no experience with anybody but eachother, but i'm not sure if you can still catch STI's?

(70)

i had sex on saturday and **he didn't wear a condom** and he didn't pull out. i am not on the pill and didn't go to get the morning after pill. i come on my period on monday, could i still be pregnant?

(71)

The other night my boyfriend asked me to give him a blow job, but i lied and told him i wasnt ready, beacause i have heard that you can catch STI's, and when his last girlfeiend gave him head they didnt use any protection! so i would feel stupid asking him to **wear a condom**! What shall i do?? please help!

These requests for advice vividly illustrate how using condoms is not simply a matter of rational decision-making between two autonomous individuals (as some sexual health promotion strategies would appear to believe) but also a discursive issue. As Holland et al. (1992: 129) observe, the notion that women are simply able to procure the most rational form of protection 'ignores the nature of systematic inequalities in the social relationships between women and men'. These emails evince a range of impedimentary circumstances surrounding sexual encounters and the instigation of condoms, including issues about whether it is right for men to wear condoms (64, 66, 67, 69, 71), concerns about the consequences of not using condoms (70), and the pressure that men put on their partners to take part in unprotected sexual activity (63, 65, 68). For a number of these young women, it is apparent that they have little or no control over the use of condoms.

Perhaps, as Gavey and McPhillips (1999) have argued, it is possible to explain the passivity or lack of agency experienced by some of the women here in terms of their being positioned in a 'discourse of heterosexual romance'. As with the 'male-sex drive discourse' encountered in Section 6.2.1, this discourse similarly constitutes men as the active, leading partners and decision makers, and women as passive recipients of the male sexual advance, which can lead to the restriction of women's agency and problems negotiating safer sex (Gavey and McPhillips 1999: 365). Consequently, for a woman to assume control of the sexual encounter, even to the extent of introducing a condom, 'would involve actions that potentially disrupt her feminine sexual identity, her sense of who she is and how she should feel and act in the context' (Gavey and McPhillips 1999: 365). This uncertainty over how women position themselves during the sexual encounter is apparent in a number of the emails above where the correspondents are pulled between, on the one hand, insisting on, or at least exploring the issue of, condom use (and thereby asserting their own autonomies) and, on the other, submitting to the sexual demands placed upon them by men: 'he wants to have sex with me bu he says he wont use a condom he wants to have a kid with me' (63), 'i would feel stupid asking him to wear a condom!' (71), 'I know he should wear a condom and i want it all to be safe, but i don't know how to do it' (67), 'ive said i would have sex with him but he wont use a condom i don't know what to do' (68).

It is further evident that for these young women their difficulties would also appear to rest in how to confront and verbally negotiate with their partners. This suggests that they may lack, or at least have difficulties in summoning, the means by which to communicate their perspectives and wishes satisfactorily to men, something which assertiveness alone would be unable to make up for (Wilton and Aggleton 1992: 155). These dilemmas thus appear to instantiate claims made by a number of sexual health researchers who have argued that there is no women's language sufficient to verbally communicate with sexual partners (Braun and Kitzinger 2001) or, more specifically, to articulate 'women's ambivalence in situations where they are reluctant to have sexual intercourse, but also reluctant to refuse it' (Holland et al. 1992: 132). It is not surprising therefore that, given their anxieties about how best to respond to the sexual demands placed upon them (for to refuse to engage in unprotected sexual activity with men potentially signifies that they do not love them) that some of the women resort to using what Miles (1993: 502) describes as 'expressions of paralysis', for example, 'What shall i do?? please help!' (71), 'i dont know what to do' (68), 'Please help!' (67), and so on.

These examples, then, serve to highlight the discursive origins of some of the profound difficulties that young women may well encounter trying to practice safer sex, not least the fear of male reprisals in the form of anger and rejection. Thus, as Cameron and Kulick (2003: 154) argue, if there is to be an effective change in young people's behaviour, not only must their knowledge about sex alter but also their norms for expressing it. For, as these young women's testimonies powerfully illustrate, neither informed knowledge about nor intention to practice safer sex are sufficient alone to ensure that adolescents will readily adopt the use of condoms.

## 6.4  Conclusion

In this chapter, the corpus analysis examined a range of themes relating to the topic of sexual health, identifying a number of patterns and commonalities in the adolescents' messages. For instance, the findings revealed how the contributors draw upon a range of common discourses in order to frame their experiences of and concerns about reproductive health. One prevailing discourse the corpus analysis identified was the 'male-sex drive discourse' which constructs women as the objects of the male sexual desire and with this the assumption that sex is something men do to women. Such a discourse was reified through the use of recurring phrasing involving the keywords *sex* and *boyfriend* and the collocate of *sex* WANTS: 'my boyfriend wants sex with me'; 'my boyfriend wants us to have sex', etc. A concern for the contributors who drew upon this discourse was that, though they communicated being under pressure to engage in sexual activity, refusal to do so would severely undermine their present relationships and result in their being rejected by their partners.

With regard to how the contributors conceptualized sexual behaviour, evidence from the corpus indicated that sexual activity, despite potentially constituting a variety of acts, was typically construed as heterosexual penetrative intercourse. The emphasis on this specific act reflects the discourse of the coital imperative which prioritizes heterosexual penetrative sexual intercourse over other forms of physical intimacy, including same-sex sexual activity. One consequence of the dominance of the coital imperative discourse, which puts coital heterosexual sex beyond question, is that it makes it difficult to promote safer sex since other forms of sexual activity are construed as being relatively marginal and peripheral to sex.

In order to make sense of issues relating to reproductive health, the contributors often appeared to work with potential folk beliefs, knowledge gaps and misinformation concerning their sexual health. For instance, it was evident that a number of the adolescents communicated a lack of knowledge concerning reproductive physiology and contraception, emphasizing, in particular, concerns relating to pregnancy over those of sexually transmitted infections. Collocational analysis of the terms *condom* and *condoms* revealed that this form of barrier contraception was commonly associated with the word *use*, or more specifically their potential or none use. Condoms were principally perceived as a form of birth control rather than as an effective form of protection against sexually transmitted diseases.

The corpus analysis, then, exposed the tension between knowledge and behaviour with regard to condom use. Even where there was evidence to suggest that the contributors were aware of the prophylactic properties of condoms, and so desired to use them, a number of adolescents described situational obstructions that impeded their introduction during sexual encounters. Contributors referred to the pressure placed on them by their (typically) male partners not to use condoms, and their fear of rejection if they resisted. On other occasions, they described both physical and emotional coercion by their partners and were thus unable to successfully negotiate condom use. These insights into adolescent sexual health support Bradley-Stevenson and Mumford's contention that the application of condoms 'requires skill and negotiation, which may be tricky at a young age' (2007: 476). The situational factors not expressly accounted for in some sexual health education explain, in part, the tendency for young people to have low adherence to health advice, and why they may be liable to participate in behaviours that put them at risk of potentially life-endangering conditions and illnesses (Wong and Tang 2005: 193).

# Questions about Sexual Transmitted Infections: HIV and AIDS

## 7.1 Introduction: HIV/AIDS stigma and discourse

In this, the second of two chapters exploring sexual health matters, we turn our attention to the theme of STIs, specifically HIV/AIDS. HIV and AIDS are the most commonly referred to sexually transmitted infection-related concerns in the AHEC. Frequency apart, there are other reasons for devoting a chapter to the analysis of questions about HIV/AIDS. Although being in its fourth decade, and despite efforts since the 1990s to naturalize the epidemic (Finn and Sarangi 2009), considerable stigma is still attached to HIV/AIDS (Turan et al. 2011). Stigma, of course, is associated with all STIs, evoking, for instance, notions of promiscuity, uncleanliness and pollution (Lawless et al. 1996: 1371), but only HIV/AIDS, for which a cure is still to be discovered, has a representational link with death, a factor which contributes to its strong emotional connotation (Graffigna and Olson 2009: 790). The stigma attached to HIV/AIDS is further heightened by its association with deviance and irresponsibility: HIV is not only transmitted by sexual activity but also by drug use, specifically the sharing of contaminated needles, an activity which is antisocial, unhygenic and reckless (Lawless et al. 1996: 1371). It is not surprising, therefore, that HIV/AIDS is liable to provoke discriminatory judgements of personal accountability and blame which are stronger than most other clinical conditions (Lawless et al. 1996: 1371).

These extremely powerful social taboos which surround HIV/AIDS make discussing the subject a complicated and hazardous affair, particularly with regard to the disclosure of personal concerns. Talking about HIV/AIDS 'imposes certain constraints upon discourse and text' (Leap 1991: 277). In other words, when speakers address HIV/AIDS concerns, they are liable to use language in unique ways, drawing on, for example, specific discursive structures such as code words and disguised subject references in order to distance themselves from the subject (Leap 1991, 1995). Moreover, individuals' formulations of HIV/AIDS matters are firmly embedded in a social context, mediated by social relationships. People do not simply passively absorb health information about HIV/AIDS. Rather it is actively taken up through interaction with others (Korner 2010: 83) and thus influenced by available social discourses. Accordingly the personal discursive production of knowledge of and beliefs about HIV/AIDS might diverge from official discourses about HIV/AIDS – hence it is vital to examine how lay language interacts with authorized discourses about HIV/AIDS (Higgins and Norton 2010: 8).

## 7.2  Sexually transmitted infections in the AHEC

The adolescent health corpus possesses a range of emails relating to STIs. As noted at the beginning of Section 6.3, the terms *STI*, *STD* and *STI's* are all collocates of the keyword *sex* (appearing 27, 10 and 9 times, respectively), as are terms referring to the specific sexually related infections and conditions of *AIDS* (24), *HIV* (16), *crabs* (10), *thrush* (5), *herpes* (5). However, these provide only a limited picture of the total extent of the adolescents' concerns with STIs. Accordingly Table 7.1 lists the total frequencies of all the STIs and related conditions that appear throughout the corpus as a whole.

The table shows that HIV/AIDS make up 42 per cent of the total number of references to specific STIs, with mention of other infections being comparatively infrequent. It is interesting to speculate whether the preference for AIDS and

**Table 7.1**  Frequencies of sexually transmitted infections and conditions in the AHEC

| Rank | Word | Frequency | % |
|------|------|-----------|---|
| 1 | AIDS | 437 | 28 |
| 2 | HIV | 243 | 16 |
| 3 | thrush | 225 | 15 |
| 4 | crabs | 203 | 13 |
| 5 | genital warts | 146 | 9 |
| 6 | herpes | 132 | 9 |
| 7 | chlamydia | 129 | 8 |
| 8 | gonorrhea | 19 | 1 |
| 9 | syphilis | 14 | 1 |

HIV is in anyway related to the mystery and aura that surround them (Heald 2005). Whatever the case, it is certain that practically all young people are aware of HIV/AIDS (Rosenthal and Moore 1994). Yet awareness, of course, is not the same as informed knowledge and understanding. Given the primacy of HIV and AIDS in the corpus, our analysis centres on the adolescent advice-seekers' knowledge and representation of these two concepts.

### 7.2.1 Conflation and the metaphorization of AIDS and HIV

As noted above, sex, with its established link to HIV/AIDS, carries 'connotations of health risk and death' (Woollett et al. 1998: 370). Although it is not possible to ascertain whether the saliency of HIV/AIDS in the corpus owes to its potential lethality – other well-known STIs, such as chlamydia and gonorrhea, are eminently treatable (Cates 1999) – the lexical preference for *HIV* and *AIDS*, the latter in particular, is revealing. Emails about HIV and AIDS (680 in total) cover a range of themes and issues, including questions relating to HIV/AIDS terminology and conceptual definitions of the terms, concerns regarding transmission and causation, and questions about symptoms and the likelihood of having HIV/AIDS.

As Table 7.1 revealed, *AIDS* appears nearly twice as regularly (437) as *HIV* (243). Of the 437 occurrences of *AIDS*, 27 co-occur with *HIV*, which suggests, on the face of it, that, in these instances, the contributors' appear to be aware of some relationship between the two concepts.

(1)
how does **HIV/AIDS** get passed on

(2)
what happens when a man or women is **hiv and has aids**

(3)
Hello, I had a couple of sexual partners a few years ago but I have now been with my boyfriend for 2 years. I was worried I may have an STI so I went to a clinic and got tested. I tested negative. However, I wasnt tested for **HIV or AIDS**. If I had a serious STI, would they have known after this?I hope you can get back to me

(4)
how are the drug manufacturers involved in the crisis (**HIV/AIDS**)

(5)
Can you be born with **HIV or AIDs** or do have to catch it?

(6)

Dr Ann I've heard alot in the newspapers about **HIV and AIDS** recently and it's gotten me very worried. In the UK how likely is it a) to come across a HIV + girl and b) to become infected from one encounter. I knows theres a chance but should I go crazy worrying about it after an unprotected experience? Many Thanks

(7)

what are the syptoms of **HIV/AIDS**?

(8)

I keep reading all peoples advice and knowledge about **HIV and AIDS** and it keeps saying infected person. How does someone innitally become infected? Please help

(9)

what is **hiv or aids**

In these messages (and in the other remaining messages in which the two terms co-occur), the adolescents clearly distinguish the concepts of HIV and AIDS, conceiving them as separate entities while also, being connected in some way (given the oblique (/) or conjuncts ('and', 'or') that co-ordinate them). However, of the remaining 410 occurrences of *AIDS* in the corpus, 385 (94 per cent) appear in isolation, that is, with no mention of reference to HIV, the virus that can cause AIDS (UNESCO 2006). This in itself, of course, doesn't necessarily mean that the adolescents do not perceive any relation between HIV and AIDS. That said, these AIDS-themed messages potentially expose some revealing insights about the questioners' knowledge and understanding of the syndrome. The following messages are typical of the range of contexts in which *AIDS* in isolation appears. As can be seen, the messages relate to a number of themes, including concerns about the likelihood of contracting of AIDS after taking part in certain kinds of activity, both sexual and non-sexual (10, 15, 16, 18, 20), questions about determining whether one has AIDS and concerns about having AIDS (11, 13), and questions about AIDS-related terminology and the concepts of AIDS (14, 19).

(10)

I want to know the dangers of getting your belly button pierced my freind told me you could die I heard somewhere else you could get **aids**! please help me I don't want to die I read other questions on this website about belly button piercing but it did not answer my question! PLEASE RESPOND!

(11)

how do i know if iv got **aids**

(12)

i know you can't get **AIDS** from saliva, just from blood or semen, but if i give oral sex to a guy without using a condom, can i get **AIDs**? what if i dont swallow?is there a safe way to give head, without the use of a condom?!

(13)

dear dr anne. i am gay and i have given someone a blowjob i think i have **aids** please help

(14)

What does **AIDS** stand for?

(15)

I had sex without using a condom and i am really scared i might be pregnant or might have **aids**

(16)

I received oral sex about 6 months ago, now i am noticing some pimple on my penis, I don't know if it is from masturbating or if it is herpes, could you help me. And also can you get genital warts, or **AIDs** from oral sex.

(17)

i am worried that i have **aids**

(18)

I had unprotected sex with a girl and ejaculated inside her. she has had many sexual partners and im not sure if she had always practiced safe sex. im worried i may have **aids**. is the risk that great?

(19)

What is **aids**?

(20)

i hace a boyfriend who told me hes been injecting drugs. i heared that drug users can get **AIDS** fron using needles is this true what should i tell my friend should i tell anyone else

The absence of any reference to HIV and the foregrounding of AIDS potentially indicate a terminological conflation of the two concepts. This failure to distinguish the two appears to result in a misconception that is liable to have profound consequences in terms of how the adolescents conceive of and understand both HIV and AIDS. For instance, in a number of the examples above, there is the underlying belief that AIDS is a communicable infection, not a syndrome or range of conditions (UNESCO 2006), with its being constructed as, and confused with, a virus or disease, something that can be readily transmitted via sexual activity: 'can you get . . . AIDS from oral sex', 'can you get AIDS by being fingered?', and so forth.

Collapsing the distinction between HIV and AIDS in this way inevitably results in confusion and reinforces 'unrealistic and unfounded fears' (Watney 1989: 184) on the part of the adolescents who may well mistakenly believe themselves to be at risk of AIDS but not HIV. Such extreme worse case scenarios conceive of AIDS as something that sets in immediately after infection, a unitary phenomenon rather than a collection of different medical conditions – beliefs which obscure, if not efface altogether, the existence of HIV, the virus which is indeed infectious. Such erroneous conflation of HIV infection with AIDS (by definition, the stage of HIV infection 'when a person's immune system can no longer cope' (Terrence Higgins Trust 2007: 1)) repeats some of the early and fundamental misconceptions and negative attitudes about AIDS that were widespread during the 1980s and 1990s (Sikand et al. 1996; Helman 2007).

For example, Warwick et al.'s (1988) in-depth study into youth beliefs about AIDS revealed that a significant number of young people, as with many adults, were unable to distinguish between HIV infection and AIDS, a finding which they attributed to the media's consistent failure to provide the public with accurate information. This fundamental misunderstanding (identifying AIDS as a transmissible disease) was 'public terror about "catching" AIDS from people in public places or during casual contact' (Grover 1990: 145). Such beliefs (and the emotive linguistic choices encoding them) prevalent during that period appear to be still evident in the adolescent health emails communicated over 20 years later. For instance, one of the central ways in which adolescents describe becoming infected with HIV or developing AIDS is through use of the lemma CATCH. CATCH occurs 30 times, the second most common verb used to describe HIV/AIDS contraction after GET (125 instances). Although relatively infrequent compared to GET, the use of CATCH as a verb encoding transmission of HIV/AIDS is telling. Whereas GET is less specific in terms of agency, of portraying personal responsibility in acquiring infection, the use of CATCH suggests a particular set of beliefs about disease contraction, implying a more active role for subjects. The use of CATCH therefore is 'revealing of the underlying psychological significance' (Johnson and Murray 1985: 152) of HIV and AIDS, as the following messages attest:

(21)
can you **catch** aids if havnt had sex?

(22)

how do you prevent **catching** h. i. v

(23)

I am very worried about **catching** HIV. Is it possible you can **catch** HIV from a sponge?

(24)

Dear Doctor Ann, I was doing one of your surveys just out of intrest and i was wondering if its true that there is a 1 in 1000 chance of **catching** AIDS if you have unprotected sex with someone who has AIDS, or if this was a mistake in the survey?

(25)

Can you **catch** HIV if you wear a earring that might have been worn by somebody else before?

(26)

out of ten what is the average to **catch** aids when having sex

(27)

Dear Doctor, Can you **catch** HIV from a person who has never had sex with anyone else before and only if any sexual fluids or blood get into your body.?? Please reply

(28)

my boyfriend went down on me the other night and i came on my period while he was. . . ya know. all abit embarassing . but can he **catch** aids, HIV etc etc?????

(29)

Can you be born with HIV or AIDs or do have to **catch** it?

(30)

the other day i had sex without using a condom i am going to take a test but i am also worried i could have **caught** an STI or AIDS or sumthing wot shall i do????!!!!!

(31)

if I have sex with someone with aids without protection can I **catch** it

(32)

is the aids virus difficult to **catch**?

Biber et al. describe 'catch' as an 'activity verb', a verb denoting actions and events 'that could be associated with choice' (1999: 361). As the above emails illustrate, 'catch' implies specific notions of agency on the part of subjects in the sense that it is within their power to avoid or prevent infection, with responsibility framed in terms of both general or universal agency – encoded via the second-person or hypothetical third-person: 'Can you catch. . ', 'how do prevent catching', 'can he catch' (21, 22, 24, 25, 27, 28, 30) – or individual control via the first-person singular pronoun: 'i could have caught . . . ', 'can i catch it', etc. (23, 30, 31). As Johnson and Murray (1985: 152) put it, 'catching' an ailment (as in catching a cold) semantically implies a degree of co-operation: 'We catch things . . . in ways which are our own fault; we blame ourselves – we should have worn galoshes, and should not have sat in a draught'.

This notion of personal agency, of being responsible for becoming infected, communicated through the verbal concept of 'catching', is made further apparent in the adolescents' questions above by their explicitly referring to prevention strategies and the likelihood of their avoiding becoming infected: 'how do you prevent catching h. i. v' (22), 'is the aids virus difficult to catch?' (32), as well as their seeking clarification as to whether specific activities are liable to result in contracting HIV/AIDS – activities which, by implication, should therefore be avoided: 'what is the average to catch aids when having sex' (26), 'if I have sex with someone with aids without protection can i catch it' (31). Here, then, both HIV and AIDS, if the requisite care is taken, are constructed as preventable through individual agency. Infection with HIV is not an inevitable outcome as, alarmingly, some young people have perceived it to be (Warwick et al. 1988).

However, despite the 'measure of participation' (Fleischman 1999: 10) entailed by use of the verb *catch* (and with this the implicit acknowledgement of responsibility on the part of adolescents for maintaining their sexual health), many commentators and public health bodies stress that neither HIV nor AIDS can be 'caught' (Watney 1989: 184). Indeed contemporary health promotion literature produced by standard-setting organizations such as UNESCO continually warns against the use of this verb to signify the way that people might become HIV positive, since it only helps to reproduce myths about HIV and AIDS (UNESCO 2006; IFJ 2006). In the messages above, for example, the various and recurring realizations of the lemma CATCH unavoidably and infelicitously conjure notions of the common cold and influenza, as evidence from the BNC attests. Consulting the 100 million word BNC, a corpus representative of both spoken and written English language as a whole, reveals that, as a transitive verb, *catch* co-occurs with the direct objects *cold* (113), *chill*, *bug* (20) and *colds* (7). As this range of collocates indicates, one typical use of the verb *catch* in general English is to describe the acquiring of relatively minor and common infections – minor in the sense of their being widespread and generally innocuous (though 'bug', of course, potentially relates to more serious infections such as MRSA, the so-called 'super bug' (Knifton 2005)). With regard to more serious viruses and illnesses, other less euphemistic constructions are used in the BNC to describe the process of becoming infected and the onset of morbidity: for example, HIV is typically *contracted, got, acquired*, while AIDS is *got, developed, contracted*. In general English, therefore, the use of *catch* to signify becoming infected is routinely associated with common and relatively trivial infections and illnesses.

Given this association, a corollary of using 'catch' to describe infection with HIV/AIDS is perhaps to assume that the virus can be acquired via casual contact, that it possesses a transmission efficacy similar to both colds and influenza. As such the adolescents' talk of 'catching' HIV/AIDS figuratively transforms the virus from something which is, in reality, difficult to transmit and is only communicable via specific routes (Terrence Higgins Trust 2007: 2) to something highly contagious, liable to spread rapidly and extensively. This underlying metaphor of HIV/AIDS as 'invisible contagion' (Helman 2007: 395) and attacking, engulfing from without (Weiss 1997) also extends to the adolescents' emails about acquiring HIV/AIDS outside of those that explicitly refer to 'catching' the virus. There are, for instance, 12 further questions concerning HIV/AIDS transmission that potentially draw on metaphors of contagion, all of which are reproduced below:

(33)
my girfreind as already kissed a boy and she wants to kiss me would I get **aids**?

(34)
Can you get **aids** from dogs?

(35)
does anyone who has **aids** have to be quarantied

(36)
I think a girl in my class has **aids**. She cut her finger by accident and i got blood on my hand. Does this mean i have aids too?

(37)
can you get **hiv** from somebody who doesn't have it?

(38)
if im zero negatif and so is my boyfriend can a get **aids**?

(39)

Hi im 14 (duh) and i have never had sex or used injection drugs (or drugs at all) but from a toothbrush is it possible for me to get **HIV**?

(40)

Dr Ann, I am food for nats and mosquitoes, they absolutely love me, but if they have bitten someone that has **AIDS**, then I am bitten, Can i be at risk of getting AIDS? Thanks Ann

(41)

can i get **aids** off my cat?

(42)

i know you said that you cant get **hiv** from kissing. but we were told in sex education that if you are french kissing and swallow the persons spit you can get **hiv**. is this true? please tell me bacause i hav been put off kissing now.

As with the emails evoking notions of 'catching' HIV/AIDS, these contributors' concerns similarly communicate fear of contagion and pollution. Here, however, ambiguity over transmission is related to not just physical intimacy with another person (e.g. 33, 42) but a wide and common range of circumstances, with, for instance, toothbrushes, insects and household pets even being potential contaminants and sources of the virus (34, 39, 40, 41). This perceived infiltration by HIV/AIDS of routine aspects of everyday and domestic life resonates with folk beliefs common in the first years of the AIDS epidemic when the virus was believed to be 'transmitted by virtually any contact with an infected person' (Helman 2007: 395). Such a conception draws on the notion of the 'miasma' theory of disease (Lupton 2004), the folk model of infection which conceives of infected persons as being surrounded as if by a miasma or contagious cloud of poisonous bad air liable to cause disease (Helman 2007: 395). In one of the examples above (35), the contributor asks whether people having AIDS need to be 'quarantied' (*sic*), a lexical choice which draws upon this miasmatic discourse, reflecting the belief that people who have acquired HIV are highly infectious and hence need to be isolated from others.

Miasmatic beliefs, as evident in the foregoing emails, where HIV/AIDS is metaphorized as something highly contagious and invisible, are closely related to what is believed to be the imperceptibility of persons with HIV infection, highlighting the difficulty for some young people of being able to identify who might or might not be infected (Warwick et al. 1988: 117). Although, against the total number of emails relating to HIV and AIDS, there are comparatively few questions from the adolescents about potential 'carriers' of the disease, the small number that are present in the corpus, and all reproduced below, expose overlapping attitudes towards to people perceived to be infected with HIV:

(43)

how do you know if a person has **hiv**? can you tell just by looking at them and if they are 16 then will any symptoms be apparent

(44)

is **AIDS** spread by homosexuals

(45)

How do gay men pass on **HIV**

(46)

Why am i surrounded by dirty lesbo's i think they all have **AIDS**!!!!!!!!! I DONT WANT **AIDS**

(47)

i have a boyfriend who told me he's been injecting drugs. i heard that drug users can get **hiv/aids** from using needles. is this true? what should i tell my friend? should i tell anyone else?

(48)

have gay men got more chance of getting **HIV**

(49)

Is there a higher risk of gays getting **HIV/Aids**

The assumption that underlies these messages is that to have HIV/AIDS is to possess characteristics or symptoms that are outwardly evident – and therefore discernible simply 'by looking' (as the contributor in example 43 expressly puts it). In addition, to have HIV/AIDS is to be deemed to belong to certain social categories – for example, to be gay (44, 45, 48, 49) or to be an injecting drug user (47). Accordingly, one way of making sense of these beliefs about HIV/AIDS is to see them as separating those individuals who are assumed to be safe and free of infection (presumably so determined through their clean, asymptomatic appearances) and those whose behaviour constitutes them as a high risk group and thus making it 'understandable' that they should have HIV/AIDS (Warwick et al. 1988: 117). This type of discursive construction draws upon an underlying 'circumscribing discourse' in which the problem of HIV/AIDS is perceived to relate only to a specific segment of the population, construing HIV/AIDS as being a confined and remote problem (Graffigna and Olson 2009: 795).

Yet such a discourse fails to take into the fact that there is no essential relation between HIV and any particular social group or category of people (Watney 1989: 185). Risk of HIV infection arises from what people do, what activities they actually participate in, not from what group they belong to or how they are labelled. Consequently, the social distance which these adolescents appear to place between themselves and the segments of society which they associate with HIV/AIDS potentially engenders complacency on their part (Wight 1993b): infection with HIV is seen as something that happens to others, specifically to the perceived 'high risk' and minority groups first associated with AIDS. Such attitudes imply that, for the adolescents who perceive HIV and AIDS to be principally confined to certain groups, groups from which they are socially distant, the likelihood of their being or becoming infected with HIV is minimal, perhaps even non-existent.

## 7.2.2  What is HIV/AIDS?

Corpus analysis so far has exposed some potential misconceptions and prejudices about HIV and AIDS on the part of some of the adolescent advice-seekers. Of particular significance is the presence of contagion and pollution metaphors which originally gave meaning to the AIDS epidemic when the syndrome was first identified in the early 1980s. The reproduction of such tropes is testament both to their power and depth of cultural internalization, with their continuing use throwing light on the still stigmatizing and alienating nature of AIDS and, especially, those individuals perceived to be at risk of infection (Lupton 2004: 62). The persistence of these metaphors, and the (mis)conceptions they engender, support the notion that AIDS has, unlike any other condition in recent times, produced 'the most extreme and extensive responses' (Nettleton 2006: 60) and so has become, according to Helman (2007: 396), 'the pre-eminent folk illness of the modern age'.

However, not all of the adolescents' emails, in the shape of distorting metaphorical transformations and alarmist folk beliefs, display such hysterical responses to HIV and AIDS. Indeed, as was detailed at the beginning of Section 7.2.1, the most commonly occurring emails about HIV and AIDS in the adolescent health corpus are fundamental questions concerning definitions and terminology, specifically: 'What is HIV/AIDS?' and 'What does HIV/AIDS stand for?' – questions that present no prior assumption about HIV or AIDS and so aim to derive a primary and informed understanding of the concepts. One way of interpreting these open and elementary types of enquiry is, of course, to regard them as emblematic of knowledge deficits and hence ignorance about sexual health.

Yet, equally, such questions might be considered vital responses to a contemporary and potentially life-threatening condition that, despite being in its fourth decade, is still commonly misunderstood (Helman 2007). AIDS did not arrive with its own vocabulary and so right from the start has been the source of linguistic difficulties (Koestenbaum 1990), particularly concerning nomenclature. As Crystal (1997: 120) observes, the unabbreviated form of AIDS is 'so specialized that it is unknown to most people'. Yet even among health experts the acronym poses problems of interpretation: although universally recognized throughout the world (Rafiquzzman 1995), its full meaning has been the source of contestation, variously understood as both 'Acquired Immune Deficiency Syndrome' and 'Acquired Immunodeficiency Syndrome', distinctions which although seemingly insignificant nevertheless demonstrate the semantic instability that surrounds the term. The acronym's irregularity is further heightened by the presence of the head word 'syndrome', which is modified by the ambiguous term 'deficiency'. As the key noun modifier, 'deficiency', somewhat counter-intuitively, indicates absence rather than presence (Leap 1995: 229). Thus, as Callen (1990: 181) argues, if to be AIDS literate involves navigating an epidemic of acronyms and mastering a specialist language of shorthand, then the questions 'What is AIDS?' and 'What does AIDS stand for?' are very well put indeed.

A further issue relating to the 'AIDS' acronym concerns its capitalization, a linguistic issue which has more than mere stylistic implications. Of the 437 occurrences of AIDS in the adolescent health corpus, 351 (80 per cent) appear entirely in lower case format ('aids'). Thus the teenagers' preference is clearly for non-capitalization of the acronym. Since lower case typography is common throughout all areas of the adolescent health corpus, the recurring instances of *aids* more likely owe to the 'lower-case default mentality' of 'Netspeak' (Crystal 2006: 92), and email especially (Baron 2000), rather than to orthographic ignorance of the term. Yet whatever the motivation for this typographical choice, one consequence of lower case usage is to undermine the strict acronymic status of the AIDS acronym and thereby transform it into a word: 'aids'. Given the many meanings that 'aids' possesses, there is the possibility that ambiguity might arise over its use: the question 'What is aids?', for example, potentially relates to a wide range of referents (though given the context of the health website, meanings other than the AIDS syndrome are unlikely).

However, potential ambiguity aside, there is a far more salutary side to this transformation of upper case AIDS to lower case aids. Sontag (2002: 179), writing about the pernicious effect that the metaphorization of AIDS has on people with the syndrome, argues that 'it is highly desirable for a specific dreaded illness to come to seem ordinary' since 'even the disease most fraught with meaning can become just an illness'. As the first major illness to be known as an acronym, and still appearing for the most part in upper case (Allan and Burridge 2006), AIDS continues to be conferred with special linguistic and emotional significance which elevates it above other illnesses. It is therefore possible to regard, in its own small way, the adolescents' wresting AIDS of its upper case status as an act of liberation: an effect, whether consciously intended or not, of suppressing the recriminatory and 'shouting' emphasis of capitalization (Crystal 2006: 37) that only serves to amplify and reinforce the notion that AIDS is 'an accusation' and therefore something 'more than simply a sickness' (Koestenbaum 1990: 164).

At the same time, the adolescents' recurrent use of lower case AIDS more broadly reflects the linguistic process whereby acronyms, once they have been in circulation for a while, shed their capitals and settle down to function as ordinary words (Allan and Burridge 2006: 219). Indeed, in losing the dots it possessed when it was first officially named in 1982 (Callen 1990: 180), the AIDS acronym has already started to undergo the process of de-acronymization to the extent that, in France at least, it now translates as lower case *sida*. Although AIDS is elsewhere not well accepted enough to become lower case *aids* (Allan and Burridge 2006), the adolescents' regular adoption of the form in their emails nevertheless instantiates this process of linguistic change. Even if universal adoption of *aids* is, on its own, unlikely to remove the prejudicial structures that surround AIDS (Koestenbaum 1990: 164), and the extreme and hysterical responses which it generates, such adoption will at least reflect the fact that HIV/AIDS is simply one more infectious disease among many others.

## 7.3 Conclusion

HIV and AIDS are the most commonly mentioned sexually transmitted diseases in the adolescent health emails. This recurring focus on HIV/AIDS over and above other sexual diseases reveals how the contributors are aware of, though at times potentially confused about, HIV/AIDS. The messages reveal the presence of folk beliefs about the way in which HIV/AIDS is transmitted and acquired, folkways that are at odds with received scientific opinion and health education initiative concerning HIV/AIDS.

In some instances, the adolescents' questions and assumptions about HIV/AIDS were redolent of some of the fundamental and hysterically inaccurate beliefs about HIV/AIDS that characterized the AIDS epidemic during the 1980s during which the syndrome was described as a plague or construed as only affecting stigmatized groups of people. Miasmic discourses of HIV/AIDS which construct the infection as being highly contagious, possessing a transmission efficiency similar to that of more common infections, were evident in the contributors' messages in which HIV/AIDS was depicted as something that could be 'caught' (a verb choice in general English typically used to encode contracting common infections). Although use of the lemma CATCH was relatively infrequent compared with the other principal verb used to describe contraction GET, other HIV/AIDS-related messages provided evidence of miasmatic discourses in which HIV is represented as a highly infectious entity. For example, a range of questions from the contributors were premised on the notion that HIV/AIDS could be contracted from merely coming into contact with objects that had been exposed to the virus and that it was even possible to acquire it from somebody that didn't have it in the first place.

What these messages reveal, then, is the abiding presence of miasmatic discourses which run counter to scientific and health information discourses about HIV/AIDS. These professional discourses construct HIV/AIDS as being contractable only through specific activities. However, no matter how dominant this modern understanding of HIV/AIDS is, miasmatic discourses still persist, remaining ineluctably present despite two decades' worth of health education designed to eradicate them and to engender more nuanced understandings of HIV/AIDS.

# Communication of Psychological Distress: Suicide and Self-harm

## 8.1 Approach to analysis

The initial survey of the AHEC as conducted in Chapter 5 identified a range of keywords that clustered under the rubric of mental health and disorder. In particular, a number of key items (reproduced in Table 8.1 below) were found to relate to the themes of depression, self-harm and suicide such that these three areas of focus can be seen as being central to, or at the very least forming a signal component of, the adolescents' mental health concerns.

The recurring focus on these three aspects of mental health may well reflect their increasing prominence in contemporary society. As was discussed in Section 3.2.1, rates of depression and self-injurious behaviours among young people have risen considerably, and are presently among the most common mental health problems likely to be experienced by today's adolescents. Although adolescent mental health is larger than the nexus of emotional disorders and self-injurious behaviour, terms in the corpus relating to other areas of mental illness, such as *schizophrenia* (which occurs only seven times), are comparatively rare. Accordingly, this chapter confines its analysis to the concerns of suicide, self-harm and depression.

Methodologically and analytically, this chapter proceeds along the lines of those laid down in Chapter 6. However, rather than principally situating analysis around one (albeit most prominent) keyword (*sex*), we are here concerned with interrogating a number of signal items in Table 8.1. The main point of departure is again by way of collocational analysis so as to explore the thematic profiles of a number of keywords relating to suicide, self-harm and depression. As with the previous two chapters, analysis centres on the dominant ways in which the adolescents communicate their health concerns, with the specific aim of

**Table 8.1** Frequency and keyness of keywords relating to depression, deliberate self-harm and suicide

| Word | Frequency | Keyness (BNC spoken) | Keyness (BNC written) |
|---|---|---|---|
| 1  depressed | 816 | 2,096.05 | 3159.41 |
| 2  die | 739 | 1,144.02 | 666.84 |
| 3  harm | 407 | 776.12 | 770.66 |
| 4  depression | 318 | 648.06 | 588.75 |
| 5  sad | 239 | 153.96 | 232.07 |
| 6  suicide | 211 | 458.82 | 341.07 |
| 7  cutting | 195 | 62.04 | 79.99 |
| 8  wrists | 98 | 273.96 | 255.82 |
| 9  unhappy | 87 | 93.06 | 34.28 |
| 10  suicidal | 75 | 196.21 | 234.38 |
| 11  overdose | 66 | 187.78 | 166.08 |
| 12  slit | 48 | 112.80 | 74.43 |
| 13  depressants | 33 | 82.24 | 158.99 |
| 14  harmer | 18 | 61.83 | 68.67 |
| 15  prozac | 12 | – | 140.64 |
| 16  selfharm | 9 | 30.92 | 66.62 |

identifying and describing underlying patterns and commonalities in the way the adolescents describe their experiences of self-injury and depression. Focusing on these patterns should, in turn, provide us with an understanding of teenagers' psychological distress from the perspectives of the young people themselves, and, in particular, how they interpret and make sense of such distress.

Although, for the sake of aetiology, it is convenient to overstate the connection between depression, suicide and self-harm (indeed much of the psychiatric literature goes to great lengths to cement the association), to collapse them into one category for analytical convenience is liable to result in passing over the uniqueness and subtleties of these related but nevertheless distinct mental health concerns. Consequently, we shall examine the adolescents' emails concerning suicide, self-harm and depression separately, describing any associations if and when they are made by the adolescents themselves, rather than assuming that such links exist *a priori*.

## 8.2  Adolescent accounts of suicidal behaviour

Table 8.1 above listed a number of keywords used by the Teenage Health Freak contributors to refer to suicide and suicidal behaviour. These included terms that relate *de facto* to the theme of suicide (*suicide, suicidal*), and terms that potentially relate to it (*die, kill, overdose, slit, cutting, wrists,* etc.). The latter expressions, however, are not solely confined to describing suicidal behaviour since they can also refer to deliberate self-harm and concerns unrelated to suicide.

What constitutes suicidal behaviour, naturally, depends on one's conceptualization of suicide. Following Fairbairn (1995), I take suicide and suicidal behaviour to refer to acts by means of which 'an individual autonomously intends and wishes to bring about his [*sic*] death because he wants to be dead or wants to die the death he enacts' (1995: 84). In other words, suicidal acts are characterized by protagonists' intentions in acting rather than by their real or apparent actions (Fairbairn 1998: 156), a definition that relies on 'inward rather than outward facts and events' (Fairbairn 1995: 2). Thus suicidal behaviour is distinguishable from self-harm since, although the intention is to injure oneself deliberately, the act of self-harm is carried out in the 'reasonably secure belief that death will not result' (Kerfoot 2000: 112). Although the outward physical act of self-harm appears to imitate and overlap with suicidal behaviour, the absence of any suicidal intent sets it apart as a separate activity.

Table 8.2 below lists all the potential references to suicide in the adolescent health corpus. Thus terms such as *cut, cuts, cutting, slit,* which in the adolescent health emails predominately relate to self-harm, are excluded (self-harm is considered in the next section), while *overdose,* which also potentially relates to self-harm, is included. As Scott and Powell (1993) observe, self-poisoning tends to be referred to psychiatrists more frequently than obvious and even admitted acts of self-mutilation.

The variety of expressions pertaining to self-destruction reveals how suicide is neither a marginal concern among the adolescents nor one that, on the face of it, is communicated tentatively and obliquely. The relative frequencies of these terms seemingly reveal a preference on the part of adolescents for expressions that are clear, bold references to suicidal behaviour. For example, the item most commonly used by the adolescents to refer to 'suicide' is the word *suicide* itself (211 occurrences), followed by the similarly explicit expressions *want to die* (74), *kill myself* (113) and *suicidal* (75). Significantly less common are metaphorical and more implicit, allusive descriptions of suicide and suicidal

**Table 8.2** Frequency of expressions relating to suicide

| | Word | Frequency |
|---|---|---|
| 1 | suicide | 211 |
| 2 | kill myself | 113 |
| 3 | want to die | 74 |
| 4 | overdose | 66 |
| 5 | suicidal | 75 |
| 6 | end it | 28 |
| 7 | way out | 24 |
| 8 | end my life | 8 |
| 9 | not worth living | 6 |
| 10 | no point to life | 5 |
| 11 | take my life | 3 |
| 12 | do myself in | 1 |

thinking: *end it* (28), *way out* (24), *not worth living* (6), *no point to life* (5), etc. When used by the adolescents, however, these implicit formulations may be used in conjunction with more explicit references to suicidal behaviour, and thus rather than avoiding any direct mention of suicide, and approaching the subject obliquely, they appear to serve a complementary function, qualifying and reinforcing the extent of the contributors' suicidal intent:

- help me I am depressed and am seeking the easy **way out** (suiccide) what can I do
- i am just so depressed the doctor wudnt give me anything and i just fell like i wanna die a keep avin daydreems bout hangin myself or cutting my wrists and i reely feel like doing it i dont no what to do at all i sometimes think the only way to **end it** is to kill myself
- dear dr Ann, i am a 13 year old girl who thinks that my life is **not worth living** any more i cant talk to any one and my mates just laugh at me whenever i tell them that im feeling very very very depressed and i have tried killing myself 3 times and ended up in hospital.
- i sometimes wish i could kill myself i thinik of taking cleaning supplies and drinking them all to **end it**
- dear dr ann, my boyfriend of 9 months got killed in a car crash a week ago and it's his funeral in a couple of day's time. I'm really dreading it. I can't

even begin to explain how devastated i feel. Now that he's gone i feel like there's **no point to life** and i really want to die to be with him.

• every day i think about killing myself. i have had alot of problems at home-my parents split up, my dad is mean, my mum acts like im stupid and my best friend is treating me like crap. i want to die, i've cut myself before and now all i want to know is a painless death method so i can **end it** all.

Here, despite the use of implicit references to suicide, there is no apparent discursive attempt on the part of these contributors to broach the subject indirectly or tentatively, let alone sidestep it altogether. On the contrary, the adolescents unabashedly communicate their suicidal intentions and behaviours, evidently insistent that the full force of their feeling should be apprehended unequivocally by the advice-giver. This bold discursive approach to the issue of suicide differs markedly from previous research (see § 3.2.4) that has described how people who experience self-destructive behaviour are, often through fear of being judged negatively, reluctant to discuss their suicidal ideation with health professionals face-to-face (Simon et al. 2006), or if they do so, are liable to express these feelings in a roundabout and implicit way (Reeves et al. 2004), avoiding the use of exposing terms that expressly relate to suicide such as 'suicide', 'killing myself', 'wanting to die'. The sidestepping of such explicit formulations in favour of euphemistic and indirect linguistic forms supports Lester and Lester's (1971: 164) observation that the 'taboo against taking one's life is so deep that the subject is avoided in speech'.

Although the adolescents' preference appears to be for communicating issues of suicide in a more open and explicit fashion (as the messages above and the terms in Table 8.2 suggest), this does not necessarily mean that the website users are not alert to, and to some extent constrained by, the societal stigmas associated with suicide, and that their attitudes towards and experiences of suicide are profoundly different to other populations. Indeed research indicates that adolescents are keenly aware of the stigma surrounding suicide and so are reluctant to discuss and explore the topic personally with others. Aware of the implications of discussing suicide, particularly the negative responses of adults, 'young people "know" that they are not supposed to admit to suicidal thoughts' (Bourke 2003: 2363).

In order to explore the adolescent contributors' perceptions and personal experiences of suicide more thoroughly, we now turn to examining the common terms in Table 8.2 restored to their original context. Our analysis will concentrate on the term *suicide* itself, for, as described above, this is the word most commonly

**Table 8.3** Lexical collocates of suicide in order of collocational strength

| | Word | Frequency | log-log score |
|---|---|---|---|
| 1 | commit | 50 | 763.25 |
| 2 | committing | 20 | 354.40 |
| 3 | attempted | 12 | 194.17 |
| 4 | think | 25 | 127.54 |
| 5 | tried | 15 | 116.91 |
| 6 | committed | 5 | 80.32 |
| 7 | thinking | 9 | 71.72 |
| 8 | attempt | 5 | 70.78 |
| 9 | feel | 15 | 69.82 |
| 10 | friends | 9 | 41.44 |
| 10 | friend | 7 | 27.35 |

used by the adolescents to describe suicidal ideation. Table 8.3 provides us with a thematic profile of *suicide*, listing the lexical lemmas, in order of collocational strength, that co-occur with this key term (for the sake of space, only the top ten are reproduced).

In terms of its lexical collocates, *suicide* is most commonly associated with the lemma COMMIT, accounting for 36 per cent of the total 211 occurrences of *suicide*. Here the adolescents' lexical preference for the formula COMMIT + *suicide* potentially reflects the 'common usage' (Lebacqz and Englehardt 1980: 672) of the construction in everyday language (for instance, according to the 100 million word BNC, COMMIT is the most common lexical collocate of *suicide* (1,835 occurrences) in general spoken and written English, co-occurring with *suicide* on 415 occasions).

Although COMMIT essentially describes the performance or doing of something (a crime, an error, a suicide), in the context of the adolescents' concerns it predominantly appears as part of constructions that speak of suicide as a contemplated or desired, but nevertheless unrealized, outcome: 'whats the best way to commit suicide', 'I've thought of committing suicide', 'im too cowardly to commit suicide', 'i . . . nearly commited suicide'. This emphasis on suicide contemplation is further borne out by a number of the remaining collocates in Table 8.3 (e.g. THINK, WANT, FEEL) which again relate to descriptions of suicidal desire and ideation rather than to attempted suicide: 'I FEEL LIKE COMMITIN SUICIDE', 'i am always thinking about commiting suicide', 'i want to commit suicide'. However, as the collocates ATTEMPT and TRY indicate, suicidal attempts, although comparatively infrequent, are also a recurring issue for the adolescents. Concerns relating to the subject of suicide thus fall across a spectrum, ranging from seemingly mild considerations of suicide through to attempts at suicide.

Of the 211 occurrences of *suicide*, 156 (74 per cent) are self-featuring (with issues concerning the contributors themselves), while the remaining 55 occurrences (28 per cent) relate to problems experienced by other people (typically a friend of the contributor) but submitted on their behalf: 'what if my friend wants to commit suicide', 'She's tried to commit suicide and I'm worried she might try again'. As the reoccurrence of the collocate *friend* and *friends* in Table 8.3 suggests, the majority of these third-party emails relate to the predicaments of peers, with contributors writing on behalf of their friends, girlfriends and boyfriends.

Although analysis will ultimately have to remain agnostic on this point, it is possible that in these instances, given the acute sensitivity and shame attached to personal disclosures of suicidal ideation and self-injury (Safer 1997), the messages are in fact 'disguised presentations' (Holmes et al. 1997), a phenomenon common in the reporting of sexual abuse, whereby disclosers substitute a third-person referent for the first-person. This observation is neither to refuse to take these emails at face value nor fail to give them serious consideration, but only to recognize the possibility that a number of the adolescents might understandably be seeking to distance themselves from impulses that are socially sanctioned and considered taboo.

Distance, moreover, allows help-seekers to think 'more clearly' about their fears and problems (Driessnack 2006: 1431), with questions of the 'I have a friend who' kind permitting them to gauge others' reactions – questions which serve as a 'dress rehearsal for a perceived life situation' (ibid.). Since there is much fear and shame in admitting to psychological pain (Pembroke 1994), not to mention the difficulty that individuals have putting their feelings into words (Clark 2002), the use of 'as if' questions to broach the subject of suicide are therefore understandable.

Unlike issues of sexual health, where, not infrequently, the sole or principal reason for the adolescents submitting their questions is to obtain information pertaining to a specific knowledge deficit, what, in general, is characteristic of the adolescents' messages concerning suicide is that they appear to serve a different pragmatic function, constituting what some suicidologists refer to as a 'cry of help', 'a way of moving toward or communicating' with someone who it is reasonably expected will be unlikely to deny them assistance (Lester and Lester 1971: 39).

However, to construe the adolescents' suicidal impulses purely as cries for help is to risk dismissing their concerns (which adolescents commonly fear happening (Coggan et al. 1997)), as mere attention seeking and fail to take them seriously (Fullagar 2001: 7). As Williams (2001) argues, suicidal behaviour is never 'merely' anything: it is, first and foremost, a profound 'cry of pain' elicited by the unbearable torment of circumstances with which the individual is unable to cope. It is not surprising, therefore, that the adolescents frequently go to considerable lengths to provide much contextual information surrounding their self-destructive impulses, in particular drawing attention to their life circumstances which they perceive as being an integral part of and inseparable from their psychological pain. For instance, in over half (60 per cent) of the 211 suicide-themed messages in total, the contributors present detailed descriptions of the circumstances that have led to their suicidal impulses (Table 8.4).

As the diversity of themes above suggest, the reasons that predispose young people to ideas of suicide are potentially complex and incorporate a range of psychological, social and psychiatric risk factors. One important observation to make here is that a number of the risk factors presented by the adolescents have been extensively identified and verified in the suicide literature. For example, there appears to be widespread psychiatric agreement that family dysfunction (Herrera et al. 2006; Gilchrist et al. 2007), depression (Kerfoot 2000), school and

**Table 8.4** Reasons cited by adolescents for suicidal impulses

| Predisposing factor | Total | % of Total |
| --- | --- | --- |
| Family dysfunction | 54 | 26 |
| Depression | 33 | 16 |
| Bullying | 25 | 12 |
| School-related pressures | 23 | 11 |
| Problems with peers/partners | 22 | 10 |
| Eating disorder and body image | 20 | 9 |
| Low self-esteem | 9 | 4 |
| Drugs and alcohol | 9 | 4 |
| Stress and anxiety | 6 | 3 |
| Illness/physical complaints | 6 | 3 |
| Sexuality | 5 | 2 |

peer-related problems (Hawton et al. 1982), sexuality (Rubenstein et al. 1998) and eating disorders (Manley and Leichner 2003) are all causes of self-injurious behaviour among adolescents.

Yet the majority of these observations are grounded in medical-based models that emphasize categorization over a concern for the perceptions and experiences of suicidal young people – individuals who cannot be divorced from their social and cultural situations (Bowen and John 2001: 257–8). Categories such as 'family dysfunction' are prone to be narrowly conceptualized and reveal little about how, at least from the perspective of the individual concerned, risk factors may be pathways to suicidal behaviour, and so fail to provide any 'individual psychological understanding' (Leenars et al. 2001: 48) of why that person sought to end their life. As Valente (1994: 322) puts it, the story of suicidal behaviour is depicted in the individuals' words, not in categories and statistics.

In contrast to much of this epidemiological strain of research, the personal insights contained in the adolescent emails afford a more contextualized picture of how risk factors are perceived by, and affect, distressed people themselves. For instance, the following messages involve the most commonly cited reason for suicidal impulses among the adolescents: family dysfunction. In terms of the adolescents' repeatedly foregrounding this predominate influence on their suicidal ideation, these examples are illustrative of the many of the problems experienced in relation to familial conflict.

(1)

Should I contact her? My mum left me and my dad when I was 1, now I'm 14 and she keeps phoneing me asking me to contact her. The problem is I don't want to see her, she hurt me real bad, and she made me think that she didn't love me, and I tried to commit **suicide** once because I was so depressed, now I'm over that, but I'm still very angry, how can I talk to someone that hurt me so bad. I have talked to my dad, he talks to her, and he said that she isn't the big bad wolf I make her out to be, but even though he doesn't see her as the 'big bad wolf' I do, what should I do, I'm so confused

(2)

Hey Dr Ann. I am very depressed, it's not a one off becuase of puberty of anything, i have massive family problems, involving police and jail, its destroying me. I want to die. i can speak to people a litle but i am forbidden to tell people my problem, nothing helps, i excersie alot, eat healthy, and try hard at thing, s but every day i am getting closer to **suicide**, but i dont want to do it, i am only alive becuase of my mum, coping throught it with her, i talk to her aswell (my parents are split up but both are involved) please help. thank you. love depressed teenager

(3)

i'm so confused. i hating life at the moment, i slit my wrists, i smoke pot (not much though), my mum is ill so i have to do loads she well strict too, i don't really know my dad even though i live with him, i think i've just lost my boyfriend, i get told off at school all the time i'm not naughty i just not on the right side of my head teacher, i fat yet i have loads of friends and stuff but sometime si want to die i dont think ill ever commit **suiside** but i almost did when i was younger i hate myself so much sometimes i can't explain how i feel other than totally crap

(4)

When i am very angry i turn to self-harm and sometimes i feel like committing **suicide**. But do you know how i can get rid of the scars i have on my right arm? I feel so lonely. My mum died when i was only 2 or 3 years old. I am in foster care but my foster family never listen to how i feel. I am Anaemic and i would like to know what food contain iron? A few months a go i was feeling depressed and i feel the same way again. PLEASE HELP!!

(5)

I've been feeling really depressed for the last few months, and after the birth of my baby sister, my parents just don't seem to notice i'm there. My attitude has lost me my boyfriend, and my grades have gone from As to Cs at school. It just doesnt feel like life is worth living. Do you think anyone cares if i'm around. What would be the quickest and least painful way to commit **suicide**?

(6)

i am clinically depressed. i have been on medication for a year now, and have received CBT sessions. things seemed to be getting better until i saw a disturbing image on the TV the other night. these usually trigger me off into a panic/depression for a short time, but i got over it after a night's sleep. but 2 days later i got into 2 huge fights with my mum, and she fell out with me and my sister (we were both on the same side). that night i almost took an overdose, which is something i'd never ever considered before. things seem ok now its the next day, but im a christian who doesnt believe in **suicide**. what is going on with me? please help, i cant talk to many people bacause when i get really upset i cant describe what happened very well to some friends.

These examples reveal how, for the adolescents, family dysfunction is a complex and multidimensional concern. The correspondents cite a number of specific problems such as parental absence and neglect, empathic failure, along with physical and emotional conflict within the household. As varied and complex as they are, these issues broadly involve interpersonal and communicative failures associated with intense feelings of confusion, hatred (both self and other directed) and, in particular, hopelessness. As Lester and Lester (1971: 69) observe, the feeling of social helplessness is especially strong in the suicidal adolescent. Here the problem appears to be compounded by the fact that the adolescents are unable to procure advice and support from someone (typically a parent) who is perceived to be a natural source of help: 'Should I contact her? My mum left me. . .The problem is I don't want to see her' (1); 'i am forbidden to tell people my problem' (2), 'my foster family never listen to how i feel' (4). Additionally, the contributors experience difficulties expressing their feelings to others: 'i can't explain how i feel other than totally crap' (3); 'i can't talk to many people because when i get really upset i cant describe what happened' (6).

The interpersonal difficulties and attendant feelings of self-violence described in these emails support the idea that adolescent suicidal behaviour is often associated with a breakdown in communication, with aggression towards the self coming into play when other channels of communication are no longer available (Kerfoot et al. 1995: 560). In their messages, the adolescents speak of their need to be noticed, listened to and understood, needs which are not fulfilled however. In the face of difficult and sometimes desperate life circumstances, and with no other apparent means of communicative redress, suicidal behaviour, for some of the young people, appears to them to be their only option. Indeed so strong is the sense of social isolation, suicide is constructed as being near-inevitable: 'every day i am getting closer to suicide' [2], 'What would be the quickest and least painful way to commit suicide?' [5].

The breakdown in communication experienced by these adolescents serves to emphasize the influence that social context has in determining whether suicidal young people seek help from others and, in particular, whether they access health services. Fullager (2005) argues that contemporary mental health policies privilege a 'calculative rationality' predicated on the understanding that young people suffering emotional turmoil will take the calculated and rational step of seeking help from professional services. Young people are thus situated in an individualized discourse that emphasizes rational choice and personal responsibility for help-seeking. For this reason professionals are liable to ask why young people don't simply talk to someone instead of risking their own lives (Fullagar 2005: 42). It is expected that distressed young people will be able to articulate their emotions to others.

However, as the emails above serve to illustrate, it is not simply a matter of emotionally afflicted individuals rationally seeking help and freely offloading their distress. Situational circumstances prevent or at the very least impede the adolescents from 'rationally' procuring assistance from sources of help including both family members and dedicated services, something which professional discourses fail to take into account or render invisible (Fullagar 2005). For instance, factors such as the adolescents' perceived inability to communicate their emotions effectively, along with concerns that no one will listen to them or empathize with how they feel, appear to serve as obstacles preventing these young people securing emotional support from their family, as well as discouraging them from pursuing outside professional help.

Although familial-interpersonal difficulty looms large in the suicide-themed emails, it is only one of the various reasons cited by the adolescents for their suicidal impulses. Moreover, as the above examples attest, issues relating to family difficulties and tensions are not presented in isolation but occur and interact with other factors such as depression, drug and alcohol abuse and self-harm. The second most common factor associated with suicide is depression (Table 8.4). Although other psychiatrically recognized mental disorders are occasionally cited, such as stress and anxiety (three occurrences), these are significantly less frequent than mention of depressive experiences. As the following examples illustrate, depression is introduced quickly during suicide-themed concerns, commonly cited at the beginning of, and often extending through, the emails. For example:

(7)

hey ann, am [first name] and i think am depressed i cry alot, i've tried **suicide** 3 times but failed and i cut myself when i just cant cope. my doctor no's about the crying and the suicide but the cuts and stuff i cant tell them am ashamed but am on anti-depressents but i dont think they help. . . . do i tell the doctor i need more help or do i just carry on like i have cause when i cut myself i feel better than i did. . . but its not healthy. . . . Help. . .

(8)

Hi, i am seriously depressed and need help. I have tried to kill myself many times since i was 13 with overdoses and alcohol but never works. I hate my life, i hate myself. I always think about death and my funeral, I know at last i will be at peace one day but I dont know if i have the guts to kill myself using more harmful ways. i need help but dont know where to start, i told my teacher tht i had depression and anxiety but didnt tell her about the **suicide**. Please help Ann.

(9)

i suffer from depression. lately i have been thinking about **suicide** really badly, its all i ever think about. i've just been in hospital because of it, i dont want to have these thoughts anymore, i want to be normal. what can i do?

(10)

i feel kinda depressed. . . . dystheria? imnot sure- i havnt been diagnosed. it seems like nothings right and my mates have all deserted me saying im a moody cow. my dad found out that i cut and tried to get a referal for a counsellor with a GP-luckiyl he failed. i dont trus them and i dont want to talk to all those people! theres no-one who understands or will even listen and its getting worse. i was getting a little better these past 3 days or so but is coming back again. . . i hate it, i really do, but im too cowardly to commit **suicide**! i wish i could. . . i dont know what you can say, but please say something if you can. but don't waste thinking time on me, get help for someone who really matters.

(11)

I've spent the past few months getting seriously depressed. I have all the symptoms, am constantly tired can't sleep, can't wake up when I do, always craving food, constant headaches, constant thoughts of **suicide**, cutting my wrists, crying for no apparent reason and loads and loads more and I know I have to stop it as recently I have been getting so close that soon I am just going to fall off the edge

(12)

I just don't know what to do I've been clinically depressed for over a year know and have been on various different meds and have been seeing a psychiatrist, psychologist etc for a year but I actually feel a whole lot worse I did a year ago. I'm being bullied at school about my weight so I stopped eating a few days ago, I have been cutting myself atleast 3 times a day in the last week and My mind is fixated on **suicide**. I know i will attempt again but now realise that 70 tablets is a pathetic amount but the thing is that I don't really want to die I just don't want to feel like this.

Despite the conceptual uncertainty that surrounds the frequently contested notion of 'depression' (Pilgrim and Bentall 1999; Stoppard 2000; Dowrick 2009), the adolescents seem here to have little hesitation embracing the concept of 'depression' and attributing it to themselves. Although individuals who suffer depression are unlikely to describe their experiences in the same way (Bentall 2003), here the adolescents' accounts of depression share characteristics in terms of both textual arrangement and lexical choice. For instance, the opening statements all contain self-diagnostic assertions ('Hi, i am seriously depressed' [8], 'i suffer from depression' [9]) which foreground the theme of depression, a theme or backdrop against which any subsequent mention of suicide needs to be considered. Thus the adolescents discursively construct a link between their experiences of depression and suicide, with mention of depression always preceding that of suicide. Since the connection between depression and suicidal behaviour is commonly recognized by both medical authority and the wider public (Bennett et al. 2003), it is possible to interpret the adolescents' foregrounding and sequencing of their depressive self-attributions as a means of legitimating and/or reinforcing their suicidal impulses.

Secondly, the adolescents couch their depressive experiences in both medico-technical terminology relating to symptomatology, diagnosis and treatments ('I have all the symptoms' [11], 'dystheria? imnot sure- i havnt been diagnosed' [10], 'am on anti-depressants' [7]) and extreme case formulations (Pomerantz 1986) through the use of intensifying adverbs ('seriously depressed', [8, 11] 'clinically depressed' [12]) which serve to emphasize the seriousness and abnormality of their psychological distress, thus distinguishing it from the emotional angst which is traditionally attributed to adolescence (Harrington 1995) or from notions of everyday sadness which are 'interpreted as a normal part of life' (Furedi 2004: 5). As we have seen, moreover, the adolescents also employ the technical term 'depression' itself ('i suffer from depression' [9], 'i told my teacher tht i had depression' [8]), use of which further privileges a medical perspective since attention is drawn to its nominal status – 'depression' as a tangible, 'singular and well-bounded entity' (Mintz 1992: 225), a distinct condition that people 'have' or something that happens to them.

Although filtered through a 'unique biographical frame of reference' (Pilgrim and Bentall 1999: 268), the adolescents clearly draw on medical, professional stances and concepts in order to reconstruct and make sense of their own depressive and suicidal experiences. They therefore situate their emotional turmoil within a medicalized discourse that constructs depression as an illness, something which can be 'diagnosed' or is made manifest by the appearance of 'symptoms'. Recasting their depressive experiences in this way is to normalize their self-destructive impulses: thoughts of suicide are only natural in the face of, and so can be explained by, their depressive disorders. It would appear, then, that these adolescents potentially construct a mechanistic link between mental illness and suicidal behaviour (Bennett et al. 2003). This has implications for the adolescents' 'subjective agency' (Bennett et al. 2003: 297) in terms of how they experience and respond to their emotional distress. For example, since depression is constructed as an overwhelming condition, something that is both hard to resist and not susceptible to personal control ('its getting worse' [10], 'i just cant cope' [7]), it has to be suffered passively. Other than recourse to ineffective psychiatric treatment ('am on anti-depressents but i don't think they help' [7], 'have been seeing a psychiatrist psychologist etc for a year but I actually feel a whole lot worse' [12]), the only other suggested means of relief is suicide, although even this course of action is perceived as being beyond the teenagers' grasp: 'im too cowardly to commit suicide!' [10], 'i've tried suicide 3 times but failed' [12], 'I don't know if i have the guts to kill myself' [8].

Given that their psychological distress is here perceived as a form of deviance or abnormal state of affairs which need to be corrected, the adolescents appear to place themselves in, or at least acknowledge, the sick role (Parsons 1951). A central component of the sick role is that the sick person should want to get better and to this end seek medical treatment (Radley 2004: 11). The desire to get well is clearly evident in the emails: 'i dont want to have these thoughts anymore, i want to be normal' [9], 'I just don't want to feel like this' [12], 'i need help but dont know where to start' [8], and the fact that they have made contact with Dr Ann, as well as, in some instances, already having received treatment, albeit unsuccessfully, is of course further testament to the adolescents actively seeking professional help.

One important consequence of being in the sick role is that the ill are not deemed responsible for their condition (Parsons 1951). Thus, despite their professed inability to take any effective personal action against depression, the adolescents' accounts above can also be seen as constructs that work to absolve them of blame for their psychological distress and hence their suicidal impulses. Indeed the mitigation of self-blame is not only characteristic of these emails that describe depressive experiences and constitute sick role criteria, but also of those that present a range of other reasons for suicidal behaviour as listed in Table 8.4. As the following illustrate:

(13)

Hello Dr Ann, sorry to bother you but I am under so much stress lately. I am 14 and I have a 19 year old boyfriend and we are so inlove, but it's a long distance relationship and I miss him so much that when I cant see him, I get so depressed and I feel like committing **suicide**. Yeah I know I'm only 14, but I don't care I cant help my feelings. Please help, what do I do?

(14)

i keep getting angry. then i get really upset. IT's usually at school. i'v got no really good mates and everyone seems to have given up on me. i'v been smoking, self harming, and nearly commited **suicide** last year i barely sleep and i feel low all the time. If i get upset my mum shouts at me and i don't no what to do. i don't exactly no why i feel like this

(15)

Dear Dr Ann, I want a boyfriend so much you don't understand. Some days when I think about how I am never going to get a boyfriend I feel like commiting **suicide**. Please help me I can't talk to anyone else I feel horrible. My friends are all starting to be noticed by boys but I feel ugly and unwanted. Please help I really beg you or I don't know what I'm going to do.

(16)

Hi I have a really really big problem. I have social anxiety disorder and I cant cope with it anymore. I have attempted **suicide** 3 times b4 but each time I have thrown up the pills. I cant stand going to school every day and it affects my life so much. I went to my doctor but he wasnt any help at al. I really want to tell some one but Im too scared and too shy to approach someone like a teacher. If someone even asks me a question on the bus I go bright red and turn away, I hate myself so much. Pls help, I am so desperate and do feel suicidal sometimes. My family dont know. Please help me.

(17)

I'm 16 years old and i'm underweight! Don't know why i don't put on weight. I have a twin sister and she puts on weight alot easier and i think she's perfect in every way. I'm scared i'm going to get anorexic. I don't know what to do. I hate myself and the way i look. I've even thought of commiting **suicide**. I was bullied about a year ago and i think about it alot, i've lost all self esteem!!!!! Please help me!!!!! Thanks

(18)

ive wrote you alot of things now about me having eating dissorders, depression, and stuff like that. now, to reveal more. . . . lately ive bin having troubles in school, with my family and friends. i've cut myself, attempted **suicide**(more than once), i dont care about myself or my life, and ive drank. but i cant help it. i dont eat, and when i do i exercise or i puke it up. its like i cant be happy with myself. im always ticked off or depressed and people say i not as fun anymore. i always ask my boyfriend and friends what is wrong with me??

As can be seen, suicidal behaviour is related to a number of causes, such as bullying, peer and relationship problems, eating disorders and family difficulties and tensions. Yet what characterizes these accounts is how the adolescents discursively mitigate culpability. Regardless of the reasons given for their self-destructive impulses, their distress is variously described as being unavoidable ('i can't help it' [18], 'I can't help my feelings' [13]), enigmatic and inexplicable ('i don't exactly no why i feel like this' [14], 'i don't no what to do' [17]) as well as being simply far too compelling and indomitable to overcome ('I can't cope with it anymore' [16]). Thus, despite efforts to influence and resist them, suicidal impulses are constructed as being outside the adolescents' personal locus of control.

The foregoing analysis of these suicide-themed messages reveals the typically elaborate and extensive descriptions of external pressures experienced by the advice-seekers. Such accounts seek to justify and explain suicidal impulses, and thus these discursive reasonings seek to give meaning to and to make sense of fraught experiences. Suicide is presented not necessarily as an irrational, senseless act but as a rational action in the face of insufferable circumstances – problems not of the adolescents' own making and problems which have escalated beyond their abilities to endure (Jacobs 1967).

## 8.3  Accounts and descriptions of self-harm

Although not the focus of the analysis, a number of the suicide-themed emails in the previous section featured references to self-harm. Given this co-occurrence, corpus evidence would, to some extent, appear to confirm the established association between suicidal ideation and self-harm (Favazza 1998; Skegg 2005). As was described in Chapter 3, there is considerable overlap between the two, which have been described as existing along a continuum (O'Connor and Sheehy 2000). However, they nevertheless remain separate behaviours motivated by distinct intentions. As Favazza points out, 'whereas a person who truly attempts suicide seeks to end all feelings, a person who self-harms seeks to feel better' (1998: 262). Indeed, on occasions, the adolescents make this distinction explicit themselves, drawing attention to the fact that their acts of self-harm are not suicide attempts but more survival strategies:

- I know **cutting** yourself is a problem for me its an addiction, but what none of my friends understand is im not doing it for **suicide** reasons. I dont want to kill myself. . . i really dont. I cut because i dont know how to deal with my pain so i take it out on my self or ill be really mad so ill just cut.
- please help its getting me down alot im not **suicidal** but i **cut** myself jus 2c if it wud help but it was only once n i no it was stupid so that was in the past. please help.
- i've tried **suicide** 3 times but failed and i **cut** myself when i just can't cope.

- i have lately beenn thinking about **suicide** now i am prettty sure i would never do it as i dont want to die and see no point in it i have been **cutiing** myself and have taled to my guidsance counsellor at school bout this a but i wont tell her about the suicide cuz she might tell my mom and i wouldnt want thta anyway
- Why does **self-harm** make everything better?
- I'm anerexic but i'm not sure. i just want to lose weight for my dancing.
  i also **self-harm** by cutting my arm when i'm angry it calms me down.

As these examples suggest, self-harm has little to do with suicidal intentions: it is, in McAllister's words, 'not about death and dying but about survival and contact' (McAllister 2003: 178). Self-harm is thus significant in and of itself and so needs to be analysed as such. To view self-harm solely through the prism of suicide is to run the risk of treating the two acts as synonymous and hence failing to recognize self-harm for the separate and alternative act that it is (Solomon and Farrand 1996). Table 8.5 lists the most frequent expressions (more than ten occurrences) in the adolescent health corpus that relate to the notion of self-harm.

Although the figure includes a range of self-harming expressions, they are all realizations of the underlying lemmas CUT, SELF-HARM, HARM, of which CUT and SELF-HARM (780 and 373 occurrences, respectively) are by far the most common. Although the act(s) constituting SELF-HARM are unspecified,

**Table 8.5** Frequency of self-harm-related lexis

|   | Word | Frequency |
|---|------|-----------|
| 1 | cut | 502 |
| 2 | self-harm | 199 |
| 3 | cutting | 195 |
| 4 | self-harming | 122 |
| 5 | cuts | 83 |
| 6 | harm | 44 |
| 7 | harming | 24 |
| 8 | self-harmed | 22 |
| 9 | self-harmer | 18 |
| 10 | self-harms | 12 |
| 11 | harms | 11 |

SELF HARM, as we shall see, is not uncommonly synonymous with 'cutting'. Given this distribution of terms, the emphasis is on what Favazza (1996) more broadly describes as 'self-mutilation', the 'deliberate destruction or alteration of one's body tissue' (1996: xviii–xix). The focus on self-mutilation is perhaps not surprising, reflecting as it does the widespread and repetitive nature of skin cutting (Favazza 1998), which is one of the most common forms of self-harm among young people (Suyemoto 1998; Dow 2004), and which has been described as the paradigm for self-harm overall (Burstow 1992: 187).

Lexis relating to, and in the context of, other recognized forms of violent self-injury (Plante 2007), such as deep-scratching, bruising and burning, hair-pulling (trichotillomania) appear infrequently, if at all, e.g. *burn* (6), *burning* (3 occurrences), *burns* (1), *trichotillomania* (5), *scratch* (4), *scratches* (3), *pluck* (2). Also comparatively infrequent are self-labelling terms: *self-harmer* occurs on 18 occasions, while the *cutter* appears only twice. The relatively infrequent use of such self-defining forms is revealing: the adolescents prioritize describing acts of self-harm and thus draw attention to the actions that they, or others, perform, rather than defining themselves in terms of their injurious behaviours. In typically eschewing labels such as *cutter* and *self-harmer*, it is possible that adolescents communicate that they are much more than their self-harming behaviours, that their lives are 'infinitely richer, their stories more complex' (Strong 1998) than these reductive labels suggest.

Although Table 8.5 provides a broad overview of the most common self-harm terms, it tells us little about any recurring themes or issues relating to the adolescents' actual experiences of self-mutilation. To discover what these thematic patterns are about, it is necessary to look at the content words associated with the most commonly occurring self-harm terms in Table 8.5. To this end, Table 8.6 lists the most common lexical items associated with CUT and SELF-HARM, occurring within a span of five sides either side of the search terms.

**Table 8.6**  Lexical collocates (log-log) of the lemmas CUT and SELF-HARM

| CUT | started, stop, help, tried, wrists, self, arm, friend, arms, feel, really, start, years, stopped, parents, depressed, harm, small, get, recently, fat, parents, worried, smoking, blood |
|---|---|
| **SELF-HARM** | help, feel, stop, depressed, think, want, know, friends, started, people, years, tried, really, used, wrists, get, self, arms, really, make, please |

From these signal collocates, a number of central themes surrounding the subject of self-harm can be seen to emerge. For instance, it is associated with notions of time, duration and cycles (*started, start, stop, stopped, years*); with low mood or anxiety (*feel, depressed, worried*); with support and assistance (*help, stop*). Further, self-harm is discussed in relation with family and peers (*parents, friend, friends*) and its physical location and enactment referred to: *wrists, arms, arm, blood.*

As a number of the collocates indicate, stopping and receiving help for injurious behaviour emerge as recurring concerns in relation to self-harm. The following messages, which contain the prominent collocates *help* and *stop*, provide insight into the adolescents' experiences of self-harm and begin to reveal what this behaviour means to them.

(1)

i tried to **stop self harming**, and i managed 5 weeks 3 days, and i failed after that, and i know ive let myself down but alot has happened to me, which made me self harm in the first place, i kept things inside me for soo long, and i have suport from skool which is gr8 help, like i have my mentor and another teacher, but recently ive started to keep it inside me and is making me self harm, and i always wrote to my teacher to say how i felt, but something stops me now, and the alternatives i used instead of **self harming** dont **help** nomore. what can i do. i know i need help, but i cant stay strong with the self harming, so much hurt is inside me and i cant get it out of my head. . please please relpy!!

(2)
i need 2 **cut** myself all the time. **help** me pls

(3)
i have recently started **cutting** myself and i want to **stop** but i cant . ive treid loads of things and im woried becase when ever i get upset i start to visualise myslef cutting . and then when im alone if i havent calmed down i start **cutting** and i want to **stop**. i hate having to hide my **cuts**/scars and i need **help**

(4)
hi i was raped last tursday and the guys in jail and im reall y depressed about it so i **cut** my wrist can u **help** or give me advice?

(5)
i smoke but im not addicted it just makes me better as i get easily stressed. have you got any suggestions for things i could do instead because i started smoking to **stop** myself from **cutting** myself

(6)

Doctor Ann: About a year ago I **stopd cutting** myself with a penknife because I'd managed to sort out my life. The other day my family had a row and I started to **cut** myself using kitchen knives, straight across my wrists. One of my friends saw the scars today, and everyone thinks I'm doing it for attention, but them thinking that partially lead to it anyway – it's a catch 22 situation **Help!**

(7)

a very good friend of mine self-harms! what can i do to **help** her **stop?**

(8)

i got sexually abused when i was 5 till 11 and i cant get over it i've had coucnelling but it doesnt **help** now i just **cut** myself all the time to try and deal with it

(9)

i get called names because i wear glasses and have ginger hair the name calling got so bad i have started to **cut** my wrists please **help**

(10)

i have been **self-harming** myself and i cant **stop** what should i do?

(11)

self harming myself i feel really upset and am **self harming** i know i want to **stop** but cant. I cant talk 2 my parents cos i dont wanna upset them

(12)

i keep going depressed. i get so upset now i start to heave, im on anti depressants but only been on them a week. i spent a year in hopsital to **help** with my **self-harming (cutting)** issues nothing has changed it has got worse and so has my ocd. just want to be happy and not so panicky and insecure

(13)

CAN YOU **HELP** ME WITH **SELF HARMING** OR NOT ITS BEEN GOING ON KNOW FOR 3 YEARS AND I JUST CARNT STOP WHAT SHOULLD I DO CAN YOU HELP ME THANK YOU FROM M R

(14)

I've started slitting my wrists, it's my way of coping with my problems. But now I really want to stop the scars are really ugly!! But i duno how 2 i feel i need to **cut** or I'll break!!! Please **Help!!!**

(15)

i self harm and i whant some **help** i hate my self for ding it it is like a vitiose circle is there any thing u can do that would help me to **stop** i do not whant to talk to my parents

(16)

Dear Dr Ann, I have been cutting and burning my self for about two or three years now and I'm worried that one day it might get too much and I might just snap and do somethign worse to me or someone else. I don't want that to happen. I really need some advice on how to **stop** cutting and burning. It's like and addiction, please help?

(17)

dear doctor i cut myself and i cant **stop** it.

In these messages, self-harm is presented as a response to physical and sexual abuse, verbal bullying, family turmoil, as well as being a reaction to feeling upset and depressed. Self-harm is constructed as a survival mechanism, a form of relief, or as one of the contributors above puts it, a means of trying 'to deal with it' [8], in this instance, the trauma of sexual abuse. Self-harm also appears to serve as a visual manifestation of distress, although the actual physical injuries that speak for those who cut (Ross 1994: 13) can also be a source of disquiet: 'I really want to stop the scars are really ugly!!' [14], 'i hate having to hide my cuts/ scars' [3]. Thus these accounts reveal some of the intolerable circumstances of young people involved in self-harm. Although the act is portrayed as a survival mechanism, a response (no matter how maladaptive) to unbearable emotional distress (Favazza 1996), its consequence of cuts and scars, which have to be treated and hidden from others, only appears to aggravate the predicaments of these young people for whom self-harm is experienced as an effective form of relief. As one of the correspondents succinctly sums up their situation, 'it's a catch 22 situation Help!' [6].

Interestingly, self-harm is also perceived to be an alternative to other risky behaviours. In an effort to avoid it, the adolescents seek participation in other harmful activities, such as smoking. Yet, such is the pull of cutting, these substitutes are comparatively less compelling and so abandoned in favour of self-harming behaviours. As one of the adolescents comments: 'the alternatives i used instead of self harming dont help no more' [1]. The pull of self-harm over and above these other risk behaviours can perhaps be further explained by the broad range of motives presented by the adolescents for the activity. As an antidote to psychological upheaval, self-harm is hard to replace since it can be caused for a number of reasons, while at the same time fulfilling different functions (Horne and Csipke 2009: 656), be it emotional release or articulating (such as visualizing) inexpressible distress.

However, as this last observation helps demonstrate, the theme that most strongly comes through in these messages is the compulsive and habitual quality of self-harm. Here the use of the simple present tense is employed to articulate a general and seemingly permanent state of affairs (Carter and McCarthy 2006: 598). For instance, self-harm is reported as being part of a repetitive, ceaseless cycle ('i just cut myself all the time' [8]) that is liable to escalate, becoming ever more acute: 'I'm worried that one day it [cutting] might get too much' [16], 'it's a catch 22 situation' [6]. Self-harm 'is like a vitiose circle' (*sic*) [15] and is described (again in the simple present) in terms of enduring desire despite there being a wish to cease the activity: 'i *need* 2 cut all the time' [2], 'i want to stop' [3]. Its persistent and cyclic nature is further emphasized by the length of time that the adolescents describe themselves as having taken part in the behaviour. In these instances, the contributors typically use the present perfect progressive to underscore the continuing, present nature of their self-injurious behaviour which commenced some time in the past: 'ITS BEEN GOING ON FOR 3 YEARS' [13], 'I have been cutting and burning myself for about two or three years' [16]. Interestingly, some contributors, using the simple past tense, draw attention to the amount of time during which they have been able to refrain from self-harming themselves, constructions which imply a sense of achievement, albeit a goal which is difficult to sustain: 'i managed 5 weeks and 3 days, and i failed after that' [1]. Formulations such as this evince the addictiveness of self-harm (Whitlock et al. 2006), a theme which we pursue in greater detail shortly.

The foregoing observations raise the question of whether self-harm is, for the adolescents, an addiction along with other risk behaviours, such as drug and alcohol dependency. The question of whether self-harm is actually addictive is a controversial and contested one (Strong 1998; Sutton 2005). Babiker and Arnold, for example, argue that formulating self-harm as an addiction, with all the negative associations that this involves, 'is to pathologize the process unnecessarily' (1997: 134). Yet despite this, the adolescents do appear to construct addict-identities for themselves, drawing consistently on the language of addiction: 'i tried to stop' [1], 'i want to stop but i cant' [3], 'i cant stop' [13], 'is there anything u can do that would help me to stop' [15], etc. In the sense that necessity replaces pleasure and dependency replaces choice (Sutton 2005), the adolescents' constitute their self-harm as addiction, or, at the very least, a behaviour that possesses a strong addictive quality.

The theme of addiction is not alone confined to these examples. In the context of self-harm, the following dependency terms also occur, *addiction* (8), *addicted* (7), *addictive* (7), *habit* (4), *habbit* (3), examples of which appear below. In these messages, the advice-seekers situate themselves in a discourse of addiction, depicting self-harm as an insuperable addiction, a form of addiction not unlike other more commonly known and understood addictions such as smoking, drinking and gambling.

(18)

I know cutting yourself is a problem for me its an **addiction**, but what none of my friends understand is im not doing it for suicide reasons. I dont want to kill myself. . . i really dont. I cut because i dont know how to deal with my pain so i take it out on my self or ill be really mad so ill just cut. Ive cut my wrists alot thats mostly where and my legs abit but i really dont know what to do about my friends or how to stop, i mean to me its not a bad thing i have the power i like that i could kill myself but iam not trying to so to me its not a problem how doi tell other people it feels good and stuff with out them thinking im crazy

(19)

I've got a really bad **habit** because evrytime my mum and I or me and my little sister have an arguement I take the scissors out from under my bed and I start slitting my wrists – I don't know what to do because after every fight I feel so depressed and the only way I feel I can get rid of this this depression is to harm myself

(20)

hey i have had a problem of cutting myself and i am worried that i am **addicted** to it cause whatever i do i cant stop its really anoying cause evrytime i am depressed i cut myself wat can i do?

(21)

Dear Dr Ann, Im am 13 years old, and im depressed & emotional. Many times to express my anger i cut myself. Although my friends get anger & tell me not to do it, i still do it anyways . Why am i cutting myself? And why is it so **addictive?** Sometimes i just cut myself for no reason. From: Depressed Teen

(22)

I have depression, and am on medication and receiving CBT. over the past few months i have developed the **habit** of pulling out the top part of my pubic hair, covering part of my mons area. It looks horrible, and I always want to pull out any growing hairs. but i'm realising it is a problem because im getting obsessed with it and have even cut the skin to get to trapped hairs. i need some advice. Please help, i think this is a form of abuse depression is to harm myself – please give me some advice – I'm really upset and I don't want my mum to find them – it will break her heart

(23)

Self Injury has always been a problem for me. It started that i NEEDED to do it. . . It made alot of the #!@%!! better for along time. I found out one of my best mates had been cutting since she was a kid – and we dediced to give up together. . . It was hard, but I gave up for 10 months before having a set back . I now dont need to do it. . . But i like it. Its a **habbit**. I Like the whole blood thing, feeling the cuts as they heal and looking after them. . . . It sounds werid but what can i do about it?! Some things trigger me off – like My boss at work. Some College teachers. . . Stress and of course arguments – but as I'm not into seein a therapist. . . is there anything else i can do!?

(24)

i self harm and it really helps me in a way i have an **addiction** to it! i cant stop but it feels good when i do it.

(25)

Right. A while back, I started cutting my wrists as a way of releasing anger, and other emotions. I had to tell my best friend and I promised her i would stop. I did, but I've recently started again, but this time, not on my wrists, but my so she doesnt notice. It's sort of becoming an **addiction** and Its all just over the usual teenage unrequited love story. It just feels so good when that razor blade goes into my leg and I feel the nip of pain and the blood slowly trickles out. I need to stop before it gets seriously out of hand. Any tips?

(26)

hey i have had a problem of cutting myself and i am worried that i am **addicted** to it cause whatever i do i cant stop its really anoying cause evrytime i am depressed i cut myself wat can i do?

Again, as with the prior set of examples, these emails illustrate, often graphically, how once a course of self-harm is started, it becomes extremely difficult to stop. Although the addictive and habitual nature of self-harm is clearly constructed as a serious concern, and therefore something that needs to be checked, it is also typically portrayed in contrary terms: cutting is 'not a problem' since it produces positive, even pleasant, effects ('it feels good and stuff' [18], 'It just feels so good when that razor blade goes into my leg [25]), while investing the self-harming adolescent with a substantial degree of 'power' ('i have the power i like that i could kill myself but iam not trying to'). In this instance (the first email in the above sequence), addiction to self-harm is not a 'bad thing'; it is only a problem in the eyes of other people. Cutting is depicted as an acceptable form of relief from intolerable pain and anger, and hence, despite the rational scientific logic which construes it as a non-understandable activity, possesses an 'internal logic' (Harris 2000: 169). The concern at the heart of the problem is responding to the negative perceptions and judgements of others, not the actual behaviour of self-harm itself. In other words, how does one reconcile self-harm, which society considers to be a disturbing and senseless act, with a non-pathological identity? As the contributor puts it, 'how doi tell other people it feels good and stuff with out them thinking im crazy' [18].

To some extent, then, these messages provide evidence of a normalizing discourse. The contributors, in other words, perceive self-harm, or aspects of self-harming behaviour, in positive terms. This normalizing discourse on self-injurious behaviour construes the activity as particularly suited to deal with emotional problems (Franzen and Gotzen 2011: 286). However, orienting to this normalizing discourse reveals tensions and contradictions in the adolescents' self-harming accounts. As can be seen in the examples above, the normalizing discourse clashes with what can be described as a 'pathologizing' discourse (Franzen and Gotzen 2011) whereby self-harm is presented as being morally wrong, a compulsive and deleterious practice.

The compulsive, addictive quality of self-harm has consequences in terms of the adolescents' representations of personal agency and control. Broadly speaking, addiction, be it to self-harm, gambling, alcohol or illicit drugs, is commonly conceived as a constraint on self-motivated actions (Bailey 2005). Thus, as an addiction, self-harm is represented as a behaviour over which the adolescents have little, if any, personal control. There are strong overlaps here with the adolescents' account of suicidal behaviour. As with the irresistible pull of suicidal impulses, self-harm is construed as a behaviour which, although recognized as a maladaptive response to psychological distress (Favazza 1996, 1998), cannot be personally overcome, and to which there are no apparent alternatives: 'whatever i do i can't stop its really annoying' [20], 'the only way I feel I can get rid of this depression is to harm myself' [19], 'is there anything else i can do!?' [23]. The perceived inability to generate personal solutions to problems here is indicative of a state of hopelessness, whether expressly stated or otherwise implied. Hopelessness is considered to be a significant factor influencing self-harming behaviours (Anderson et al. 2004), and as the above examples attest, the adolescents appear to have reached such states of despair where the only way out is by recourse to 'maladaptive problem-solving techniques' (McLaughlin et al. 1996: 524), such as cutting.

Again these accounts of self-harm dependency can, to some extent, be seen as echoing the adolescents' accounts of suicidal behaviour in which they situate themselves within a restricted locus of personal control which, in turn, serves to mitigate culpability for their self-destructive impulses. In constructing self-harm as an overpowering addiction, the adolescents also foreground the minimization of their personal agency. As Davies (1998: 270) observes, a discourse of addiction 'translates behaviour that is "bad" and "purposive" into behaviour that is "non-volitional"'. Therefore if their behaviour is portrayed as being beyond their control, then it is, by extension, also non-culpable: for one, so the logic suggests, cannot be blamed for something over which one has no personal influence.

However, there is a sad irony at work here. Participating in self-harm is widely acknowledged as a means of being in control of one's life and feelings (Babiker and Arnold 1997; Strong 1998; Plante 2007). If individuals are powerless to act against the often appalling life events that have affected and continue to affect them, events that include sexual and physical abuse, family trauma, bullying, as well as the experience of crippling mood disorders such as depression, they are at least still able to exert a degree of control over their own bodies. As the emails in this section have illustrated, self-harm functions as a method of coping with internal rage, grief or pain, relieving the adolescents of oppressive feelings and enabling them, if only momentarily, to 'reclaim something of themselves' (Babiker and Arnold 1997). No matter how destructive their acts of self-harm might appear to them (and to other people), in taking part in such behaviours they are at least able to convert their chaos into calm, powerlessness into control (Favazza 1996).

Yet although self-harm undeniably provides a sense of control, the adolescents, ironically, have very little self-control over their self-mutilation, over this unique form of personal agency. Thus they appear to be in a double-bind, having little control over the only behaviour which, paradoxically, affords them some degree of empowerment over their life situations. Plante (2007: 56) argues that the power to cut or not to cut rests entirely with those who self-harm. However, as the foregoing analysis has broadly demonstrated, the adolescents consistently articulate a contrary view: self-harm is an activity from which it is impossible or at least very difficult to escape. Rather than being a symbol of autonomy and power, as is so commonly described in the mental health literature, self-harm is, at least for these young people, more symbolic of the absence of control, something which exerts a considerable influence over them.

## 8.4 Conclusion

This chapter has examined adolescents' questions relating to self-harm and suicide, providing discourse-based insights into young people's accounts of self-harming behaviours. With regard to suicide-related concerns, a recurring theme involved the issue of communication breakdown. A number of contributors expressed having no outlet available to them through which to disclose their emotional turmoil to other people. These adolescents appeared to be reacting against the prominent individualized discourse that promotes individual responsibility for help-seeking, that one will seek help when one needs it. Such a discourse is premised on the understanding that distressed people will be able to straightforwardly express their concerns and emotions to others. Yet such a discourse does not take into account the situational factors that are liable to present people from seeking advice.

This sense of hopelessness, the inability to help oneself, was also evident in the self-harming messages. Rather than finding another safer outlet for their distress, such as seeking professional psychological support, self-harm was described as an effective means of emotional release and venting uncontainable turmoil. Self-harm was, moreover, presented as act of habituation (indeed an addiction) which was difficult if not impossible to stop. In some instances the adolescents drew upon a normalizing discourse in order to make sense of and justify their self-injurious behaviours: acts such as cutting were construed positively, presenting a quick, if temporary, solution to their problems.

What these messages (both suicide and self-harm-related) have in common is that they reveal the difficulties which the contributors experience communicating their emotional turmoil to other people. Attention to the discursive processes of the contributors revealed that their inability to share concerns with others owed not to any personal disinclination to disclose their feelings (on the contrary they expressed a strong desire to talk with others), but rather to the perceived consequences of doing so: they feared the hostile reactions or indifference of their families; the presumed inability of health providers to respond effectively to their distress; breeches in confidentiality after disclosure (in particular, GPs informing their parents of their problems); and doubts about their own abilities to authentically communicate how they feel.

Professional health services, however, are predicated on the 'rational' assumption that young people experiencing suicidal thoughts, self-harm or depression will seek professional help for their problems, and that, consequently, they will freely and openly express their emotional distress to others (Fullagar 2005). This chapter has demonstrated how social and cultural influences are likely to dissuade adolescents from obtaining emotional support since they may perceive their disclosures as being too exposing and potentially subject to dismissal by advice-givers. Consequently, even if young people are aware that they have a problem for which they need to seek professional help, they may not undertake the so-called logical step of consulting others and so keep their problems dangerously confined to themselves.

# Adolescent Accounts of Depression

## 9.1 Introduction: Defining depression

In the previous chapter, the corpus exploration of both suicide and self-harm related emails revealed that, at every step of the way, depression was a prominent theme in the adolescents' mental health concerns. In the analysis so far, the adolescents have described depression in a variety of ways, constructing it variously as a disease, the course of which inevitably leads to suicidal impulses, and, less specifically, but no less powerfully, as a form of insufferable and inexplicable psychological distress, relief from which is only afforded by extreme and injurious courses of action, such as cutting. Having considered depression through the prism of suicide and self-harm, we now turn our attention to the topic of depression in and of itself.

Table 8.1 in Chapter 8 listed a number of keywords in the AHEC that broadly relate to the subject of depression: *depressed* (816 occurrences), *depression* (318), *sad* (239), *unhappy* (87), *Prozac* (12). As this selection of terms indicates, the adolescents refer to depression in a variety of ways, adopting diction which directly and lexically describe the theme of depression (*depressed* and *depression* itself), as well as more general and less pathologically-freighted terms (*sad, upset*). Given their precise lexical relations with the concept of depression, our analysis in this chapter principally focuses on the keywords *depressed* and *depression*.

Yet, first, a caveat. Although these two terms possess the same lexical root, both springing from the base-form 'depress', it should be recognized that *depression* (and by semantic association its counterpart *depressed*) is not a single, rigid state of being, a uniquely definable condition that is both universally recognized and accepted. 'Depression', as a descriptive noun, is a vague term for a variety of states, a blanket expression that is used widely and with little care (Leader 2007: 7), meaning different things to different people (Wittink et al. 2008).

Applied as it is to a variety of emotional states that can both be seen as normal or pathological (Lewis 1993), 'depression' is thus extremely difficult to pin down and comprehend (Karp 1996).

Moreover, although here is not the place to pursue such a complex debate, it also needs to be observed that the clinical validity of depression has been and continues to be questioned (Bentall 2003; Leader 2007; Dowrick 2009). In western societies at least, 'depression' is clinically determined on the basis of criteria currently set out in the American Medical Association's diagnostic and statistical manual (DMS-IV) and the World Health Organisation's international classification of disease (ICD-10). These diagnostic categories assume, however, that depression, in the sense it refers to a specific and unitary entity, is a valid, objectively defined concept (Dowrick 2009), albeit one that is acknowledged as being variable in severity: for instance, depending on the number of symptoms experienced, one can either be diagnosed with a minor or major depressive episode. Yet even this gradation is statistically arbitrary, with the boundaries between different types of depression being 'far from clear cut' (Busfield 1996: 91).

Therefore we need to be aware that when the adolescents refer to *depression* or being *depressed* they will not necessarily be describing a clearly bounded condition, a unitary state of being. Unlike other conditions that are considered to originate from a biological disorder within the body, and for which a straightforward diagnostic test can be carried out (such as a scan or blood test), there is no comparable procedure, outside of subjective or independent clinical judgement, to determine whether an individual should be diagnosed with depression (Ross and Pam 1995; Stoppard 2000). Thus when the adolescents report themselves as experiencing depressive symptoms, it does not necessarily follow that they will actually be suffering from clinically definable depression. Indeed, as Coyne (1994) argues, when individuals self-report psychological distress, the symptoms so reported may well be conceptually distinct from those consistent with diagnosable depression. Studies that depend on self-report inventories to test questions about clinical depression, for instance, tend to overlook the prevalence of normal unhappiness or 'ersatz depression', mistaking it for pathology (Coyne 1994: 29). As Karp (1996: 28) reminds us, 'Unlike most illnesses that we either do or do not have, everyone feels "depressed" periodically'.

However, the aim of the analysis in this chapter is not diagnostic: it is neither to determine whether the adolescents are actually suffering from depression nor how statistically valid their symptoms are (if and where presented) – whether they can be ticked off against DSM-IV and ICD-10 criteria and be epidemiologically counted. Rather, as experiences of depression are profoundly subjective (Rogers et al. 2001), the corpus analysis is here directed at identifying and describing underlying patterns in the adolescents' mental health experiences. I am interested in what and how the adolescents report as depression and how they themselves make sense of their depressive experiences, without assuming that the symptoms and complaints that they describe necessarily signify an underlying depressive disorder.

## 9.2 The corpus approach to depression-related concerns: How do adolescents formulate their distress?

Although, as noted above, the keywords *depressed* and *depression* derive from the same lexical origin, they possess distinct lexicogrammatical characteristics. For instance, in the context of personal disclosure, *depression*, as a noun, can follow what Lipták and Reintges (2006) refer to as the 'possessive auxiliary' ('I *have* depression'), and the lexical verb 'suffer' ('I *suffer* from depression'), while the participial adjective *depressed* can follow the substantive verb ('I *am* depressed') or a lexical verb such as 'feel' ('I *feel* depressed'). These lexicogrammatical options and distinctions are important, since preference for a certain form encodes a particular version of events which, in turn, will have consequences for how experiences are constructed and understood. For instance, the common statements 'I have [depression]' and 'I am [depressed]' are indications of how individuals situate themselves in relation to their illness experiences, and as such are aspects of an illness discourse that, as well as revealing a self-labelling position, also provides a potential illness explanation (Estroff et al. 1991: 339). Thus the keywords *depressed* and *depression*, in terms of their collocational profiles, require a fine discrimination that accounts for their syntactical profiles.

Accordingly, Table 9.1 lists the most salient collocates that surround *depressed* and *depression*. As with previous collocational analyses I have used the log-likelihood measure to generate collocates since it is liable to yield a mixture of both functional and lexical words (Baker 2006: 102). Considering both the functional and lexical collocates affords a grammatical and semantic profile of *depressed* and *depression*, which serves as a useful point of entry into a subsequent concordance analysis. For reasons of space, I have listed only the 30 most salient collocates.

**Table 9.1** Functional and lexical collocates of 'depressed' and 'depression' in order of overall collocation strength. (The numbers alongside each collocate represent the number of times the word occurs within a span of five words to the left and right of the node.)

---

### *depressed*

---

#### left collocates

---

I (464), and (158), really (169), feel (126), am (169), get (70), feeling (45), so (64), very (56), think (57), I'm (51), been (48), me (77), my (44), is (74), because (17), about (9), the (13), all (6), but (28), always (26), time (8), have (32), to (33), getting (28), making (19), it (39) stressed (16), know (14), she (24)

---

#### right collocates

---

I (313), and (244), really (17), feel (131), am (29), get (23), feeling (4), so (13), very (55), think (16), I'm (12), been (11), me (17), my (83), is (28), because (35), about (52), the (76), all (46), but (43), always (8), time (31), have (52), to (59), getting (3), making (1), it (34), stressed (16), know (26), she (14)

---

### *depression*

---

#### left collocates

---

I (126), and (34), have (61), from (40), suffering (18), of (43), suffer (15), the (38), think (29), for (19), is (52), manic (9), to (22), about (19), my (35), into (15), with (25), anxiety (3), am (15), suffered (6), what (17), has (16), can (16), stress (7), been (11), symptoms (7), severe (5), do (17), got (10), mental (6)

---

#### right collocates

---

I (95), and (94), have (18), from (40), suffering (1), of (11), suffer (1), the (17), think (4), for 13, is (22), manic (6), to (32), about (9), my (18), into (0), with (4), anxiety (6), am (15), suffered (0), what (14), has (6), can (9), stress (3), been (6), symptoms (1), severe (1), do (4), got (10), mental (0)

---

As the high salience of the first-person singular form ('I') in Table 9.1 suggests, both *depressed* and *depression* typically occur within self-featuring emails, detailing the subjective experiences of the writers themselves. Other prominent functional collocates include the words include *and, have, am.* Whereas the collocate *and* varies widely in terms of its position (appearing with similar regularity as a left- and right-sided collocate), both *am* and *have* predominantly feature as left-sided collocates. Consequently, the most common syntactical structures in which *depressed* and *depression* are situated are, respectively, constructions of the type 'I + am + depressed' and 'I + have + depression'.

These two central, underlying syntactic patterns reflect two essential means of representing experience, that of 'being' and 'having' (Fromm 1979), which give rise to both distinct and similar recurring themes and concerns in the adolescents' discourse. If we first consider the existential statement 'I am depressed', what is striking about this form of linguistic representation is that being *depressed* is commonly described as a response to negative personal and social circumstances. Given the range of adverse life events reproduced, the following randomly selected examples (1–7) describe this depressive reaction:

(1)
**I'm really depressed** about splitting up with my boyfriend. I still like him and its getting me down.

(2)
i'm not sure if its because of my spots but i've been a little **depressed** recently. Is this normal?

(3)
i cant stop eating **i am depressed** and stuf but i need to know how to stop eating choclates and crisps as i am forever hungry i may have a habit of eating i dont know wot is wrong with me and i am not fat i am skinny kind of just rite really

(4)
i am not happy with myself i am fat i get bullied and **i am depressed**

(5)
**im so depressed**, i think i am because i cant stop crying and i feel so worthless, im 17 and my boyfriend upsets me alot, ive been with him for 2 years now and he means the world to me, i just feel so sad, my friends and family say its him, but without him id b so much worse than i am now. help!

(6)
**i am just feeling depressed**. i feel so allone, i have fallen out with my best m8 and now she is threating to get some big hard ppl on me at school. i feel like everyone is getting on with their life and i dont matter, my friends and family all rush around with their lives and i m just left here.

(7)

**im depressed**, im very worried about my gcse and always feel like a failure and letting my parents down. i feel guilty and miss my sister very much. what can i do to help all this

These messages fix just as firmly and extensively on the problems encountered by the adolescents as they do on the disclosure and subject of depression itself. De Shazer (1997: 138) observes that the statement 'I am depressed' is akin to instinctively and uncontrollably exclaiming 'Ouch!' after stubbing one's toe in the dark. Indeed being depressed can here be seen as a corollary of adverse circumstances (a stubbing of one's toe in the dark), in particular the difficulty of coping with the pressures of fraught but not uncommon life events. The questions asked of Dr Ann seek not so much medical advice but practical, social instruction, questions that can be interpreted as asking: How do I deal with bereavement? What do I do about my family problems? How can I get a girlfriend? And so on.

The state of being depressed, therefore, is not something that happens without reason. Although, on occasions, the adolescents do in fact reproach themselves, their depressed states are attributed in the main to circumstances over which they have little influence, for instance, the culpable behaviour of others ('my boyfriend upsets me a lot' (example 5), 'i get bullied' (4), 'she is threating to get some big hard ppl on me at school' (6)) or the intractable nature of their bodies ('I am really chubby for ma age and . . . i eat a healthy diet and get loads of exercise' (2), 'i am forever hungry . . . i dont know wot is wrong with me' (3). The implication is that, in the face of such difficulties, these teenagers are powerless or at the very least severely restricted in regulating their emotional well-being, and hence situate themselves in a 'victim discourse' (Drew et al. 1999) where they cannot be held personally and morally accountable for their depressed states of being.

Moreover these emails also convey the sense that the emotional distress so reported is transient in nature. Arising as they do not from a fixed, internal flaw, specifically an essentially ' "weak" or "flawed" personality' (Cornford et al. 2007), but principally from adverse circumstances, it follows that the adolescents' depressed states are impermanent, dependent on changeable social contexts, and hence liable to disappear. Consequently, the depressed experience is constructed as non-pathological. This is potentially further reflected in the adolescents' preference for the underlying construction 'I + am + depressed' over alternative forms of linguistic representation. Whereas 'depressed' is a state that an individual can be, 'depression' is something that 'enters' (Cassell 1976) and transforms the individual into the problem (Fromm 1979: 22). Thus, unlike the sequence 'I have depression' which implies that pathology 'has been incorporated into the self' (Fleischman 1999: 7), to state that 'I am depressed' does not necessarily convey the sense that one's psychological pain is tantamount or akin to illness, pathology that has occupied and become an enlargement of the self. As opposed to 'being depressed', however, when the adolescents report 'having depression', they invariably filter their depressive experiences through a medical perspective, construing their emotional distress as pathological, as in examples 8–14:

(8)

A boy I Instant message just told me **I have manic depression** were everynow and again I feel good then go back to being down again, its very true and I know I need help, but I am scared to ask about it. 'Manic Depression' is something new to me and I dont really understand what it means?!

(9)

**I have depression**, and it seems to be getting worse lately. i've been feeling horrible through most of the hols, and i still do even though im back at school. i was thinking of dropping out, but ive decided to stay and drop a subject instead. but how can i make myself feel better? i'm putting my family through a lot of grief.

(10)

dear Dr Ann, **i have had depression** since the age of 11/12 but have never spoken to anyone about it. recently this depression has got to me more and I have started cuttin my wrist. . . . with some intent to kill myself. At good times i don't want to do this so is there anything i can do to prevent it happening next time i have another long spell of depression?

(11)

**i have depression** alot of people say and they also say im becoming anorexic. my parents are saying i have an eating disorder. ive looked at websites about anorexia and i have alot of the symptoms. such as:always exercising, thinking your fat and afraid to gain weight, getting cold, depression, emotional issues, and some other things. i dont know what to do, i think im fat and overweight, but ive tried not eating and exercising, but it i only lose weight when i don't eat for periods of time. like i usually eat 1 meal a day at the most because my mom forces me to. i want to lose weight fast.

(12)

**i have severe clinical depression.** i feel so bad i dont know what to do anymore. i took an overdose but my friend found out and told someone so now i'm alive.

i wish she never found out, i'd much rather be dead than living a life that i hate. why do i feel like this? why do i have these terrible thoughts?

(13)

dear dr ann **i have got depression** and i self-harm! am i weird? and have you got any advice on what to do when i feel like self-harming?

(14)

I am seriously messed up. **I have had depression** for 18 months now. A year ago, I started councilling but it didn't help. I was also put on Prozac but that did nothing. In January, I was sent to an adolescent acute psychiatric unit, but I didn't feel better and took an overdose of 64 paracetamal. Hospital unfortunately saved me from that, but I tried to drown myself, poison myself, slit my wrists. I also stopped eating. In a month, I only ate 3 yoghurts and 2 fruit salads. Now I am in an eating disorder unit but I only get 3 hours of therapy a week and I used to get 16, so how is such a short amount going to help me recover from depression, especially as I don't get on with my therapist? My depression came before my eating problem I'm 95% sure. I've got to be in the EDU until November at the earliest and that just makes me more depressed. Please help me before I try to take my life again.

Whether having received a prior diagnosis or otherwise, these contributors appear to have no hesitation embracing the technical concept of 'depression'. As with Epstein et al's (2010) research into how distressed people name their turmoil, embracing the term 'depression' evidently communicates something beyond sad, an experience that lexis relating to ordinary sadness are insufficiently able to capture. Using the term 'depression' privileges a medical perspective since attention is drawn to its nominal status: depression is perceived as a discrete, definitive entity which is both possessed by, and appears to possess, the contributors. This idea of possession, communicated metaphorically in the verbal sense of 'having depression', emphasizes the burden of the depressive experience – the debilitating weight that restricts the adolescents' freedom of action (Semino 2008: 182).

Even if some of the writers claim to have undergone medical diagnosis, thereby medicalizing their distress, depression in the foregoing examples clearly takes on an objectified, ontological status, not unlike other disease entities which are popularly conceived of as objects that intrude on the self (Cassell 1976). Note, for example, how depression is described as being an 'it' ('it seems to be getting worse lately' [9]), is something that is 'got', and is an entity that can be precisely and clinically refined through the use of modifiers, thus becoming ever more discrete ('I have manic depression' [8], 'I have severe clinical depression' [12]). Similarly, depression is qualified by the determiner 'this' and on 12 other occasions (though not appearing in the above) by the definite article, both of which are a form of definitive modification which again further confer depression an objective quality: 'recently the depression has got to me more', 'what can i do about the depression', 'what i can take for the depression', etc.

A consequence of these objectifying descriptions is that they impart a sense of depression as being a fixed, continuous lived experience, with little prospect of resolution. In their discourse the adolescents, sometimes very precisely, point up the enduring and persistent element of their depression: 'I have had depression for 18 months now' (14), 'i have had depression since the age of 11/12' (10), 'it seems to be getting worse lately' (9), the latter example suggesting that, owing to the change in intensity, depression has been a stable feature in the contributor's life, although has only recently become severe enough to indicate that something is wrong (thus illustrating the difficulty for people who may have felt for a time that something was wrong with them but, in the absence of a set of triggering feelings, along with the 'conceptual apparatus' to recognize and give them meaning (Karp 1996: 39), have perhaps been unable to make sense of and articulate their trouble).

Both Warner (1976) and Mintz (1992) observe that the English language, which characterizes diseases as nouns rather than verbs, promotes a mind-body dualism which tends to marginalize the role of the individual in their illness experience. This is exemplified, according to Warner (1976: 65), by the possessive construction of 'to have + illness' forms, use of which constrains us from readily accepting that individuals, their personalities, and social and environmental processes are factors in the development of their condition. Considering the above messages, it can be seen that the adolescents do indeed situate themselves passively in relation to their depressive experiences. Depression is not generally attributed to some identifiable and recognizable cause, such as adverse personal and social factors: in these instances 'to have depression' can be translated as being, as Lewis (1993: 27) puts it, 'when you don't have a reason for feeling as you do', for example: 'why do I feel like this? why do i have these terrible thoughts?' (12). Even the messages in which depression is explicitly associated with other problems (principally eating disorders and self-harm) suggest that depression is the pre-eminent, constant condition, preceding other difficulties, such as in examples 11, 13, 14.

It is not surprising, therefore, that when the adolescents speak of 'having depression', they are liable to adopt a clinical perspective, viewing their condition through the lens of medical understanding (although equally, of course, it might be that a clinical perspective encourages the use of such objectifying linguistic features). Whatever the case, it is certainly evident that the adolescents appear to pathologize their complaints, drawing on, as we have seen, a medical register in order to frame their depressive experiences. As was noted in the analysis of suicide-related emails in Chapter 8, where depression was constructed as an illness giving rise to irresistible self-destructive impulses, the pathologizing of depression similarly implies here that the problem is intrinsic and uncontrollable (McLeod 1997), a condition requiring expert clinical intervention so as to rid the self of pathology.

## 9.3  Mitigating expressions of distress: 'I think I have depression'

Telles and Pollack (1981) argue that, in western societies, people adhere to a set of socially sanctioned beliefs that deem illness an internal matter legitimated only by a medical perspective. Accordingly, it is possible to interpret these possessive 'I have depression' constructions, along with the clinical perspectives in which they are situated, as a way of legitimating the adolescents' depression experiences, and hence constructing concerns that justify medical attention. Moreover, these unmitigated possessive constructions (i.e. bald statements shorn of any qualifying modality, for example, 'I could have depression', 'I might have depression', etc.) reveal the readiness with which the diagnostic label of depression is adopted, the certainty with which depression is attributed to the self. In other words, these adolescents appear to have reached a point along their depressive career paths where they have negotiated and come to settle on a particular illness identity for themselves.

However, evidence from the corpus suggests that a number of the adolescents are still exploring and testing out a depression identity. For example, both the key terms *depressed* and *depression* collocate with the word *think* (see Table 9.1). *Think* co-occurs with *depressed* and *depression* 73 and 33 times respectively, appearing predominantly as a left-sided collocate, that is, within a span of five words before *depressed* and *depression*: 'I think I could be depressed', 'I think I have depression', etc. Thus *think* predominantly performs a hedging function, qualifying the self-attribution of psychological disturbance. The following examples (15–20) illustrate the uncertainty associated with depressive attribution:

(15)

**i think i have depression** but i dont want to tell my family about it because the one thing that makes me happy they will take away and make me wear different clothes i dont want that to hapen what should i do?

(16)

**I think i suffer from depression**, *i always feel sad, i am having trouble sleeping*, and i cut myself. some friends do know of my problem, but they prefer me 2 hide it because i bring them all down! and i don't trust anyone else that i know. i can't tell my parents, as they won't understand (my dad believes depression is something peopl make up, and i tend to just argue with my mum)and i am too afraid to see a doctor because i don't know what to tell them, or how to word things. i have tried to find other ways to deal with the way i feel, other than cutting, but the only other option for me is heavy drinking, smoking, and i sometimes experiment with drugs. *i think depression has already caused me to do poorly in my GCSE's* help.

(17)

**I think im depressed** but im not 100% sure, at school people see me confident and bubbly but deep down i feel lonely, fed up, always tired, *upset for no reason* and sometimes i feel like i cant go on or cope and i just cry! am I really depressed? and what should i do now? i dont want to talk to someone about it because everyone just forgets about it like it doesnt matter

(18)

**i think im depressed** i think thats why my grades are slipping but my parents think im just being a drama queen. how do i know for sure if i do?

(19)

Hey Dr Ann, I'm 15 and **i think i am depressed**, I dont have all the symptoms but *I feel really down and just can't feel good*. I used to feel like this all the time but it seemed to go away for about 6 months now it has hit me again I just feel like im useless and i don't want to do anything. Its weird because *I actually have nothing to get stressed about* we aren't doing exams in school and I cant think what could be getting me like this, *Am i depressed and could I get anti-depressents?* what shall I do?

(20)

**I think i am depressed** yet *i dont feel i have a particular reason*, so im kind of stuck with a repeated image of previous self harm, having to wear clothes with sleeves to hide the marks if there is no reason is there no solution?

These messages evince the difficulty experienced by the adolescents in negotiating and validating an illness identity for themselves and, with this, the ambiguity of the depressive state. The contributors cite a range of factors that prevent their being able to establish whether or not they may be suffering from a recognizable depressive disorder and sanction their emotional distress. For example, they are impeded by the scepticism of others towards the clinical validity of depression. As Pollock (2007) observes, many people do not regard the experience of psychological distress as an appropriate topic for medical scrutiny. Consequently the refusal of others to accept depressive illness makes it very difficult to have one's distress socially validated, a predicament that, potentially results in their addressing questions to Dr Ann as a way of securing a medical response and social validity for their problem.

Allied to this bar on legitimization is the prime difficulty of actually communicating one's emotional distress to other people. Depression is perceived as a subject that others are liable to treat as relatively insignificant (perhaps owing again to the scepticism that surrounds its clinical provenance): 'i don't want to talk to someone about it because everyone just forgets about it like it doesnt matter' (17). It is not surprising, then, that depression resists disclosure even to parents: 'i can't tell my parents, as they won't understand' (16). Moreover, since depression is essentially a private, internal experience, it cannot be readily translated into discourse, which in turn serves as an obstacle to seeking medical help: 'i am too afraid to see a doctor because i don't know what to tell them, or how to word things' (16).

Throughout these accounts of depressive experiences, the adolescents can be seen to adopt what Kessler et al. (1999) describe as a 'psychologising' style of symptom presentation, a style in which, rather than normalizing, that is, explaining away one's symptoms, their pathological significance is heightened. Given the various obstacles that prevent the adolescents from resolving their depressive illness identities, the harnessing of such a discourse style can perhaps be seen as a way of anticipating and heading off potential doubt on the part of Dr Ann, pre-empting (no matter how unlikely) the 'pull yourself up by the bootstraps' type of response which construes emotional distress as mere self-indulgence and weakness of character (Switzer et al. 2006).

For example, this psychologizing style – instances of which are italicized in examples 15–20 – is evident in the way in which the adolescents refrain from normalizing their emotional distress, such as attributing it to some environmental irritant: 'i feel . . . upset for no reason' (17), 'i actually have nothing to get stressed about' (19), 'i don't feel i have a particular reason' (20). Although the adolescents do describe situational difficulties in relation to their emotional distress, these appear to be secondary, construed not as giving rise to depression, but rather being caused by it: 'i think i am depressed i think that's why my grades are slipping' (18), 'i think depression has already caused me to do poorly in my GCSE's' (16).

The psychologizing style of discourse is further apparent in the presentation of symptoms which are described in pathological terms such that their significance is difficult to downplay or normalize: 'i always feel sad, i am having trouble sleeping' (16), 'i feel really down and just can't feel good' (19). As with the adolescents who, without mitigation, assert that they 'have depression', these teenagers similarly adopt organic rather than situational explanations for depression. Thus, in spite of their mitigated claims to a depressive identity ('I think i suffer from depression'), these contributors appear, in fact, to be very much on the verge of self-diagnosis, for which, by extension, medical action is the most appropriate solution. As one of the correspondents puts it, 'Am i depressed and could I get anti-depressants?' (19).

## 9.4 The incommunicability of depression: 'Feel and feeling depressed'

The foregoing analysis has shown how the adolescents are liable to conceptualize their emotional distress as depression, assuming medical and individualistic explanations which construe the condition as inherent and pathological. What is also apparent in these emails, and not just those which manifestly adopt this kind of perspective, is the incommunicability of depression, the difficulty of conveying how one feels to other people, of accurately, authentically describing one's inner turmoil. Perhaps the ready adoption of the terms *depressed* and *depression* (convenient tailor made labels for signalling one's distress) can be seen as a way of addressing the inherent difficulty with communication. However, as Karp (1996: 40) argues, even these terms are code words that cannot bridge the chasm of feelings that separate the worlds of those experiencing depression from the worlds of others. In short, there is no language that covers the lived experience of depression (Lewis 1993).

The official 'objective' diagnostic criteria for depressive disorder (both the *Diagnostic and Statistical Manual of Mental Disorders* (DSM-IV) and the *International Statistical Classification of Diseases* (ICD-10)) are similarly inadequate for describing subjective experiences of depression (Stoppard 2000) and, consequently, fail to represent the diversity and idiosyncrasy of human distress (Dundon 2006). As a point of comparison to the adolescents' personal accounts of depression, let us briefly consider these clinical criteria. Table 9.2 below (adapted from Dowrick 2009: 16) summarizes depressive symptoms as currently set out in DSM-IV and ICD-10.

**Table 9.2** Summary of depressive symptoms in DSM-IV and ICD-10

|   | Symptoms of depression | DSM-IV | ICD-10 |
|---|---|---|---|
| 1 | Depressed mood | + | + |
| 2 | Markedly diminished interest or pleasure in activities | + | + |
| 3 | Loss of energy or fatigue | + | + |
| 4 | Loss of confidence or self-esteem | – | + |
| 5 | Unreasonable self-reproach or guilt | + | + |
| 6 | Recurrent thoughts of death or suicide, or any suicidal behaviour | + | + |
| 7 | Diminished ability to think or concentrate | + | + |
| 8 | Psychomotor agitation or retardation | + | + |
| 9 | Insomnia or hypersomnia | + | + |
| 10 | Change in appetite | + | + |

What is immediately noticeable about these diagnostic criteria is their abstract and impersonal quality. Although helping to produce 'an impression of detached scientific objectivity' (Stoppard 2000: 26), the criteria, arguably, are vague and ambiguous. For instance, the intensifier 'markedly' (in the criterion 'markedly diminished interest or pleasure in activities') is open to contestation. As Stoppard (2000) argues, how markedly is 'markedly'? Just how diminished should one's 'interest or pleasure in activities' have to be for it to become statistically significant, a pathological symptom indicative of depression? It is not clear. Likewise, how disabling, if disabling, should one's 'psychomotor agitation or retardation' have to be? (As I write these words, owing to a variety of situational pressures, I am presently experiencing a mild irritability which might vaguely approximate to 'psychomotor agitation', but, in the absence of other symptoms, is this any reliable indication that I am officially, if only partially, experiencing depressive symptomatology and am, by extension, quasi-depressed?)

The limited vocabulary available for describing depression perhaps helps to account for the adolescents' common use of a stock of recurring lexical items to express their emotional distress. So far in our corpus analysis, we have already considered patterns of use surrounding the common terms *depressed*, *depression* and *think*. Other emotion lexis upon which the adolescents regularly draw are *feel* and its related form *feeling*, both of which collocate with *depressed* 257 and 49 times, respectively (see Table 9.1 above). Given that depression is a condition characterized by negative affect and feeling, it is not surprising that these emotion terms are salient in the adolescents' depressive accounts.

Of the 257 occurrences of *feel*, 126 of these appear as left-sided collocates, while 45 of the 49 occurrences of *feeling* also appear before the node *depressed*. The most common position of *feel* and *feeling* is at L2, that is, the penultimate position prior to *depressed*, with the L1 position being occupied by an intensifier, for example 'I feel *so* depressed', 'I'm feeling *really* depressed'. This type of construction (*feel* + intensifier + *depressed*/*feeling* + intensifier + *depressed*) occurs 53 and 23 times, respectively. Thus both *feel* and *feeling* most typically occur with some degree of intensification.

This is a significant communicative pattern. Intensifiers are used to modify adjectives (in this case, the participial adjective *depressed*) by making their meaning stronger and by amplifying and emphasizing their meaning (Stenström 1999: 74). The adolescents' recurring use of intensifiers in the context of feeling depressed can thus be seen as a way of seeking linguistically to do justice to, and perhaps reify, the severity of their depressed states. The following examples can be considered typical examples of how the adolescents employ intensifying constructions:

(21)
i **feel really depressed** and duno what to do i dont want to tell my mum or dad & its all because of like. . problems such as how much i love my girlfriend & i hate myself & i dont feel good or anything! please help i feel weird all the time

(22)
i **feel really depressed**, but im not, i feel like im being left out off things at school but im not, i get that **feeling** like im losing my friends every day, but im not. and i have my sats next week, do you know whats wrong with me? can you help me please?

(23)
i keep getting really bad headaches behind my eyes n im constantly takin nurofen, ive just started college but dnt find it to stressful sometimes i **feel really depressed** and if one little thing happens ill jst cry or want to scream n scream or really hurt something but then sometimes i can be fine could this be related to my headaches

(24)

Things are really getting me down lately i **feel so depressed** and don't know how to snap out of it. I lay awake at night thinking about things

(25)

I **feel really depressed** but do not know why. There is something bugging my brain, making me feel this why but i am not sure what. Can you give me tips on relieving this kind of stress or depression please? Thanks

(26)

Hi Dr Ann, i really need help, im a self harmer, i recently tried to stop and managed 5 weeks and 3 days, but then i failed, and ive made it 2 days so far without it, i know it isnt much, but its trying, but i cant go onw anymore, i feel so empty, i have support from school which is great help, but i just cant cope with life nomore, and i dont want to be here! I dont tlk to my mom or any family, my mom sed i spend to much time feeling sorry formyself which hurt, but she dont know how hard it is, and how everyday is difficult with the self harm, i just **feel so depressed**, i have since decmeber!

(27)

Dear Dr Ann, recently i have been **feeling very depressed** im unhappy about every aspect of my life, I have nothing going for me I'm so unhappy and i'm not sure what to do.

(28)

I'm **feeling really depressed** is self harming normal in these circumstances I was living in a house with some mates at college but I got really depressed and they got sick of me because I wasn't "any fun anymore". I got kicked out, I was gonna fight to stay but as they kicked me out I didn't see a point in staying where I wasn't wanted. Problem is 3 of my mates have been killed in 2 years, and my best mate hung himself 11 months ago, i've had other big problems in my life for the past 7 years, i feel so alone. I've got no one to talk to because I can't get to see a psychiatrist because i've never tried to kill myself, so therefore i'm not deemed to be at significant risk. I'm scared i'm gonna do something really stupid, because I'm missing my mate so much, i often wish i was dead so the pain could end and I could be with my best mate again. But i'm scared of dying, i dunno what to do???!!!

(29)

i am **feeling really depressed** all the time and i dont know what to do about it could you help? i havent told anyone about this because i dont have a best friend and i dont want to talk to my doctor about it this is really upsetting me and i feel that all my friends are just gonna leave me because im just so miserable and upset

(30)

I am **feeling really depressed** at the moment, but I am really happy. I mainly feel depressed because its close to Christmas, and my nanna died last January. No one seems to care about this, because I still haven't grieved properly and its hitting me hard. I want to cry, but if I cry alone, it doesn't help. What should I do?

(31)

For a while now I have been **feeling really depressed**. I want to talk my GP because I think I might have a mental health problem but i'm worried that i might end up talking to a doctor who i know won't understand and I won't be able to say anything to them and I'll get really upset about it. How can i talk to a doctor who I know will understand? Otherwise I can't take the risk.

(32)

im **feeling really depressed** lately and i can't help feeling trapped inside my own mind. i don't know what to do. no one seems to believe me, they all blame it on 'hormones'. I think its more. Please help.

(33)

hi, i really need your help. recently ive been **feeling really depressed** about everything in lfe. i always start crying at the wrong times even when there is absolutely no reasons for it. whats wrong with me, and should i go and see a doctor?

In striving to authentically convey their lived experiences of depression, the adolescents produce highly charged and manneristic descriptions which cannot be very readily resolved into either the DSM-IV or ICD-10 checklists of statistically significant symptoms. These subjective experiential vignettes are rich in idiosyncratic meaning, conveying a level of affect that is absent in the impersonal abstractions of de-contextualized assessment criteria. For example, where official checklists describe 'psychomotor agitation or retardation', the adolescents present a far greater vivid realization of the symptom. As one of the contributors (example 23) puts it, 'if one little thing happens ill just cry or want to scream n scream or really hurt something'. 'Psychomotor agitation' is here stylistically rendered with a graphic vivacity that makes it much more significant than its DSM-IV and ICD-10 equivalents, and as such goes way beyond, and thus bears little resemblance to, the text books' definition.

As with other research exploring young people's accounts of psychological distress (e.g. Wisdom and Green 2004; Dundon 2006), these emails reveal how the adolescents' experiences of depression admit much more than the clinical formulations of the disorder. The adolescents describe themselves as feeling depressed regardless of whether their symptoms and behaviours match those of the official criteria. For example, other than in relation to dementia and factitious disorder, self-harm does not feature in DSM-IV. Although 'recurrent thoughts of death or suicide, or any suicidal behaviour' are a customary symptom of depression, suicidal thoughts and behaviour, as the previous chapter has shown, are often distinct from acts of self-harm. For the adolescents, part of their unique experience of depression often involves the intimately associated behaviour of self-harm: 'I'm feeling really depressed is self harming normal in these circumstances' [28], 'everyday is difficult with the self harm, i just feel so depressed' [26].

Furthermore, unlike the precise and orderly statistical requirements of DSM and ICD approaches, which assume that depression, in a detached objective fashion, can be unambiguously identified in an individual, the adolescents' accounts of depression are chaotic, bewildering and, sometimes, contradictory. They are testament to the complexity and diffuseness of their depressive experiences, and the linguistic struggle to recount them. For instance:

> **i feel really depressed**, but im not, i feel like im being left out off things at school but im not, i get that feeling like im losing my friends every day, but im not. and i have my sats next week, do you know whats wrong with me? can you help me please?

> **I am feeling really depressed** at the moment, but I am really happy

> I feel like I have a relly bad problem! One minute I will be mucking around with my friends, perfectly happy, and the next **I feel depressed** and moody! what's wrong with me? I don't think it is mood swings because it happens every day and it is always the same! I hate doing it because I feel like my friends hate me for it! What is it and how can i stop?

> I dont know why but **I feel depressed** a lot of the time. Nothing particularly bad has happened in my life but i still feel this way. I feel alone even though I have quite good friends . . . I went to the doctor about it but I find it hard explaining exactly whats going on in my mind . . . Have you got any suggestions of what I can do cos I dont want to carry on like this. – from confused and depressed my life is good i gt a gr8 bf my mum n dad split up n i had trouble with that but they are ok with each other now i have plenty of friends & a great family but i feel like crying all they time **i feel depressed** n i duno y?????

Although feelings of low mood are intensely and keenly felt, the contributors seem here to be mistrustful of their perceptions (or else aware of the contradictory nature of their situations), struggling to reconcile their personal, social contexts with their emotional distress. Depression is thus a paradox, an inconstant, the personal experience of which is far removed from the essential and fixed nature of the condition as clinically constituted. The literal, technical rendering of depressive symptoms in DSM-IV and ICD-10 contributes, in part, to their abstract and vague character. Yet personal accounts of depression not infrequently employ metaphorical language (Karp 1996; McMullen and Conway 2002). Mental states, for which there are no ready-made linguistic formulae (Morrow 2006), are hard to reproduce literally. By contrast metaphor, as Gibbs (1994: 125) observes, allows us to 'communicate configurations of information that better capture the rich, continuous nature of experience than does literal discourse alone'.

As the above examples illustrate, when the adolescents talk of feeling depressed, they are liable to present their depressive symptoms as acute and inexplicable. It is not surprising, then, that, given the indescribable nature of these symptoms to which they are striving to give voice, they should tend to figurative language and vivid imagery to pin down the experience of their inner torment. A recurring image in the foregoing emails draws on the underlying metaphor that depression is isolation and incarceration:

> I feel so depressed I don't know how to snap out of it
>
> i can't help feeling trapped inside my own mind
>
> i just can't cope. . .I don't want to be here!
>
> i feel so alone. . .i often wish I was dead so the pain could end

To experience depression is to suffer an intolerable, suffocating sense of personal isolation and abstraction; it as though these adolescents were living in another world, irrevocably and helplessly sealed off from other people. Depression is enforced disconnection from others, to be locked within oneself. Consequently, depression is something from which the adolescents' desperately crave release, though the means by which this might be achieved seem elusive and not within their power to bring about, which can only aggravate and reinforce the sense of the loss of social connection. For example, although the adolescents intimate that release might be brought about by sharing their distress, they are reluctant or unable to talk to other people: 'i haven't told anyone about this because i dont have a best friend and i dont want to talk to my doctor', 'i don't tlk to my mom or any family', 'I've got no one to talk to because I can't get to see a psychiatrist'.

Another metaphor that provides similar concrete power is that which compares depression to a physical force and/or a living organism:

its hitting me hard

There is something bugging my brain, making me feel this why but i am not sure what

Here depression takes on a physical, animate character; it has become an entity possessing its own agency, mysteriously and potently attacking its victims. As with many of the adolescents' conceptualizations of depression examined throughout this section, the notion of one's brain being 'bugged' suggests that depression is an organic, inherent aspect of the individual, a biological assault on the brain that results in depressive malfunction, in the same way that, say, a lung or kidney might be subject to infectious invasion.

More broadly, these constructions exemplify the underlying metaphor 'medicine is war', which is often the trope of choice in medical language (Gwyn 2002), a figure of speech common to both professionals and patients alike (Skelton et al. 2002a, 2002b). However, the use of the military metaphor has serious consequences for the agency of the sufferer. As the foregoing illustrate, the adolescents perceive themselves to be at the mercy of an invasive, hard-hitting entity which they appear unable to resist, a perception which is engendered by the choice of figurative representation.

For example, Hodgkin (1985) argues that the 'medicine is war' metaphor is liable to passively position patients, for the main protagonists in the 'conflict' are doctors and diseases (as in the above examples, the adolescents appear to be mere onlookers, helpless witnesses to their own personal distress). Doctors harness a range of technologies or 'weapons' (to continue the military analogy), such as an ever increasing arsenal of psychotropic medication. If depression is formulated as being biochemical in origin, a disturbance or 'bugging' of the brain, then, by extension, licence is granted to neuroleptic intervention, with the consequent removal of the individual from the treatment regime. Thus the military metaphor has a determinative function (McMullen and Conway 2002), use of which may unwittingly contribute to the sense of powerlessness experienced by the adolescents.

Overall, then, the foregoing metaphoric extracts provide a vivid sense of what depression feels like from the inside rather than, as in the diagnostic manuals, what it looks like from the outside. Broadly, these metaphoric accounts construct depression as an indubitably negative state. Indeed so intolerable is this mode of being that, in some instances, it is akin to and described in terms of, actual physical pain and distress.

## 9.5 Conclusion

In this chapter I have shown how the adolescents principally formulate their accounts of and questions about depression through two recurring syntactical structures: 'I am [depressed]' and 'I have [depression]'. These structures are not arbitrary but appear to encode two distinct motivated ways of perceiving and perhaps even experiencing depressive states.

The formulation 'I am depressed' typically involved the contributors describing their distress in situational terms, that is, relating their low mood to adverse external circumstances (bullying, splitting up with partners, pressure of exams). The depressive state was thus a reaction to the personal and social context of the contributors' lives, a momentary state of distress. In contrast, the messages in which the adolescents described themselves as 'having depression' generally articulated a more enduring and deep-grained psychological problem, situating their problems in a medicalized discourse of emotional distress. In these 'I have depression' messages, the depressive state was discursively formulated as being organic and pathological, drawing on technical, medical terms in order to convey the clinical nature of the problem. These self-pathologizing formulations, in turn, had consequences for the adolescents' personal agency, with depression being portrayed as an irresistible impulse that the contributors reported being unable to personally overcome and hence their having to rely medical intervention. In some instances, professional interventions for depression, such as the use of antidepressant medication, were presented as ineffectual, having little effect in ameliorating psychological distress. (The potential consequences of adopting clinical, proto-professional register to formulate depression-related concerns are explored further in the concluding chapter).

What the analysis also made apparent was the incommunicability of the depressive experience: the contributors' reported difficulties in putting their distress into words. One way of responding to this problem of communicating depression was for the contributors to employ the emotion words *feel* and *feeling*. In these messages, the contributors' accounts of the depressive state admitted much more than official, clinical formulations of depression, such as the criteria set out in the DSM-IV. Moreover, rather than describing their accounts in the detached objectified discourse of the statistical checklist, the adolescents' experiences were bewilderingly chaotic, reflecting the inexpressible complexity of their predicaments.

# 10

# Conclusions

This study has sought to demonstrate how a corpus approach to health communication can productively combine both quantitative and qualitative approaches, a combination which can be seen as part of the currently ongoing rapprochement between the two methodologies (Whitley 2007). Such a mixed-method approach was able to yield rich and complementary findings that 'stretch and enrich the topic under investigation' (Whitley 2007: 697), with the use of frequency lists and, in particular, keywords lending quantitative validity to more fine-grained qualitative work exploring adolescents' perceptions and constructions of sexual and mental health. The harnessing of a number of staple computational and analytical procedures, such as collocation and concordances, was able to produce original textual and thematic insights which both add to our understanding of young people's health discourses, while supporting and challenging findings presented by existing studies.

In the following sections I draw together various methodological, analytical and practical underpinnings, outlining the key thematic findings and practical insights generated by this corpus study of health communication. I then describe the utility of online health forums for engaging with adolescents, a population less likely to access, and much more likely to be critical of, traditional face-to-face sources of health provision (Rees-Lewis 1994). The remaining part of the discussion describes some of the limitations of the corpus approach to interrogating adolescent health communication, addressing the issue of how future corpus studies might address these potential shortfalls, and build on the existing findings newly emerging from this study.

## 10.1  What does corpus analysis tell us about adolescent health? Insights for practitioners

### 10.1.1  Sexual health

The corpus analysis of the adolescent health emails both supports and contradicts findings from previous research into the sexual health of young people. Across a range of themes and topics, the adolescents' emails provided *prima facie* evidence of apparent knowledge deficits and misconceptions about the subject. This was particularly the case with matters relating to the topic of conception, with the adolescents' emails commonly betraying misinformation regarding the biology and physiology of reproduction, and their fears of pregnancy over and above the risk of STI, findings which have been consistently reported elsewhere in the adolescent health literature (e.g. Holland et al. 2000; Mason 2005). It was further evident that the adolescents communicated a number of uncertainties about HIV and AIDS. A recurring issue was the tendency for some of the advice-seekers to potentially conflate HIV and AIDS, thereby reinforcing the idea that the two entities are synonymous. And as the analysis demonstrated, such a conflation is liable to obscure awareness of the ways the virus is transmitted, thereby potentially impeding accurate assessment of degrees of risk in relation to young people's sexual behaviour (Aggleton et al. 1989: 59).

Yet the picture of adolescent sexual health communication was not solely characterized by the articulation of lay beliefs and irrational prejudices. Recurring throughout the corpus were questions and concerns that aimed at deriving prime understandings of a range of sexual health subjects, in particular fundamental questions of the 'What is . . . ?' type (e.g. 'What is sex?', 'What is AIDS?', etc.). Although possible to interpret such questions as indicative of information gaps, they can also be seen as aiming to deconstruct sexual health concepts which are commonly taken for granted. Thus, given the contested and often contradictory answers it widely receives, the question 'What is sex?' commonly posed by the adolescents is a necessary, critical enquiry and indeed one which many researchers in sexual health have themselves asked and continue to ask (e.g. Richters and Song 1999; Randall and Byers 2003).

However, it is important to realize that these findings regarding adolescents' beliefs about sexual health cannot simply be generalized to the adolescent population at large. The young people who contribute to the Teenage Health Freak website constitute a specific group of users who articulate certain feelings and thoughts, and therefore their potential knowledge gaps cannot be said to be representative of adolescents more widely. Many young people are well-informed about matters of sexual health and have no need to seek online health advice. Not all young people have questions about HIV and AIDS and other reproductive health concerns.

That said, corpus-conducted health discourse analysis is able to yield potentially new and significant insights into adolescent sexual health and so has much to contribute to the subject. Indeed the research literature has paid little attention to the naturally-occurring discursive routines of young people and what these potentially reveal about how adolescents communicate their knowledge, attitudes and beliefs about sexual health. Studies of young people's sexuality have been dominated by self-report methodologies (Moore, Rosenthal and Mitchell 1996) which typically involve the use of questionnaires in order to explore sexual health concerns. One of the limitations of the questionnaire method is that it is often used in conjunction with problem-focused research agendas dictated by researchers themselves. Consequently, respondents may feel pressured into supplying information and therefore may decline to provide answers, or substitute random replies for earnest and accurate responses (Moore et al. 1996: 186).

Additionally, respondents may display euphemistic constraint when providing answers, under-representing their sexual behaviours and attitudes towards sexual health (ibid.). This is, of course, not to suggest that the adolescent health emails analysed in this book are entirely free of fabrication or understatement. However, the fact that they are non-elicited, originating, in the first instance, from the adolescents themselves rather than researchers' agendas, means that at least the concerns so communicated are principally motivated by what young people deem to be personally relevant to them – a factor which perhaps helps in part to account for the often frank and meticulous detail of their self-disclosures.

Another facility of the corpus approach is that, as a novel and unique approach for researching sexual health communication, it constitutes both a fresh methodological and analytical perspective and responds to calls for new and multiple modes of research into sexual behaviour (Dockrell and Joffe 1992). Such a call for new approaches underscores the difficulty of providing an adequate depiction of adolescent sexual health, a challenge which is due, in no small part, to the fact that the right to privacy is, understandably, jealously guarded in this sensitive area of research (Moore et al. 1996: 186). It is not surprising, therefore, that, despite the increasing amount of surveys and epidemiological work on the subject, there is a lack of data concerning how people communicate sexual health issues in naturally-occurring situations (Silverman 1997). Given the context in which the adolescents submit their concerns to the Teenage Health Freak website, a naturally occurring form of online advice-seeking, the health email corpus (and internet-based data more broadly) constitutes a unique discourse source with which to survey personal, sensitive health concerns, complementing more traditional methodological approaches such as questionnaires and interviews.

This study, then, highlights the role and value of the Web-based forum as a means of eliciting sexual health problems from a generation who have often been reluctant to consult practitioners, peers and others for personal health advice and information (Suzuki and Calzo 2004). Apart from contributing to theoretical perspectives of adolescent sexual health, the findings should therefore be of interest to health professionals and educators working with young people. In particular, the corpus approach affords an effective means of identifying the 'incremental effect' (Baker 2006: 13) of discursive patterns, allowing (among many other communicative trends) the discovery, for example, of discourses such of the 'male sex drive' and 'heterosexual romance', discourses which are liable to prevent young people from practicing safer sex. As with lay beliefs about sexual health, the subtle presence and full implication of these discourses in the communicative routines of adolescents may well be overlooked by health professionals and policymakers unaccustomed to considering the significance of discourse in the shaping of interventions and policy. If educational initiatives are to be successful, then language, as Cameron and Kulick (2003: 154) argue, must not simply be regarded as 'a medium for sex and health education but something that must be discussed explicitly as part of the process'.

### 10.1.2  Mental health

By focusing on a number of keywords (and their collocates) relating to suicide, self-harm and depression and themes and issues surrounding these signal terms, the corpus analysis provided important insights into how young people interpret and conceptualize mental health concerns which they report as most commonly affecting them. Although the emails examined in this study serve more as vignettes – little, though cumulatively substantial, windows into the fraught lives of the contributors to Teenage Health Freak, rather than, say, sustained interview accounts – the messages collectively provided an insightful picture of the lived experiences of adolescents suffering psychological disturbance.

Wissow and Platt (2006) note that research into adolescents' perceptions and understanding of mental health indicates that young people are liable to possess limited knowledge about what constitutes a treatable mental health problem. Adolescents, for instance, have been shown to conflate mental health and mental 'retardation', while regarding only very serious disorders as something for which it is proper to seek medical help (Secker et al. 1999; Smith 2004). Much of the data in this study appears to contradict this finding. For the adolescents seeking online support for their emotional problems, what they deem to be mental health issues necessitating professional help or at least enquiring about appear to be broader than those elicited in previous studies.

For instance, a number of the contributors to the website believed the experience of feeling temporarily and reactively depressed to be worthy of medical intervention, even when it was directly attributed to and equated with 'normal' day-to-day life trials and problems, including issues with families, relationships with peers, educational pressures and bullying. There was, moreover, a tendency to medicalize the depressive experience, to situate emotional distress within a medical discourse, thereby construing it as an objective, clearly bounded clinical phenomenon. Such a formulation contradicts a number of previous studies into adolescent beliefs about mental health in which depression is considered not to constitute mental illness, but is merely something encountered as part of everyday life, something located within the bounds of normal life (Secker et al. 1999). It may well be that the common adoption of a clinical perspective by the Teenage Health contributors reflects the current and increasing trend in western societies to medicalize complaints that previously have been considered to be inevitable aspects of human experience (Moynihan et al. 2002).

Taking the adolescents' subjective experiences of suicide, self-harm and depression together, several underlying themes were seen to emerge. Although analysis from the onset did not *a priori* presume links among the three, and consequently I examined each in isolation, what emerged during the course of corpus interrogation was the recurring presence of depression in the adolescents' suicide and self-harm concerns. For example, depression (after family disruption) was given as the second most common reason for the adolescents experiencing suicidal impulses. The attribution of depression to themselves could be seen as a means of explaining and justifying their suicidal impulses, while reinforcing the irresistibility of the pull towards self-destruction.

Depression similarly loomed large in accounts of self-harm. Here depression was portrayed as a source of inexorable psychological pain, relief from which was only afforded by self-injurious courses of action, particularly self-mutilation. Although the act of cutting appeared to grant them a degree of relief, the persistent and ineluctable presence of depression meant that self-harm provided only temporary respite for the adolescents and therefore had to be resorted to on a regular basis to sustain its effect. The repetitive nature of self-harm reflects its habitual nature. Indeed a recurring issue identified by the adolescents was that self-harm was akin to an addiction and hence an activity which they are unable to cease.

However, as with suicide, evidence from the corpus suggested that, despite the signal influence of depression, there is no one single explanation for self-injurious behaviours. For example, self-harm functioned as a coping mechanism, a response to physical and sexual abuse, bullying and familial turmoil, and therefore, as with suicidal impulses, was related to social and cultural influences, as well as to psychological disorders, including depression.

Consequently, interventions for self-harm that focus on correcting the behaviour in the individual may be incomplete or misdirected (McAllister 2003: 183). The assorted meanings which the adolescents associate with self-harm suggest that health providers, so McAllister argues, need to have flexible responses to young people who self-injure, knowing that there are often many reasons for the activity and that it cannot simply be reduced to a problem residing within the individual (Johnstone 1997). Therefore, unless multiple meanings are noticed and shared with colleagues, then the likelihood is that conventional and ill-fitting beliefs will be maintained and unsatisfactory outcomes will continue (McAllister 2003: 183). Allowing that self-harm could possibly be a venting of anger towards society reinforces, McAllister suggests, the view that it is not sufficient to restrict health care to the individual – a need to address broader concerns such as social and cultural inequities, and to develop primary care to prevent and respond early to childhood abuse, is also important (ibid.).

Although the analysis focused principally on the subjective experiences of psychological distress (as was observed, the majority of the emails were written from first-person perspectives), a number of the messages relating to suicide, self-harm and depression described the behaviour and/or predicaments of third parties, particularly friends. It was possible that, given the extremely face-threatening act of personally disclosing and admitting to self-injurious behaviours, a number of these third-party accounts were potentially disguised presentations in which references to friends were substituted for the first-person (i.e. the contributors themselves). Analysis, however, could not be certain and thus remained agnostic on this point.

Another salient theme which the corpus analysis of mental health concerns revealed was the repeated sense of helplessness and hopelessness conveyed by the advice-seekers. Depressive experiences and the pull of suicidal and self-harming impulses were regularly constructed as being overwhelming, and so could not be very readily, if at all, resisted. Consequently, the adolescents perceived themselves to be passively situated in relation to their psychological distress, with little prospect of personal amelioration.

This was particularly evident in relation to depression, which was commonly presented and understood in medical terms. Depression was construed as something solid or tangible, a clinical condition which one has, one possesses, and hence inheres within the individual, a condition which, like physical, infectious disease, is amenable to pharmacological intervention (even if such treatment was sometimes described by the adolescents as being ineffectual). Even in the instances where the adolescents mitigated attributing depression to themselves through the use of modalizing terms (e.g. 'I think I have depression'), they were still liable to medicalize their depressive experiences, adopting a psychologizing style of symptom presentation rather than normalizing or playing down their emotional distress. In adopting a psychologizing approach to symptom presentation, the adolescents could also be seen to frame their experiences of depression in what de Swaan (1990) describes as 'proto-professional' terms, where the emphasis on clinical symptoms and a medical, technical understanding of psychological distress mixes lay and professional beliefs.

More broadly, the adolescents' adoption of a clinical understanding of depression, and the readiness with which distressful symptoms are pathologized, may reflect the western medical practice of treating depression as a discrete disease concept (Dowrick 2009), as well as reflecting the increasing trend of medicalizing distress and suffering which could be considered to be everyday and unavoidable facets of human life (Moynihan et al. 2002). Rose (2006), for example, describes a current climate in which the problems of living are becomingly increasingly psychiatrized. With the proliferation of self-help internet forums, depressive checklists and inventories in schools and surgeries, and the widespread presence of screening programmes, individuals are coming under increasing pressure to partake in self-diagnosis, to consider whether their emotional stresses might be pathological.

Perhaps, then, the trend of psychiatrization helps to account for the adolescents' commonly articulating their distress in clinical terms and their seeking to pathologize depressive symptomatology. The appeal of psychiatrizing one's distress is that it gives form to, and helps to make sense of, a set of inexplicably complex and chaotic symptoms. Thus adopting the clinical label of depression can be seen as a way of accounting for and, in turn, absolving the adolescents of their personal problems. As Lewis (1995) points out, in categorizing oneself as depressed, depression itself becomes the problem, not the individual who, by extension, becomes no longer personally responsible for their existing state of affairs. Putting a clinically validated name to their suffering, moreover, also meets the demand of justifying that they are deserving of help (Drew et al. 1999). It may well be therefore that the adolescents' adoption of a depressive identity is, somewhat paradoxically, empowering, encouraging them to act to resolve it (Lewis 1995).

Given that the way in which people conceptualize psychological distress and present their symptoms to practitioners influences whether they are diagnosed with an emotional disorder (Kessler et al. 1999), it is important for health professionals to be aware of the medical discourses in which young people are inclined to situate themselves when communicating their depression to others (Bennett et al. 2003). If adolescents, as this study suggests, are prone to using a proto-professional medical register and so psychologizing their distress, that is treating it as pathological rather than attributing it to the problems of everyday experience, then it may be that they are more susceptible to diagnosis regardless of whether their 'depression' is actually in fact clinical or not. This, arguably, is even more of a concern in the current context of mental health, with a number of practitioners, for example Parker (2007) and, more recently, Spence (2013), claiming that depression is being overdiagnosed and antidepressants overprescribed to people in the United Kingdom. According to Spence, the clinical threshold for depression has been lowered in recent years (owing to revisions in DSM criteria), with the consequence that normal emotional states are being treated as illness, which in turn has led to increasing inappropriate management of depressive conditions.

A potential risk, therefore, is that young people and practitioners may possibly collude in medicalizing normal human distress, considering 'any expression of depression as mandating treatment' (Parker 2007: 335). As Dowrick (2009) observes, GPs are liable to seize a problem that contains a straightforward solution: the concept of depression thus becomes a protective strategy for health practitioners through which order and understanding can be conveniently imposed on communicated emotional confusion and chaos. Consequently, when responding to young people's accounts of psychological distress, practitioners need to take carefully into account self-pathologization, particularly as young people may be influenced, as this study has shown, by medical models of depression which restrict the role of personal agency and therefore downplay, or even exclude altogether, the personal and social context in which their distress is embedded. As Switzer et al. (2006: 1214) argue, primary care practitioners should incorporate an understanding of the role of personal responsibility during the consultation, especially if they are to increase the likelihood of their patients discussing depressive symptoms and considering appropriate interventions for depression.

## 10.2  Potential limitations of the corpus approach

Despite the range of insights into adolescent sexual and mental health which the corpus approach was able to generate, it is important to emphasize that the analysis was principally confined to a number of prominent keywords and their associated collocates. In following the principle of pursuing the strongest available linguistic patterns, a number of other analytical avenues were, unavoidably, left unexplored. For example, with regard to the corpus examination of suicide-themed concerns, analysis focused principally on the relatively frequent term 'suicide' at the expense of other less commonly occurring expressions. Analysis of these comparatively infrequent terms might have yielded contrary themes and patterns. Whatever the insights so derived, whether they contradict or confirm the findings presented in this study, pursuing these alternative avenues of enquiry would most likely diversify and enrich the present line of enquiry.

Moreover, centring analysis on and around the strongest patterns, specifically the items which recur most commonly, points up the selective nature of corpus analysis and the fact that, like other forms of textual analysis, it can never be exhaustive. Although quantificational data derived from statistically robust frequency and keyword measures are objective (in the sense that such data are generated mechanically as opposed to being selected by the researcher), the application of frequency and keyword lists nevertheless entails a degree of subjectivity and selectivity (Moon 2007). As Stubbs (2005) observes, although the corpus researcher is restricted to features that the corpus software can locate, these features still need to be selected and require interpreting.

The interrogation of adolescent accounts of depression, for instance, involved the analytical step of isolating the lexical items *depressed* and *depression* in preference to equally topically relevant, if less common, terms, such as *sad* and *unhappy*. Although the selection was justified in terms of saliency and lexical overlap with the theme under investigation, it still remains a partial decision on the part of the researcher, a subjective intervention common to many other qualitative methods of textual analysis.

Of course, selectivity is, to some extent, precipitated by practical convenience, a corollary of working with extensive data sets. Interrogating a two million word corpus of health emails is, regardless of how far-reaching the analysis

(Baker 2006: 178), necessarily a selective and subjective endeavour. Although, as Baker (ibid.) points out, the corpus approach provides a very effective means of reducing substantial amounts of linguistic material into more manageable portions, thereby making the task of analysis humanly achievable, the data computationally singled out for interrogation may still be too extensive to make sense of. The range of keywords relating to sexual health as identified in Chapter 6, for example, were far too numerous to be interrogated one by one and given the individual attention that they ideally deserve. Consequently, it was necessary to restrict analysis relating to the theme of reproductive health to the solitary, though essential, term *sex* (and its collocates), the most common lexical item in the corpus, with other key items remaining in the background.

In practically limiting analysis to a number of the most common keywords relating to sexual and mental health, the corpus approach adopted in this study potentially runs the risk of obscuring or overlooking any individual variation from the central patterns surrounding these dominant signal items. In aggregating the messages produced by many adolescents, the corpus method is more suited to identifying only what is common and universal to all contributors (Seale et al. 2006). The perceptions and experiences of sexual and mental health of a number of individual adolescents may be significantly different from the collection of young people 'with whom they have been aggregated' (Seale et al. 2006: 2588).

It should further be emphasized that the common patterns of communication unearthed by the corpus analysis are not necessarily universal and once-for-all, that is, they are unlikely to be reproduced in different contexts or on other occasions. The nature of the experiences communicated by the contributors to the Teenage Health Freak website, including their attitudes towards and conceptualizations of sexual and mental health, along with the language used to articulate these concerns, would almost certainly vary if produced in different communicative and research settings. The young people who have expressed their sensitive concerns so frankly through the visual anonymity of the internet health forum are unlikely to exhibit the same characteristically high levels of candour and openness if they were to disclose these same problems face-to-face (i.e. if they were prepared to so disclose them in the first place!).

Similarly, if the adolescent health discourse derived from alternative research methods, say, questionnaires or focus groups, with the data originating from an investigator rather than a participant-directed agenda, the nature and construction of the responses may well differ from the patient-initiated actions in Web forums that place the responsibility and the main say in the hands of users themselves. Participants who utilize Web forums to disclose their problems to others, for instance, are liable to exercise elevated levels of emotional expressivity, with details of their illness experiences being discussed more intimately and freely than they would during research interviews (Seale et al. 2010).

The results of this study provide a substantial snapshot of contemporary sexual and mental health problems experienced and communicated by young people. The Teenage Health Freak Website itself is very popular with adolescents, receiving on average 52,864 visits a day. Although this study does not make precise demographic claims about the nature of the population visiting the website, it is likely to be accessed by a wide range of young people, predominantly from Anglophone countries. Of course, the material here does not necessarily tell us how Asian or Australasian teenagers would talk about the issues, nor does the data collection process allow the questions and problems to be traced to particular class, ethnic or faith subgroups. This would have to wait upon the creation of corpora where researchers have proactively collected demographic and contextual information to accompany the language itself.

However, the issues raised by researchers on internet health in different countries have been shown to be intriguingly similar, especially given the differentiation in face-to-face health care cross-nationally. Nations with substantial public provision yield similar concerns to those with largely insurance-funded systems. On both sides of the Atlantic, and even as far afield as China, the anonymity afforded by the internet is valued (Lou et al. 2006; Rogers and Mead 2004), and this is particularly important for adolescents, since, as we have seen, they are often reluctant to request health advice from their doctors in person.

## 10.3 Electronic health communication: Some implications for care

A characteristic feature of both the sexual and mental health concerns communicated by the adolescents in this study was their candid, personally exposing quality. Analysis revealed how embarrassing and taboo topics were typically explored freely and explicitly, articulated without apparent inhibition. Although this is not to deny that the adolescents were also, on occasions, reluctant to impart personally exposing information and prone to indirect expression (as was observed in Chapter 8, it is likely that some contributors may well have resorted to disguising their identities when communicating suicide-related concerns), a preference for unflinching and vivid expression was clearly in evidence throughout the analysis, with the adolescents typically eschewing euphemism in favour of more orthophemisitic (direct or neutral) language.

Research into sexual and mental health has brought into focus the communicative difficulties that participants (both patients and professionals alike) experience when discussing these highly sensitive topics face-to-face (Weijts et al. 1993; Reeves et al. 2004; Stewart 2005; Pollock 2007). Although not confined to the age group alone, the problem is particularly acute for adolescents, who have consistently been shown to report poor communication between themselves and doctors (Jacobson et al. 1996; Beresford and Sloper 2003), particularly the disclosure of embarrassing and delicate issues owing to a poor understanding of patient confidentiality (Jacobson et al. 2001).

Young people, for instance, are reluctant to articulate their depressive feelings and suicidal impulses to health professionals, counsellors and teachers for fear of breaches of confidence (Coggan et al. 1997). Moreover, the adolescent patient is, during encounters with clinicians, liable to have difficulties recognizing and expressing his or her feelings (Manley and Leichner 2003). Young people in face-to-face exchanges have been found to discuss suicide in an oblique, general fashion, distancing themselves from the subject and being acutely aware of the implications of discussing such a tabooed topic (Bourke 2003). Owing to the stigma surrounding suicide and other mental health concerns, young people are liable to resist confiding in others, knowing that they are not supposed to admit to having suicidal thoughts (Bourke 2003: 2363).

In communicating their concerns to the Teenage Health Freak website, the adolescents in this study have taken the calculated step of seeking an alternative, non-interventional source of assistance. The online medium provides them with a venue in which they can deal with the same developmental and psychological issues as in their offline lives (Subrahmanyam et al. 2004). In the case of sexuality and mental health, the electronic forum provides 'a safe place to vent feelings and express negative emotions' (Sullivan 2003: 86), a place wherein such delicate and exposing themes can be communicated in an anonymous and disembodied social context. Indeed young people themselves have described the importance of anonymity as a factor determining whether they seek support or not (Coggan et al. 1997).

The dissociative anonymity and invisibility which make the internet such an effective vehicle for self-disclosure help to account for the candid and explicit nature of the adolescents' electronic health emails. As was described in Section 2.3.1, the factors of anonymity, invisibility and asynchronicity create an 'online disinhibition effect' (Suler 2004) whereby people self-disclose or act out more intensely than they would in person. As McKenna and Bargh (1998: 62) put it, 'under the protective cloak of anonymity users can express the way they truly feel and think'. Moreover, as Suler suggests (2004), anonymity enables individuals to separate their online personae and actions from their offline realities. Consequently, whatever the adolescents communicate to Dr Ann cannot be linked directly to the rest of their lives: no one needs know that they have sought medical assistance. This is a vital consideration for young people: to approach others for help, particularly family members or people known to the adolescent, would be to validate any sense of failure and weakness experienced by the help-seeker, for, in the eyes of other people, seeking assistance 'could be perceived as a shameful act' (Scourfield et al. 2007: 252).

The 'hyperpersonal' (Walter 1996) nature of the adolescents' online communiqués can also be attributed to invisibility and disembodiment. The fact that participants in an electronic exchange cannot see and hear each other, even if their identities are known to one another, significantly amplifies the effect of disinhibition (Suler 2004). When the adolescents transmit their concerns into cyberspace, they will not have had to concern themselves with broader paralinguistic signs, such as how others will respond facially, whether, for instance, their messages will be greeted with a grimace or a frown, or how others will sound in response – dismissed, say, by a disapproving grunt or a gasp of horrified surprise. As Suler (2004: 322) observes, to witness the shake of a head, a bored expression or a sigh in response to a personal disclosure is to suffer rejection and further inhibit what one is willing to reveal.

This study has demonstrated how computer-mediated communication constitutes a practical resource for eliciting emotionally rich disclosures from psychologically disturbed and worried young people. Given the fraught nature of the contributors' experiences so vividly recounted in their emails, the research reinforces the need to ensure that, in the effort to communicate distress, open and preferred lines of communication are available between adolescents and sources of help. The availability of such channels of communication plays an important part in reducing the need for the adolescent to engage in suicidal behaviour (Manley and Leichner 2003: 35), allowing young people to discuss difficult feelings which otherwise might remain dangerously bottled up.

Further, analysis revealed that the adolescents frequently described breakdowns in communication with other people, particularly their difficulties disclosing problems to others and hence having their need to be noticed, listened to and understood go unfulfilled. Their experiences of communicating problems to others involved descriptions of the difficulty and inability to talk to family and friends, as well as a reluctance to share health problems through established institutional routes and traditional face-to-face service networks. Such breakdowns highlight the influence that social context has in determining whether distressed young people access health care. As Fullager (2005) observes, contemporary health provision privileges a rationality predicated on the belief that young people will take the decided and rational step of acquiring professional help, and that young people will be able to express their problems and emotions freely to others. Yet, as this study has shown, it is, for the adolescents, not simply a matter of rationally seeking professional assistance and readily disclosing one's distress. Contextual factors are liable to impede young people from procuring professional assistance, not least their perceived inability to express their emotions effectively face-to-face, along with the belief that no one will empathize with how they feel.

Consequently, recourse to internet sources of health provision may be their prime or, in some cases, their sole source of support when in need of emotional and medical assistance – the only source of help they feel able to utilize in times of turmoil. As described above, the anonymity afforded by the internet, specifically its facility of providing advice without the risk of parents finding out about their concerns, make it a valuable source of health and advice information for adolescents (Kanuga and Rosenfeld 2004; Gray et al. 2005a, 2005b). The assurance of confidentiality has been shown to increase young people's willingness to disclose sensitive information to doctors, while concerns about parental notification have the opposite effect (Ford et al. 1997).

Unlike traditional health care services, where the emphasis is on the client attending an unfamiliar environment, typically at a time dictated by the professional (Gray et al. 2005a, 2005b), the internet provides convenient unconstrained access to health services. In terms of communicating with professionals online, electronic communication allows young people to formulate their problems in their own terms, space and time, affording them a platform from which to ask awkward, sensitive or detailed questions without the fear of being judged or stigmatized (Cotton and Gupta 2004) – a negative outcome at times referred to in both the adolescents' sexual and mental health concerns.

This study's findings demonstrate that young people are adept at articulating their health concerns electronically (concerns that they otherwise might not have communicated to others), doing so with high degrees of openness and directness and employing orthophemistic and, not infrequently, precise unflinching medical terminology. Given the regularity with which electronic forms of communication are used by young people, with, for example,

75 per cent of today's youth having used the internet to seek health advice (Kanuga and Rosenfeld 2004), there is arguably greater scope for more extensive and systematic use of email in health care. As the popularity of interactive websites specializing in adolescent health testifies, email and online messaging have the potential to reach out to and connect with young people who might be reluctant to engage with more traditional face-to-face health services (Harvey et al. 2007).

Despite health services being slow to use email for doctor-patient communication (Committee on Quality Health Care in America 2001), it is important in the digital age for health care professionals to understand that their role is changing in that 'they increasingly have to act as health guides, mediators, and information brokers for patients and consumers' (Eysenbach 2004: 439). Professional resistance to the application of online services in health care remains a substantial obstacle to the realization of the internet's therapeutic potential (Anderson et al. 2004). Part of this potential lies in the opportunities to connect with people who may have health needs but find other kinds of communication embarrassing or difficult to initiate.

It is important, then, for health professionals to understand and respond to not just how new information services are affecting the delivery of health care but also how digital technologies are rapidly shaping and changing contemporary communicative practices. Awareness of these impacts is particularly important in relation to adolescent health since today's teenagers, the so-called Millennial or net generation, have grown up with digital technologies in a world mediated by digital texts – distinctly different from adults' ideas about literacies (Hagood et al. 2002). Some adolescents feel that their communicative practices and literacies are not being recognized and accommodated by mainstream educational institutions (Phelps 1998). Such lack of accommodation parallels the complaints that adolescents have in relation to the lack of specialized health services and the lack of recognition of them as a distinct group with specific needs and as individuals (Beresford and Sloper 2003). In utilizing their preferred medium of communication, on-line health advice may promote better engagement with adolescents.

## 10.4 Health communication and corpora: Some final words

With its focus on a range of individual, subjective descriptions of what it is like for young people to experience concerns about their well-being, the study offers a timely counterweight to much mainstream positivistic research that has rarely considered the lived health and illness experiences of young people, particularly in relation to sensitive concerns such as mental health. As Nicolson (1995: 339) argues, 'no amount of experimental rigour, sophisticated statistical techniques or large-scale application of psychometric testing' affords an understanding of what it actually feels like to personally experience psychological distress. Such an appreciation comes about through close consideration of the actual language used by young people to articulate their health experiences, rather than through decontextualized research that fails to give attention to the linguistic construction of their concerns (McQueen and Henwood 2002). Corpus enquiry into the communicative repertoires of adolescents thus provides discursive insights into the meaning of their worlds, as well as the social and cultural contexts in which their concerns are situated.

From the practitioner's perspective (and indeed any professional working with young people), the findings from this study emphasize the importance of appreciating and responding to adolescents' subjective experiences of health and illness. Adolescents are a specific client group at a unique stage of emotional, neurological, physical and social development (McPherson 2005), and thus exhibit complex help-seeking behaviours which are different from other age groups (Boldero and Fallon 1995). If professionals are to tailor support that reflects the uniqueness of adolescence, it is important for them to be aware of young people's accounts of and attitudes towards health, since these will inevitably influence how adolescents respond to health advice and so modify their behaviour. Accordingly, it has hoped that the insights generated by this study will be of practical interest to health professionals, educationalists and people working with young people, providing an important alternative insider perspective to much of the more impersonal, experimental research that characterizes adolescent health.

As I have sought to demonstrate throughout this book, an effective and innovative way to explore lay theories and folk beliefs about health is to interrogate corpora of naturalistic data. As Crawford et al. (2014) argue, a data-driven learning approach to health communication reliably provides practitioners with a novel opportunity to learn more about the types of issues that they are likely to encounter in health care exchanges, facilitating, in particular, an understanding of the folkways clients use to interpret what has gone wrong and appreciating the rhythms of complaint. In terms of learning activities, the use of naturally-occurring data, moreover, constitutes a more fully evidence-based experience for health service personnel that adds significant value to what is achievable through more commonly used staged material featuring in role-plays, hypothetical examples and similar 'artificial' educational activities (Brown et al. 2006).

The systematic interrogation of corpus data explicates the many and diverse forms of health care language, such as the linguistic routines of adolescents, yielding greater insight into the meaning of health care communication. The promise of the corpus approach is that it affords a detailed analysis of a range of health care language styles and routines, which can then be utilized in communication training programmes. This creative synthesis between health care and corpus linguistics has the potential to provide a wide variety of health practitioners with the information they need to make substantial improvements in care delivery in a range of settings. Corpus-based research, such as the present study, has identified recurring patterns of medical communication and, consequently, can provide medical educators with linguistic information with which to more evidentially inform communication training and development.

This study has highlighted how the linguistic exploration of naturalistic health data sets of this kind is a valuable source of insight into the vocabularies, registers and lexicogrammatical features used, the concerns raised, and issues attended to by adolescents seeking health advice and information online. As was demonstrated, the corpus of adolescent health emails can be used to examine participants' own accounts of their experiences and perceptions of delicate issues such as sexual and mental health, issues which are extremely difficult to broach in face-to-face encounters with practitioners. The difficulty of obtaining the naturally-occurring health discourse of teenagers is well-known, a factor which accounts for the limited amount of research in this area of study (Stenström et al. 2002). Thus, to professionals concerned with the health care of adolescents, such a data set is a valuable resource to help get to grips effectively with this client group.

# References

Abrams, D., Abraham, C., Spears, R., Marks, D. (1990) 'AIDS invulnerability: Relationships, sexual behaviour and attitudes among 16–19-year-olds'. In P. Aggleton, P. Davies and G. Hart (eds), *AIDS: Rights, Risk and Reason*. London: The Falmer Press, 35–51.

Abrams, L., Gordon, A. (2003) 'Self-harm narratives of urban and suburban young women'. *AFFILIA, 18*: 429–44.

Ackard, D., Neumark-Sztainer, D. (2001) 'Health care information sources for adolescents: Age and gender differences on use, concerns, and needs'. *Journal of Adolescent Health, 29*: 170–76.

Adolphs, S. (2006) *Introducing Electronic Text Analysis*. London: Routledge.

Adolphs, S., Brown, B., Carter, R., Crawford, P., Sahota, O. (2004) 'Applied clinical linguistics: Corpus linguistics in health care settings'. *Journal of Applied Linguistics, 1*: 9–28.

Advocates for Youth (2010) *Adolescents and Sexually Transmitted Infections: A Costly and Dangerous Global Phenomenon*. Washington, DC: Advocates for Youth.

Aggleton, P., Homans, H. (1987) 'Teaching about AIDS'. *Social Science Teacher, 17*: 24–8.

Aggleton, P., Homans, H., Mojsa, J., Watson, S., Watson, S. (1989) *AIDS: Scientific and Social Issues: A Resource for Health Educators*. Edinburgh: Churchill Livingstone.

Aggleton, P., Oliver, C., Rivers, K. (1998) *The Implications of Research into Young People, Sex, Sexuality and Relationships*. London: Health Education and Authority.

Allan, K., Burridge, K. (2006) *Forbidden Words: Taboo and the Censoring of Language*. Cambridge: Cambridge University Press.

Ammerman, S., Perelli, E., Adler, N., Irwin, C. (1992) 'Do adolescents understand what physicians say about sexuality and health?'. *Clinical Pediatrics, 76*: 590–95.

Anderson, M., Woodward, L., Armstrong, M. (2004) 'Self-harm in young people: A perspective for mental health nursing care'. *International Nursing Review, 51*: 222–28.

Anderson, M., Standen, P., Noon, J. (2005) 'A social semiotic interpretation of suicidal behaviour in young people'. *Journal of Health Psychology, 10*: 317–31.

Apter, A., Freudenstein, O. (2000) 'Adolescent suicidal behaviour: Psychiatric populations'. In K. Hawton (ed.), *The International Handbook of Suicide and Attempted Suicide*. Chichester: Wiley, 261–73.

Arnett, J. (2007) 'Suffering, selfish, slackers? Myths and reality about emerging adults'. *Journal of Youth and Adolescence, 36*: 23–9.

Aronsson, K., Rundstrom, B. (1988) 'Child discourse and parental control in pediatric consultations'. *Text, 8*: 159–84.

Aston, G. (2002) 'The learner as corpus designer'. In B. Kettemann and G. Marko (eds), *Language and Computers: Studies in Practical Linguistics*. Amsterdam: Rodopi, 9–25.

Atkins, S., Harvey, K. (2010) 'How to use corpus linguistics in the study of health communication'. In M. McCarthy and A. O'Keefe (eds), *The Routledge Handbook of Corpus Linguistics*. Abingdon, UK: Routledge, 605–19.

Aynsley-Green, A., Barker, M., Burr, S., Macfarlane, A., Morgan, J., Sibert, J., Turner, T., Russell, V., Waterston, T., Hall, D. (2000) 'Who is speaking for children and adolescents and for their health at the policy level?' *British Medical Journal, 321*: 229–32.

Babiker, G., Arnold, L. (1997) *The Language of Injury: Comprehending Self-Mutilation*. Oxford: Blackwell.

Bailey, L. (2005) 'Control and desire: The issue of identity in popular discourses of addiction'. *Addiction Research and Theory, 13*: 535–43.

Baker, P. (2004) 'Querying keywords: Questions of difference, frequency, and sense in keywords analysis'. *Journal of English Linguistics, 32*: 346–59.

—. (2005) *Public Discourses of Gay Men*. London: Routledge.

—. (2006) *Using Corpora in Discourse Analysis*. London: Continuum.

—. (2010) *Sociolinguistics and Corpus Linguistics*. Edinburgh: Edinburgh University Press.

Baker, P., Gabrielatos, C., Khosravinik, M., Krzyzanowski, M., McEnery, A., Wodak, R. (2008) 'A useful methodological synergy? Combining critical discourse analysis and corpus linguistics to examine discourses of refugees and asylum seekers in the UK press'. *Discourse & Society, 19.3*: 273–306.

Barak, A. (2007) 'Emotional support and suicide prevention through the internet: A field project report'. *Computers in Human Behaviour, 23*: 971–84.

Baron, N. (1998) 'Letters by phone or speech by other means: The linguistics of email'. *Language and Communication, 18*: 133–70.

—. (2000) *Alphabet to Email: How Written English Evolved and Where It's Heading*. London and New York: Routledge.

—. (2003) 'Why email looks like speech'. In J. Aitchison and D. Lewis (eds), *New Media Language*. London: Routledge, 85–94.

Barrington, M. (1969) 'Apologia for suicide'. In A. Downing (ed.), *Euthanasia and the Right to Death*. London: Peter Owen, 90–103.

Bennett, S., Coggan, C., Adams, P. (2003) 'Problematising depression: Young people, mental health and suicidal behaviours'. *Social Science & Medicine, 57*: 289–99.

Bentall, R. (2003) *Madness Explained: Psychosis and Human Nature*. London: Penguin.

Berber-Sardinha, T. (2000) 'Comparing corpora with WordSmith Tools: How large must the reference corpus be?'. *Proceedings of the Workshop on Comparing Corpora, Annual Meeting of the ACL*, 1–8 October 2000, Hong Kong, 7–13.

Beresford, B., Sloper, P. (2003) 'Chronically ill adolescents' experiences of communicating with doctors: A qualitative study'. *Journal of Adolescent Health, 33*: 172–79.

Bergstrom L., Roberts J., Skillman L., Seidel J. (1992). "You'll feel me touching you, sweetie': Vaginal examinations during the second stage of labour'. *Birth,19*: 10–18.

Biber, D. (1993) 'Representativeness in corpus design'. *Literary and Linguistics Computing, 5*: 243–57.

Biber, D., Conrad, S. (2004) 'Corpus-Based Comparisons of Registers'. In C. Coffin, A. Hewings and K. O'Halloran (eds), *Applying English Grammar: Functional and Corpus Approaches*. London: Arnold, 40–56.

Biber, D., Conrad, S., Reppen, R. (1998) *Corpus Linguistics: Investigating Language Structure and Use*. Cambridge: Cambridge University Press.

Biber, D., Johansson, S., Leech, G., Conrad, S., Finegan, E. (1999) *Longman Grammar of Spoken and Written English*. London: Longman.

Boldero, J., Fallon, B. (1995) 'Adolescent help-seeking: What do they get help for and from whom?'. *Journal of Adolescence, 18*: 193–209.

Bondi, M. (2010) 'Perspectives on keywords and keyness'. In M. Bondi and M. Scott (eds), *Keyness in Texts*. Amsterdam: John Benjamins, 1–18.

Bourke, L. (2003) 'Toward understanding youth suicide in an Australian rural community'. *Social Science & Medicine, 57*: 2355–65.

Bowen, A., John, A. (2001) 'Gender differences in presentation and conceptualization of adolescent self-injurious behaviour: Implications for therapeutic practice'. *Counselling Psychological Quarterly, 14*: 357–79.

Bradley-Stevenson, C., Mumford, J. (2007) 'Adolescent sexual health'. *Paediatric and Child Health, 17*: 474–79.

Braun, V., Kitzinger, C. (2001) '"snatch," "hole" or "honey-pot?" Semantic categories and the problem of nonspecificity in female genital slang'. *The Journal of Sex Research, 38*: 146–58.

British Medical Association. (2003) *Adolescent Health*. London: BMA Publications.

—. (2005) *Sexual Health June 2005*. Available at http://www.bma.org.uk/ap.nsf/Content/ sexualhealthjune05. Accessed on 13 March, 2006.

—. (2006) *Child and Adolescent Mental Health: A Guide for Healthcare Professionals*. BMA: London.

Brown, B., Crawford, P., Carter, R. (2006) *Evidence-Based Health Communication*. Maidenhead: Open University Press.

Burack, R. (2000) 'Young teenagers' attitudes towards general practitioners and their provision of sexual health care'. *British Journal of General Practice, 50*: 550–54.

Burgess, S., Hawton, K., Loveday, G. (1998) 'Adolescents who take overdoses: Outcome in terms of changes in psychopathology and the adolescents' attitudes to care and their overdoses'. *Journal of Adolescence, 21*: 209–18.

Burstow, J. (1992) *Radical Feminist Therapy*. Newbury Park, CA: Sage.

Busfield, J. (1996) *Men, Women and Madness*. London: Macmillan Press.

Butler, C. (1998) 'Using computers to study texts'. In A. Wray, K. Trott and A. Bloomer (eds), *Projects in Linguistics: A Practical Guide to Researching Language*. London: Arnold, 213–23.

Callen, M. (1990) 'AIDS: The linguistic battlefield'. In C. Ricks and L. Michaels (eds), *The State of the Language: 1990s Edition*. London and Boston: Faber and Faber, 171–81.

Cameron, D. (2001) *Working with Spoken Discourse*. London: Sage.

Cameron, D., Kulick, D. (2003) *Language and Sexuality*. Cambridge: Cambridge University Press.

Candlin, S. (2000) 'New dynamics in the nurse-patient relationship?'. In S. Sarangi and M. Coulthard (eds), *Discourse and Social Life*. London: Longman.

Cape, J. (2002) 'Consultation length, patient-estimated consultation length, and satisfaction with the consultation'. *British Journal of General Practice, 52*: 1004–06.

Car, J., Sheikh, A. (2004a) 'Email consultations in health care: 1 – scope and effectiveness'. *British Medical Journal, 329*: 435–38.

—. (2004b) 'Email consultations in health care: 2 – acceptability and safe application'. *British Medical Journal, 329*: 439–42.

Carter, R. (2004) *Language and Creativity: The Art of Common Talk*. London: Routledge.

Carter, R., McCarthy, M. (2006) *Cambridge Grammar of English*. Cambridge: Cambridge University Press.

Cassell, E. (1976) 'Disease as an 'it': Concepts of disease revealed by patients' presentation of symptoms'. *Social Science and Medicine, 10*: 143–46.

Cates, W. (1999) 'Estimates of the incidence and prevalence of sexually transmitted diseases in the United States'. *Sexually Transmitted Diseases, 26*: 2–7.

Centre for Disease Control. (2011) *HIV Among Youth*. USA: Department of Health and Human Services.

Cheek, J. (2004) 'At the margins? Discourse analysis and qualitative research'. *Qualitative Health Research, 14*: 1140–150.

Churchill, R. Allen, J., Denman S. (2000) 'Do the attitudes and beliefs of young teenagers towards general practice influence actual consultation behaviour?'. *British Journal of General Practice, 50*: 953–57.

Clark, A. (2002) 'Language of self harm is somatic and needs to be learnt'. *British Medical Journal, 324*: 788.

Clerehan, R., Buchbinder, R. (2006) 'Toward a more valid account of functional text quality: The case of the patient information leaflet'. *Text and Talk, 26*: 39–68.

Coggan, C., Patterson, P., Fill, J. (1997) 'Suicide: Qualitative data from focus group interviews with youth'. *Social Science and Medicine, 45*: 1563–70.

Coleman, J. (1974) *Relationships in Adolescence* (London: Routledge).

Coleman, J., Hendry, L. (2000) *The Nature of Adolescence* (3rd ed). London: Routledge.

Collste, G. (2002) 'The internet doctor and medical ethics: Ethical implications of the introduction of the internet into medical encounters'. *Medicine, Health Care and Philosophy, 5*: 121–25.

Committee on Quality Health Care in America. (2001) *Crossing the Quality Chasm: A New Health System for the 21st Century*. Washington, DC: National Academy Press.

Connor, U., Upton, T. (2004) 'Introduction'. In U. Connor and T. Upton (eds), *Discourse in the Professions: Perspectives from Corpus Linguistics*. Amsterdam: John Benjamins, 1–8.

Cook, R. J. (1984) *Women's Health and Human Rights*. Geneva: World Health Organization.

Cornford, C., Hill, A., Reilly, J. (2007) 'How patients with depressive symptoms view their condition: A qualitative study'. *Family Practice, 24*: 358–64.

Cotton, S., Gupta, S. (2004) 'Characteristics of online and offline health information seekers and factors that discriminate between them'. *Social Science and Medicine, 59*: 1795–806.

Coyne, J. (1994) 'Self-reported distress: Analog or ersatz depression?'. *Psychological Bulletin, 116*: 29–45.

Crawford, P., Brown, B. (2010) 'Health communication: Corpus linguistics, data driven learning and education for health professionals'. *Taiwan International ESP Journal, 2*: 1–26.

Crawford, P., Brown, B., Harvey, K. (2014) 'Corpus linguistics and evidence-based health communication'. In H. Hamilton and W. S. Chou (eds), *The Routledge Handbook of Language and Health Communication*. London: Routledge.

Crystal, D. (1997) *The Cambridge Encyclopedia of The English Language*. Cambridge: Cambridge University Press.

—. (2006) *Language and the Internet*. Cambridge: Cambridge University Press.

—. (2011) *Internet Linguistics*. London: Routledge.

Culp, A., Clyman, M., Culp, R. (1995) 'Adolescent depressed mood, reports of suicide attempts, and asking for help'. *Adolescence, 30*: 827–37.

Daube, D. (1972) 'The linguistics of suicide'. *Philosophy and Public Affairs, 1*: 387–437.

Davies, J. (1998) 'Pharmacology versus social process: Competing or complementary views on the nature of addiction?'. *Pharmacological Theory, 80*: 265–75.

De Beaugrande, R. (2001) 'Large corpora, small corpora, and the learning of language'. In M. Ghadessy, A. Henry and R. Roseberry (eds), *Small Corpus Studies and ELT* Amsterdam: John Benjamins, 3–28.

De Shazer, S. (1997) 'Some thoughts on language use in therapy'. *Contemporary Family Therapy, 19*: 133–41.

De Swaan, A. (1990) *The Management of Normality: Critical Essays in Health and Welfare*. London: Routledge.

DiClemente, R., Zorn, J., Temoshok, L. (1986) 'Adolescents and AIDS: A survey of knowledge, beliefs, and attitudes about AIDS in San Francisco'. *American Journal of Public Health, 77*: 1443–45.

Dockrell, J., Joffe, H. (1992) 'Methodological issues involved in the study of young people and HIV/AIDS: A social psychological view'. *Health Education Research, 7*: 509–16.

Donovan, C., Mellanby, A., Jacobson, L., Taylor, B., Tripp, J. (1997) 'Teenagers' views on the general practice consultation and provision of contraception'. *British Journal of General Practice, 47*: 715–18.

Dow, P. (2004) *'I Feel Like I'm Invisible': Children Talking to ChildLine about Self-Harm.* London: ChildLine.

Dowrick, C. (2009) *Beyond Depression* (2nd ed). Oxford: Oxford University Press.

Drew, M., Dobson, K., Stam, H. (1999) 'The negative self-concept in clinical depression'. *Canadian Psychology, 40*: 192–204.

Driessnack, M. (2006) 'Draw-and-tell conversations with children about fear'. *Qualitative Health Research, 16*: 1414–35.

Dundon, E. (2006) 'Adolescent depression: A metasynthesis'. *Journal of Pediatric Care, 20*: 384–92.

Durkheim, E. (2006) *On Suicide.* London: Penguin.

Eckersley, R., Dear, K. (2002) 'Cultural correlates of youth suicide'. *Social Science and Medicine, 55*: 1891–904.

Epstein, R., Duberstein, P., Feldman, M., Rochlen, A., Bell, R., Kravitz, R., Cipri, C., Becker, J., Bamonti, P., Paterniti, D. (2010) '"I didn't know what was wrong:" How people with undiagnosed depression recognize, name and explain their distress'. *Journal of General Internal Medicine, 25*: 954–61.

Estroff, S., Lachicotte, W., Illingworth, L., Johnston, A. (1991) 'Everybody's got a little mental illness: Accounts of illness and Self among people with severe, persistent mental illnesses'. *Medical Anthropology Quarterly, 5*: 331–69.

Eysenbach, G. (2004) 'Deja-vu'. *British Medical Journal, 328*: 439.

Eysenbach, G., Diepgen, T. (1998) 'Towards quality management of medical informationon the internet: Evaluation, labelling, and filtering of information'. *British Medical Journal, 317*: 1496–502.

Fairbairn, G. (1995) *Contemplating Suicide: The Language and Ethics of Self Harm* London: Routledge.

—. (1998) 'Suicide, language, and clinical practice'. *Philosophy, Psychiatry, and Psychology, 5*: 157–69.

Fairclough, N. (2000) *New Labour, New Language?*. London: Routledge.

Family Planning Association. (2010a) *Teenage Pregnancy Factsheet*. London: The Family Planning Association.

—. (2010b) *Sexually Transmitted Infections Factsheet*. London: The Family Planning Association.

Favazza, A. (1996) *Bodies Under Siege: Self-Mutilation and Body Modification in Culture* (2nd ed). Baltimore: The John Hopkins University Press.

—. (1998) 'The coming of age of self-mutilation'. *The Journal of Nervous and Mental Disorders, 186*: 259–68.

Feldman, M., Franks, Duberstein, P., Vannoy, S., Epstein, R., Kravitz, R. (2007) 'Let's not talk about it: Suicide inquiry in primary care'. *Annals of Family Medicine, 5*: 412–18.

Finn, M., Sarangi, S. (2009) 'Humanizing HIV/AIDS and its (re)stigmatizing effects: HIV public "positive" speaking in India'. *Health, 13*: 47–65.

Fleischman, S. (1999) 'A linguist on illness and disease'. *Journal of Medical Humanities, 20*: 3–31.

Flowerdew, L. (2004) 'The argument for using English specialized corpora to understand academic and professional language'. In U. Connor and T. Upton (eds), *Discourse in the Professions: Perspectives from Corpus Linguistics*. Amsterdam: John Benjamins, 11–33.

Ford, C. A., Millstein, S. G., Halpern-Felsher, B. L. (1997) Influence of physician confidentiality assurances on adolescents' willingness to disclose information and seek future health care. *Journal of American Medical Association, 278*: 1029–34.

Foucault, M. (1972) *The Archaeology of Knowledge*. London: Tavistock.

Fox, N. (1993) *Postmodernism, Sociology and Health*. Buckingham: Open University Press.

Francis, G., Kramer-Dahl, A. (2004) 'Grammar in the construction of medical case histories'. In C. Coffin, A. Hewings and K. O' Halloran (eds), *Applying English Grammar: Functional and Corpus Approaches*. London: Arnold, 172–90.

Franzen, A. G., Gotzen, L. (2011) 'The beauty of blood? Self-injury and ambivalence in an Internet community'. *Journal of Youth Studies, 4*: 279–94.

Freud, A. (1958) 'Adolescence'. *Psychoanalytic Study of the Child, 15*: 255–78.

Friedman, H. (1989) 'The health of adolescents: Beliefs and behaviour'. *Social Science and Medicine, 29*: 309–15.

Fromm, E. (1979) *To Have or To Be?*. London: Abacus.

Fujimura, L., Weis, D., Cochran, J. (1985) 'Suicide: Dynamics and implications for counselling'. *Journal of Counselling and Development, 63*: 612–15.

Fullagar, S. (2001) 'Towards a sociocultural analysis of youth suicide: Researching the everyday narratives of urban and regional communities' *Youth Suicide Prevention Bulletin, 5*: 7–9.

—. (2003) 'Wasted lives: The social dynamics of shame and youth suicide'. *Journal of Sociology, 39*: 291–307.

—. (2005) 'The paradox of promoting help-seeking: A critical analysis of risk, rurality and youth suicide'. *Critical Psychology, 14*: 31–51.

Furedi, F. (2004) *Therapy Culture: Cultivating Vulnerability in an Uncertain Age*. London: Routledge.

Gains, J. (1999) 'Electronic mail – a new style of communication or just a new medium? An investigation into the text features of email'. *English for Specific Purposes, 18*: 81–101.

Gardner, D., Chowdry, R. (1985) 'Suicidal and parasuicidal behaviour in borderline personality disorders'. *Psychiatric Clinics in North America, 8*: 389–403.

Gavey, N., McPhillips, K. (1999) 'Subject to romance: Heterosexual passivity as an obstacle to women initiating condom use'. *Psychology of Women Quarterly, 23*: 349–67.

Gavin, M., Rogers, A. (2006) 'Narratives of suicide in psychological autopsy: Bringing lay knowledge back in'. *Journal of Mental Health, 15*: 135–44.

Gibbs, R. (1994) *The Poetics of Mind: Figurative Thought, Language, and Understanding.* Cambridge: Cambridge University Press.

Gilchrist, H., Howarth, G., Sullivan, G. (2007) 'The cultural context of youth suicide in Australia: Unemployment, identity and gender'. *Social Policy and Society, 6*: 151–63.

Gilfoyle, J., Wilson, J., Brown, B. (1992) 'Sex, organs and audiotape: A discourse analytic approach to talking about heterosexual sex and relationships'. *Feminism and Psychology, 2*: 209–30.

Graffigna, G., Olson, K. (2009) 'The ineffable disease: Exploring young people's discourses about HIV/AIDS in Alberta, Canada'. *Qualitative Health Research, 19*: 790–801.

Grashoff, U. (2006) *Let Me Finish.* London: Headline.

Gray, N., Klein, J. (2006) 'Adolescents and the internet: Health and sexuality information'. *Current Opinion in Obstetrics and Gynaecology, 18*: 519–24.

Gray, N., Klein, J., Cantrill, J., Noyce, P. (2002) 'Adolescents girls' use of the internet for health information: Issues beyond access'. *Journal of Medical Systems, 26*: 545–53.

Gray, N., Klein, J., Noyce, P. (2005a) 'The internet: A window on adolescent health literacy'. *Journal of Adolescent Health, 37*: 243–47.

Gray, N., Klein, J., Noyce, P., Sesselberg, T., Cantrill, J. (2005b) 'Health information-seeking behaviour in adolescence: The place of the internet'. *Social Science and Medicine, 60*: 1467–78.

Gray, N., Harvey, K., McPherson, A., Macfarlane, A. (2008a) 'Medicine dilemmas in adolescents' email messages'. *The International Journal of Pharmacy Practice,1*: 34–5.

Gray, N., Harvey, K., Macfarlane, A., McPherson, A. (2008b) "Help! Adolescent Health Language in Email Messages'. *Journal of Adolescent Health, 42*: 5–6.

Griffiths, L. (2004) 'Electronic text-based communication – assumptions and illusions created by the transference phenomena'. In G. Bolton, S. Howlett, C. Lago and J. Wright (eds), *Writing Cures: An Introductory Handbook of Writing in Counselling and Therapy.* London: Routledge, 137–41.

Groom, N. (2010) 'Closed-class keywords and corpus-driven discourse analysis'. In M. Bondi and M. Scott (eds), *Keyness in Texts.* Amsterdam: John Benjamins, 59–78.

Grover, J. (1990) 'AIDS: Keywords'. In C. Ricks and L. Michaels (eds), *The State of the Language: 1990s Edition.* London and Boston: Faber and Faber, 142–62.

Gunnell, D., Frankel, S. (1994) 'Prevention of suicide: Aspirations and evidence'. *British Medical Journal, 308*: 1227–33.

Gwyn, R. (2002) *Communicating Health and Illness.* London: Sage.

Hadlow, J., Pitts, M. (1991) 'The understanding of common health terms by doctors, nurses and patients'. *Social Science and Medicine, 32*: 193–96.

Hagood, M., Stevens, L., Reinking, D. (2002) 'What do *they* have to teach us? Talkin' 'cross generations!'. In D. Alvermann (ed.), *Adolescents and Literacies in a Digital World.* New York: Peter Lang, 68–83.

Harden, A., Willig, C. (1998) 'An exploration of the discursive constructions used in young adults' memories and accounts of contraception'. *Journal of Health Psychology, 3*: 429–45.

Harrington, R. (1995) 'Depressive disorder in adolescence'. *Archives of Diseases in Childhood, 72*: 193–95.

Harris, J. (2000) 'Self-harm: Cutting the bad out of me'. *Qualitative Health Research, 10*: 164–73.

Harvey, K. (2012) 'Disclosures of depression: Using corpus linguistics methods to examine young people's online health concerns'. *International Journal of Corpus Linguistics, 17*: 349–79.

Harvey, K., Koteyko, N. (2012) *Exploring Health Communication*. London: Routledge.

Harvey, K., Brown, B., Crawford, P., Macfarlane, A., McPherson, A. (2007) 'Am I normal? Teenagers, sexual health and the internet'. *Social Science and Medicine, 65*: 771–81.

Harvey, K., Churchill, D., Crawford, P., Brown, B., Mullany, L., Macfarlane, A., McPherson, A. (2008) 'Health communication and adolescents: What do their emails tell us?'. *Family Practice, 25*: 1–8.

Handwerk, M., Larzelerre, R., Friman, P. (1998) 'The relationship between lethality of attempted suicide and prior suicide communication in a sample of residential youths'. *J Adolescence, 21*: 438.

Hawton, K., Fagg, J. (1992) 'Deliberate self-poisoning and self-injury in adolescents. A Study of characteristics and trends in Oxford, 1976–1989'. *British Journal of Psychiatry, 162*: 816–23.

Hawton, K., O'Grady, J., Osborn, M., and Cole, D. (1982) Adolescents who take overdoses: their characteristics, problems and contacts with helping agencies. *British Journal of Psychiatry, 140*: 118–23.

Heald, S. (2005) 'Abstain or die: The development of HIV/AIDS policy in Botswana'. *Journal of Biosocial Science, 38*: 29–41.

Health Protection Agency. (2011) *HIV in the United Kingdom: 2011 Report*. London: Health Protection Agency.

Helman, C. (2007) *Culture, Health and Illness* (5th ed). London: Hodder Arnold.

Heritage, J., Maynard, D. (eds) (2006) *Communication in Medical Care: Interaction between Primary Care Physicians and Patients*. Cambridge, UK: Cambridge University Press.

Herrera, A., Dahlblom, K., Dahlgren, L., Kullgren, G. (2006) 'Pathways to suicidal behaviour among adolescent girls in Nicaragua'. *Social Science and Medicine, 62*: 805–14.

Herring, S. (2001) 'Computer-mediated discourse'. In D. Schiffrin, D. Tannen and H. Hamilton (eds), *The Handbook of Discourse Analysis*. Oxford: Blackwell, 612–34.

Herzlich, C. and Pierret, J. (1986) 'Illness: From causes to meaning'. In C. Currer and M. Stacey (eds), *Concepts of Health, Illness and Healing*. Leamington Spa: Berg, 73–96.

Hewings, A., Coffin, C. (2004) 'Grammar in the construction of online discussion messages'. In C. Coffin, A. Hewings and K. O' Halloran (eds), *Applying English Grammar: Functional and Corpus Approaches*. London: Edward Arnold.

Hewitt, P., Stokes, R. (1975) 'Disclaimers'. *American Sociological Review, 40*: 1–11.

Higgins, C., Norton, B. (2010) 'Applied linguistics, local knowledge and HIV/AIDS'. In C. Higgins and B. Norton (eds), *Language and HIV/AIDS*. Bristol: Multilingual Matters, 1–19.

Hillier, L., Harrison, L., Warr, D. (1998) "When you carry condoms all the boys think you want it': Negotiating competing discourses about safe sex'. *Journal of Adolescence, 21*: 15–29.

Hodgkin, P. (1985) 'Medicine is war: And other medical metaphors'. *British Medical Journal, 291*: 1820–21.

Holland, J., Ramazanoglu, C., Scott, S., Sharpe, S., Thompson, R. (1992) 'Pressure, resistance, empowerment: Young women and the negotiation of safer sex'. In P. Aggleton, P. Davies and G. Hart (eds), *AIDS: Rights, Risk and Reason*. London: The Falmer Press, 142–62.

Holland, J., Ramazanoglu, C., Sharpe, S., Thomson, R. (1996) *The Male in the Head: Young People, Heterosexuality and Power*. London: Tufnell Press.

—. (2000) 'Deconstructing virginity – young people's accounts of first sex'. *Sexual and Relationship Therapy, 3*: 221–32.

Hollway, W. (1984) 'Gender difference and the production of subjectivity'. In J. Henriques, W. Hollway, C. Urwin, C. Venn and V. Walkerdine (eds), *Changing the Subject: Psychology, Social Regulation and Subjectivity*. London: Methuen, 227–63.

Holmes, G., Offen., L., Waller, G. (1997) 'See no evil, hear no evil, speak no evil: Why do relatively male victims of childhood sexual abuse receive help for abuse-related issues in adulthood?'. *Clinical Psychology Review, 17*: 69–88.

Horne, O., Csipke, E. (2009) From feeling too little and too much, to feeling more and less? A nonparadoxical theory of the functions of self-harm. *Qualitative Health Research, 19*(5): 655–67.

Hunston, S. (2002) *Corpora in Applied Linguistics*. Cambridge: Cambridge University Press.

Hunston, S., Thompson, G. (2000) 'Editors' Introduction'. In S. Hunston and G. Thompson (eds), *Evaluation in Text: Authorial Stance and the Construction of Discourse*. Oxford: Oxford University Press, 1–8.

Hurry, J., Aggleton, P., Warwick, I. (2000) 'Introduction'. In P. Aggleton, J. Hurry and I. Warwick (eds), *Young People and Mental Health*. Wiley: Chichester, 1–8.

Hutchinson, M., Cooney, T. (1998) 'Patterns of parent-teen sexual risk communication: Implications for interventions'. *Family Relations, 47*: 185–94.

Hyde, A., Howlett, E., Drennan, J., Brady, D. (2005) 'Masculinities and young men's sex education needs in Ireland: Problematizing client-centred health promotion approaches'. *Health Promotion International,20*: 334–41.

Ingham, R. (1993) 'Older bodies in older clothes'. *Health Psychology Update, 14*: 31–6.

Ingham, R., Woodcock, A., Stenner, K. (1992) 'The limitations of rational decision-making models as applied to young people's sexual behaviour'. In P. Aggleton, P. Davies and G. Hart (eds), *AIDS: Rights, Risk and Reason*, London: Falmer Press, 163–73.

Jack, R. (1992) *Women and Attempted Suicide*. Hove: Lawrence Erlbaum.

Jackson, M. (1984) 'Sex research and the construction of sexuality: A tool of male supremacy?'. *Women's Studies International Forum*, 7: 43–51.

Jackson, S. (1982) 'Femininity, masculinity and sexuality'. In S. Friedman and E. Sarah (eds), *On the Problem of Men*. London: The Women's Press.

—. (2005a) '"Dear girlfriend. . .": Constructions of sexual health problems and sexual identities in letters to a teenage magazine'. *Sexualities*, 8: 282–305.

—. (2005b) '"I'm 15 and desperate for sex": "Doing" and "undoing" desire in letters to a teenage magazine'. *Feminism and Psychology*, 15: 295–313.

Jacobs, J. (1967) 'A phenomenological study of suicide notes'. *Social Problems*, 15: 60–72.

Jacobson, L., Wilkinson, C., Owen, P. (1994) 'Is the potential of the teenage consultations being missed?: A study of consultation times in primary care'. *Family Practice*, 11: 296–99.

Jacobson, L., Wilkinson, C., Pill, R., Hackett, P. (1996) 'Communication between teenagers and British general practitioners: A preliminary study of the teenage perspective'. *Ambulatory Child Health*, 1: 291–301.

Jacobson, L., Richardson, G., Parry-Langdon, N., Donovan, C. (2001) 'How do teenagers and primary healthcare providers view each other? An overview of key themes'. *British Journal of General Practice*, 51: 811–16.

Jan de Wilde, E. (2000) 'Adolescent suicidal behaviour: A general population perspective'. In K. Hawton (ed.), *The International Handbook of Suicide and Attempted Suicide*. Chichester: Wiley, 249–59.

Jeffries, L. (2000) 'Don't throw out the baby with the bathwater: In defence of theoretical eclecticism in stylistics'. *PALA Occasional Papers*, 12: 1–16.

Johnson, D., Murray, J. (1985) 'Do doctors mean what they say?'. In D. Enright (ed.), *Fair of Speech: The Uses of Euphemism*. Oxford: Oxford University Press, 151–58.

Johnstone, L. (1997) 'Self-injury and the psychiatric response'. *Feminism and Psychology*, 7: 421–26.

Johnstone, B. (2008) *Discourse Analysis* (2nd ed). Oxford: Blackwell.

Joinson, A. (2001) 'Self-disclosure in computer-mediated communication: The role of self-awareness and visual anonymity'. *European Journal of Social Psychology*, 31: 177–92.

Jones, A. (2007) 'Admitting hospital patients: A qualitative study of an everyday nursing task'. *Nursing Inquiry*, 14: 212–23.

Jones, R., Finlay, N., Simpson, N., Kreitman, T. (1997) 'How can adolescents' health needs and concerns best be met?'. *British Journal of General Practice*, 47: 631–34.

Kanuga, M., Rosenfeld, W. (2004) 'Adolescent sexuality and the internet: The good, the bad, and the url'. *Journal of Pediatric and Adolescent Genecology*, 17: 117–24.

Karp, D. (1996) *Speaking of Sadness: Depression, Disconnection, and the Meanings of Illness*. Oxford, New York: Oxford University Press.

Kegeles, S., Adler, N., Irwin, C. (1988) 'Sexually active adolescents and condoms: Changes over one year in knowledge, attitudes and use'. *American Journal of Public Health, 78*: 460–61.

Kennedy, G. (1998) *An Introduction to Corpus Linguistics*. London: Longman.

Kerfoot, M. (2000) 'Youth suicide and deliberate self-harm'. In K. Hawton (ed.), *The International Handbook of Suicide and Attempted Suicide*. Chichester: Wiley, 111–30.

Kerfoot, M., Harrington, R., Dyer, E. (1995) 'Brief home-based intervention with young suicide attempters and their families'. *Journal of Adolescence, 18*: 557–68.

Kerfoot, M., Dyer, E., Harrington, V., Woodham, A., Harrington, R. (1996) 'Correlates and short-term course of self-poisoning in adolescents'. *British Journal of Psychiatry, 168*: 38–42.

Kessler, D., Lloyd, K., Lewis, G., Gray, D. P. (1999) 'Cross sectional study of symptom attribution and recognition of depression and anxiety in primary care'. *British Medical Journal, 318*: 436–40.

Kirkman, M., Rosenthal, D., Smith, A. (1998) 'Adolescent sex and the romantic narrative: Why some young heterosexuals use condoms to prevent pregnancy but not disease'. *Psychology, Health and Medicine, 3*: 355–67.

Klein, J., Wilson, K. (2002a) 'Delivering quality care: Adolescents' discussion of health risks with their providers'. *Journal of Adolescent Health, 30*: 190–95.

Klein, J., Rossbach, C., Nijher, H., Geist, M., Wilson, K., Cohn, S., Siegel, D., Weitzman, M. (2001) 'Where do adolescents get thier condoms?'. *Journal of Adolescent Health,29*: 186–93.

Kleiner, K., Akers, R., Burke, B., Werner, J. (2002) 'Parent and physician attitudes regarding electronic communication in pediatric practices'. *Pediatrics, 109*: 740–44.

Knifton, C. (2005) 'Social work and the rise of the MRSA "super bug"'. *Practice, 17*: 39–42.

Koestenbaum, W. (1990) 'Speaking in the shadow of AIDS'. In C. Ricks and L. Michaels (eds), *The State of the Language: 1990s Edition*. London and Boston: Faber and Faber, 163–70.

Korner, H. (2010) 'Safe sex – not so straightforward: Intersubjective positioning in gay men's accounts of sexual exposure to HIV'. In C. Higgins and B. Norton (eds), *Language and HIV/AIDS*. Bristol: Multilingual Matters. pp. 83–112.

Kraft, P. (1993) 'Sexual knowledge among Norwegian adolescents'. *Journal of Adolescence, 16*: 3–21.

Kreitman, N., Smith, P., Tan, E. (1970) 'Attempted suicide as language: An empirical study'. *British Journal of Psychiatry, 116*: 465–73.

Kreyer, R. (2003) 'Genitive and *of*-construction in modern written English: Processability and human involvement'. *International Journal of Corpus Linguistics, 8*: 169–207.

Kvalem, I. and Traeen, B. (2000) 'Self-efficacy, scripts of love and intention to use condoms among Norwegian adolescents'. *Journal of Youth and Adolescence, 29*: 337–53.

Lawless, S., Kippax, S., Crawford, J. (1996) 'Dirty, diseased and undeserving: The positioning of HIV positive women'. *Social Science and Medicine, 43*: 1371–77.

Lawrence, J. (1993) 'African-American adolescents' knowledge, health-related attitudes, sexual behavior, and contraceptive decisions: Implications for the prevention of adolescent HIV infection'. *Journal of Consulting and Clinical Psychology, 61*: 104–12.

Leader, D. (2007) *The New Black: Mourning, Melancholia and Depression*. London: Hamish Hamilton.

Leap, W. (1991) 'AIDS, linguistics, and the study of non-neutral discourse'. *The Journal of Sex Research, 28*: 275–87.

—. (1995) 'Talking about AIDS: Linguistic perspectives on non-neutral discourse'. In H. ten Brummelhuis and G. Herdt (eds), *Culture and Sexual Risk: Anthropological Perspectives of AIDS*. Sydney: Gordon and Breach, 227–38.

Lebacqz, K., Englehardt, H. (1980) 'Suicide'. In D. Horan and D. Mall (eds), *Death, Dying and Euthanasia*. Maryland: Aletheia Books, 688–96.

Leech, G. (1992) 'Corpora and theories of linguistic performance'. In J. Svartvik (ed.), *Directions in Corpus Linguistics*. Berlin: Mouton de Gruyter, 105–22.

Leenars, A., De Wilde, E., Wenckstern, S., Kral, M. (2001) 'Suicide notes of adolescents: A life-span comparison'. *Canadian Journal of Behavioural Science, 33*: 47–57.

Leone, P. (2010) 'General spoken language and school language: Key words and discourse patterns in history textbooks'. In M. Bondi and M. Scott (eds), *Keyness in Texts*. Amsterdam: John Benjamins, 235–49.

Lester, G., Lester, D. (1971) *Suicide: The Gamble with Death*. New Jersey: Prentice-Hall.

Lewis, S. (1993) 'Talking blues'. *Nursing Times, 11*: 26–8.

—. (1995) 'A search for meaning: Making sense of depression'. *Journal of Mental Health, 4*: 369–82.

Lipták, A. K., Reintges, C. H. (2006) 'Have = be+P. New evidence for the preposition incorporation analysis'. In M. Frascarelli (ed.), *Phases of interpretation*. Berlin: Mouton de Gruyter, 107–32.

Lobley, J. (2001) 'Whose personality is it anyway? The production of "personality" in a diagnostic interview'. In A. McHoul and M. Rapley (eds), *How to Analyse Talk in Institutional Settings*. London: Continuum, 113–23.

Lou, C., Zhao, Q., Gao, E., Shah, I. (2006) 'Can the internet be used effectively to provide sex education to young people in China?'. *Journal of Adolescent Health, 39*: 720–28.

Lupton, D. (2004) *Medicine as Culture* (2nd ed). London: Sage.

Madge, N., Harvey, J. (1999) 'Suicide among the young – the size of the problem'. *Journal of Adolescence, 22*: 145–55.

Mahlberg, M. (2007) 'Lexical items in discourse: Identifying local textual functions of *sustainable development*'. In M. Hoey, M. Mahlberg, M. Stubbs and T. Teubert (eds), *Text, Discourse and Corpora*. London: Continuum, 191–218.

Mandl, K., Kohane, I., Brandt, A. (1998) 'Electronic patient-physician communication: Problems and promise'. *Ann Intern Med,129*: 495–500.

Manley, R., Leichner, P. (2003) 'Anguish and despair in adolescents with eating disorders: Helping to manage suicidal ideation and impulses'. *Crisis, 24*: 32–6.

Manning, E. (1997) 'Kissing and Cuddling: The reciprocity of romantic and sexual activity'. In K. Harvey and C. Shalom (eds), *Language and Desire: Encoding Sex, Romance and Intimacy*. London: Routledge, 43–59.

Mason, L. (2005) 'They haven't a clue!' A qualitative study of the self-perceptions of 11–14-year old clinic attenders'. *Primary Health Care Research and Development, 6*: 199–207.

Maughan, B., Kim-Cohen, J. (2005) 'Continuities between childhood and adult life'. *British Journal of Psychiatry, 187*: 301–03.

Mautner, G. (2007) 'Mining corpora for social information: The case of the elderly'. *Language in Society, 36*: 51–72.

—. (2009) 'Corpora and critical discourse analysis'. In P. Baker (ed.), *Contemporary Corpus Linguistics*. London: Continuum, 32–46.

—. (2010) *Language and the Market Society. Critical Reflections on Discourse and Dominance*. London and New York: Routledge.

McAllister, M. (2003) 'Multiple meaning of self-harm: A critical review'. *International Journal of Mental Health Nursing, 12*: 177–85.

McCabe, J. (2005) 'Who are the experts? Medicalization in teen magazine advice columns'. *Sociological Studies of Children and Youth, 11*: 153–91.

McCarthy, M., Handford, M. (2004) 'Invisible to us': A preliminary corpus-based study of spoken business English'. In U. Connor and T. Upton (eds), *Discourse in the Professions: Perspectives from Corpus Linguistics*. Amsterdam: John Benjamins, 167–201.

McCarthy, D., Rapley, M. (2001) 'Far from the madding crowd: psychiatric diagnosis as the management of moral accountability'. In A. McHoul and Rapley, M. (eds), *How to Analyse Talk in Institutional Settings*. London: Continuum, 159–67.

McEnery, A. (2005) *Swearing in English: Bad Language, Purity and Power from 1856 to the Present*. London: Routledge.

McEnery, A., Baker, P., Cheepen, C. (2002) 'Lexis, indirectness and politeness in operator calls'. In Peters, P., Collins, P., and Smith, A. (eds), *New Frontiers in Corpus Research*. Amsterdam: Rodopi, 53–69.

McEnery, A., Wilson, A. (2001) *Corpus Linguistics*. Edinburgh: Edinburgh University Press.

McEnery, A., Xiao, R., Tono, Y. (2006) *Corpus-Based Language Studies*. London: Routledge.

McHoul, A., Rapley, M. (2001) 'Preface: With a little help from our friends'. In A. McHoul and M. Rapley (eds), *How to Analyse Talk in Institutional Settings*. London: Continuum, 2–9.

McKay, S. (2003) 'Adolescent risk behaviours and communication research: Current directions'. *Journal of Language and Social Psychology, 22*: 74–82.

McKenna, K., Bargh, J. (1998) 'Plan 9 from cyberspace: The implications of the internet for personality and social psychological research'. *Journal of Personality and Social Psychology, 75*: 681–94.

—(2000) 'Plan 9 from cyberspace: The implications of the internet for personality and social psychological research'. *Journal of Personality and Social Psychology, 75*: 681–94.

McLaughlin, J., Miller, P., Warwick, H. (1996) 'Deliberate self-harm in adolescents: Hopelessness, depression, problems and problem-solving'. *Journal of Adolescence, 19*: 523–32.

McLeod, A. (1997) 'Resisting invitations to depression: A narrative approach to family nursing'. *Journal of Family Nursing, 3*: 394–406.

McMullen, L., Conway, J. (2002) 'Conventional metaphors for depression'. In S. Fussell (ed.), *Verbal Communication of Emotions: Interdisciplinary Perspectives*. Mahwah, New Jersey: Lawrence Erlbaum, 167–81.

McPherson, A. (2005) 'ABC of adolescence: Adolescents in primary care'. *British Medical Journal, 330*: 465–67.

McPhillips, K., Braun, V., Gavey, N. (2001) 'Defining (hetero)sex: How imperative is the "coital imperative"'. *Women's Studies International Forum, 24*: 229–40.

McQueen, C., Henwood, K. (2002) 'Young men in 'crisis': Attending to the language of teenage boys' distress'. *Social Science and Medicine, 55*: 1493–509.

McRobbie, A. (1996) 'More! New sexualities in girls' and women's magazines'. In J. Curran, D. Morley and V. Walkerdine (eds), *Cultural Studies and Communications* London: Arnold, 172–95.

Mechanic, D. (2001) 'How should hamsters run? Some observations about sufficient patient time in primary care'. *British Medical Journal, 232*: 266–68.

Mental Health Foundation. (2006) *Truth Hurts:Report of the National Inquiry into Self-Harm among Young People*. London: Mental Health Foundation.

Michaud, P., Suris, J. C., McPherson, A., Macfarlane, A. (2004) 'Alice in cyberland: Use and abuse of health websites by young people'. *Italian Journal of Pediatrics, 30*: 198–204.

Miles, L. (1993) 'Women, AIDS, and power in heterosexual sex: A discourse analysis'. *Women's Studies International Forum, 6*: 497–511.

Mintz, D. (1992) 'What's in a word: The distancing function of language in medicine'. *The Journal of Medical Humanities, 13*: 223–33.

Mishan, F. (2004) 'Authenticating corpora for language learning: A problem and its resolution'. *ELT Journal, 58*: 219–27.

Mondimore, F. (2002) *Adolescent Depression: A Guide for Parents*. Baltimore and London: The John Hopkins University Press.

Moon, R. (2007) 'Words, frequencies, and texts (particularly Conrad): A stratified approach'. *Journal of Literary Semantics, 36*: 1–33.

Moore, S., Rosenthal, D. (1993) *Sexuality in Adolescence*. London and New York: Routledge.

Moore, S., Rosenthal, D., Mitchell, A. (1996) *Youth, AIDS and Sexually Transmitted Diseases*. London and New York: Routledge.

Morrison, A., Love, A. (1996) 'A discourse of disillusionment: Letters to the Editor in two Zimbabwean magazines 10 years after independence'. *Discourse and Society, 7*: 39–76.

Morrow, P. (2006) 'Telling about problems and giving advice in an internet discussion forum: Some discourse features'. *Discourse Studies, 8*: 531–48.

Moynihan, R., Heath, I., Henry, D. (2002) 'Selling sickness: The pharmaceutical industry and disease mongering'. *Britsh Medical Journal, 324*: 886–91.

Nettleton, S. (2006) *The Sociology of Health and Illness* (2nd ed). Cambridge: Polity Press.

Nicolson, P. (1995) 'Qualitative research, psychology and mental health: Analysing subjectivity'. *Journal of Mental Health, 4*: 337–45.

Noon, G. (1978) 'On Suicide'. *Journal of the History of Ideas, 39*: 371–86.

Ogle, S., Glaiser, A., Riley, S. (2008) 'Communication between parents and their children about sexual health'. *Contraception, 77*: 283–88.

O'Connor, R., Sheehy, N. (2000) *Understanding Suicidal Behaviour*. Leicester: BPS Books.

O'Halloran, K. A. (2009) 'Inferencing and cultural reproduction: A corpus-based critical discourse analysis'. *Text and Talk, 29*: 21–51.

Orpin, D, (2005) 'Corpus Linguistics and Critical Discourse Analysis: Examining the ideology of sleaze'. *International Journal of Corpus Linguistics, 10*: 37–61.

Parker, I. (1992) *Discourse Dynamics: Critical Analysis for Social and Individual Psychology*. London: Routledge.

Parker, G. (2007) 'Is depression overdiagnosed?' *British Medical Journal, 335*: 328.

Parry, R. (2004) 'Communication during goal-setting in physiotherapy treatment settings'. *Clinical Rehabilitation, 18*: 668–82.

Parsons, T. (1951) *The Social System*. Glencoe: The Free Press.

Partington, A. (2003) *The Linguistics of Political Argument: The Spin-Doctor and the Wolf-Pack at the White House*. Abingdon: Routledge.

Pearce, M. (2005) 'Informalization in UK party election broadcasts 1966–1997'. *Language and Literature, 14*: 65–90.

Pembroke, L. (ed.) (1994) *Self-Harm: Perspectives from Personal Experience*. Survivors Speak Out: London.

Peremans, L., Hermann, D., Avonts, P., Van Royen, S., Denekens, J. (2000) 'Contraceptive knowledge and expectations by adolescents: an explanation by focus groups'. *Patient Education and Counselling, 40*: 133–41.

Phelps, S. (1998) 'Adolescents and their multiple literacies'. In D. Alverman, K., Hinchman, D. Moore, S. Phelps and D. Waff (eds), *Reconceptualising the Literacies in Adolescents' Lives*. New Jersey: Erlbaum, 1–2.

Pilgrim, D., Bentall, R. (1999) 'The medicalisation of misery: A critical realist analysis of the concept of depression'. *Journal of Mental Health, 8*: 261–74.

Pilnick, A. (1999) '"Patient counselling" by pharmacists: Advice, information or instruction?'. *The Sociological Quarterly, 40*: 613–22.

Plante, L. (2007) *Bleeding to Ease the Pain: Cutting, Self-Injury and the Adolescent Search for Self*. Connecticut: Praeger.

Pollock, K. (2007) 'Maintaining face in the presentation of depression: Constraining the therapeutic potential of the consultation'. *Health, 11*: 163–80.

Pomerantz, A. (1986) 'Extreme case formulations: a way of legitimizing claims'. *Human Studies, 9*: 219–29.

Powers, S., Hauser, S., Kilner, L. (1989) 'Adolescent mental health'. *American Psychologist, 44*: 200–08.

Pretzel, P. (1972) *Understanding and Counselling the Suicidal Person*. Nashville: Abingdon.

Radley, A. (2004) *Making Sense of Illness*. London: Sage.

Rafiquzzman, M. (1995) 'AIDS' nomenclature's spelling or style'. *Journal of the Royal Society of Health, 15*: 331.

Randall, H., Byers, E. (2003) 'What is sex? Students' definitions of having sex, sexual partner, and unfaithful sexual behaviour'. *The Canadian Journal of Human Sexuality, 12*: 87–96.

Rees-Lewis, J. (1994) 'Patient views on quality in general practice: Literature review'. *Social Science and Medicine, 39*: 655–70.

Reeves, A., Bowl, R., Wheeler, S., Guthrie, E. (2004) 'The hardest words: Exploring the dialogue of suicide in the counselling process – a discourse analysis'. *Counselling and Psychotherapy Research, 4*: 62–71.

Rich, M., Lamola, S., Gordon, J., Chalfen, R. (2000) 'Video intervention/prevention assessment: A patient-centered methodology for understanding the adolescent illness experience'. *Journal of Adolescent Health, 21*: 155–65.

Richters, J., Song, A. (1999). 'Australian university students agree with Clinton's definition of sex'. *British Medical Journal, 318*: 1011–12.

Riley, D. (2004) 'All mouth and no trousers: Linguistic embarrassments'. *Critical Quarterly, 46*: 26–32.

Rogers, A., Mead, N. (2004) 'More than technology and access: Primary care patients' views on the use and non-use of health information in the internet age'. *Health and Social Care in the Community, 12*: 102–10.

Rogers, A., Pilgrim, D. (2005) *A Sociology of Mental Health and Illness* (3rd ed). Maidenhead, UK: Open University Press.

Rogers, A., May, C., Oliver, D. (2001) 'Experiencing depression, experiencing the depressed: The separate worlds of patients and doctors'. *Journal of Mental Health, 10*: 317–33.

Rose, N. (2006) 'Disorders without borders? The expanding scope of psychiatric practice'. *BioSocieties, 1*: 465–84.

Rosenthal, D., Moore, S. (1994) 'Stigma and ignorance: Young people's beliefs about STDs'. *Venereology, 7*: 62–6.

Rosenthal, D., Feldman, D. (2002) *Talking Sexuality: Parent-Adolescent Communication*. San Fransisco: Jossey-Bass.

Ross, M. (1994) 'Maggy Ross'. In L. Pembroke (ed.), *Self-Harm: Perspectives from Personal Experience*. Survivors Speak Out: London, 14–16.

Ross, C., Pam, A. (1995) *Pseudoscience in Biological Psychiatry: Blaming the Body*. New York: Wiley.

Rubenstein, J., Halton, Kasten, L., Rubin, C., Stechler, G. (1998) 'Suicidal behaviour in adolescents: Stress and protection in different family contexts'. *American Journal of Orthopsychiatry, 68*: 274–84.

Ruusuvuori, J. (2005) 'Comparing homeopathic and general practice consultations: The case of problem presentation'. *Communication and Medicine, 2*: 123–35.

Safer, D. (1997) 'Self-reported suicide attempts by adolescents'. *Annals of Clinical Psychiatry, 9*: 263–69.

Samaritans. (1996) *Key Facts: Young People and Suicide*. Slough: Samaritans.

—. (2009) *Young People's Emotional Health*. Slough: Samaritans.

Sarangi, S. (2004) 'Editorial: Towards a communicative mentality in medical and healthcare practice'. *Communication and Medicine, 1*: 1–11.

Sauntson, H., Morrish, L. (2011) 'Vision, values and international excellence: The 'products' that university mission statements sell to students'. In M. Molesworth, R. Scullion and E. Nixon (eds), *The Marketisation of Higher Education and the Student as Consumer*. Abingdon: Routledge, 73–85.

Schouten, B., Van Den Putte, B., Pasmans, M., Meeuwesen, L. (2007) 'Parent-adolescent communication about sexuality: The role of adolescents' beliefs, subjective norm and behaviral control'. *Patient Education and Counselling, 66*: 75–83.

Scott, M. (2000) 'Focussing on the text and its key words'. In L. Burnard and T. McEnery (eds), *Rethinking Language Pedagogy from a Corpus Perspective*. Frankfurt: Peter Lang, 103–22.

—. (2001) 'Comparing corpora and identifying keywords, collocations, frequency distributions through the WordSmith Tools suite of computer programs'. In M. Ghadessy (ed.), *Small Corpus Studies and ELT. Theory and Practice*. Philadelphia: John Benjamins, 47–67.

—. (2008) *WordSmith Tools Help Manual*. Version 5. Oxford: Oxford University Press.

—. (2009) 'In search of a bad reference corpus'. In D. Archer (ed.), *What's in a Wordlist? Investigating Word Frequency and Keyword Extraction*. Farnham: Ashgate, 77–90.

—. (2010) 'Problems in investigating keyness, or clearing the undergrowth and marking out trails'. In M. Bondi and M. Scott (eds), *Keyness in Texts*. Amsterdam: John Benjamins, 43–57.

Scott, S., Powell, J. (1993) 'Brief report: Adolescent self-mutilation in a rural area'. *Journal of Adolescence, 16*: 101–10.

Scourfield, J., Jacob, N., Smalley, N., Prior, L., Greenland, K. (2007) 'Young people's gendered interpretations of suicide and attempted suicide'. *Child and Family Work, 12*: 248–57.

Seale, C. (2006) 'Gender accommodation in online cancer support groups'. *Health, 10*: 345–60.

Seale, C., Charteris-Black, J. (2010) 'Keyword analysis: A new tool for qualitative research'. In I. Bourgeault, R. Dingwall and R. de Vries (eds), *The Sage Handbook of Qualitative Methods in Health Research*. London: Sage, 536–55.

Seale, C., Ziebland, S., Charteris-Black, J. (2006) 'Gender, cancer experience and internet use: A comparative keyword analysis of interviews and online cancer support groups'. *Social Science and Medicine, 62*: 2577–90.

Seale, C., Boden, S., Williams, S., Lowe, P., Steinberg, D. (2007) 'Media constructions of sleep and sleep disorders: A study of UK national newspapers'. *Social Science and Medicine, 65*: 418–30.

Seale, C., Charteris-Black, J., Macfarlane, A., Mcpherson, A. (2010) 'Interviews and internet forums: A comparison of two sources of qualitative data'. *Qualitative Health Research, 20*: 595–606.

Secker, J., Armstrong, C., Hill, M. (1999) 'Young people's understanding of mental illness'. *Health Education Research, 14*: 729–39.

Semino, E. (2008) *Metaphor in Discourse*. Cambridge: Cambridge University Press.

Shrier, L., Shih, M., Hacker, B., de Moor, C. (2007) 'A momentary sampling study of the affective experience following coital events in adolescents'. *Journal of Adolescent Health, 40*: 357–64.

Sikand, A., Fisher, M., Friedman, S. (1996) 'AIDS knowledge, concerns, and behavioural changes among inner-city high school students'. *Journal of Adolescent Health, 18*: 325–28.

Silberg, W., Lundberg, G., Musacchio, R. (1997) 'Assessing, controlling, and assurring the quality of medical information on the internet: Caveat lector et viewer –let the reader and viewer beware'. *Journal of the American Medical Association, 277*: 1244–45.

Silverman, D. (1997) *Discourses of Counselling: HIV Counselling as Social Interaction* London: Sage.

Simon, T., Mercy, J., Barker, L. (2006) 'Can we talk?' Importance of random-digit-dial surveys for injury prevention research'. *American Journal of Preventive Medicine, 31*: 406–10.

Sinclair, J. (1991) *Corpus, Concordance, Collocation*. Oxford: Oxford University Press.

—. (1999) 'A way with common words'. In H. Hasselgard and S. Oskefjell (eds), *Out of Corpora: Studies in Honour of Stig Johnasson*. Amsterdam: Rodopi, 157–79.

Skegg, K. (2005) 'Self-harm'. *The Lancet, 366*: 1471–83.

Skelton, J., Hobbs, F. (1999a) 'Descriptive study of cooperative language in primary care consultations by male and female doctors'. *British Medical Journal, 318*: 576–79.

—. (1999b) 'Concordancing: Use of language-based research in medical communication'. *Lancet, 353*: 108–11.

Skelton, J., Murray, J., Hobbs, F. (1999) 'Imprecision in medical communication: Study of a doctor talking to patients with serious illness'. *Journal of the Royal Society of Medicine, 92*: 620–25.

Skelton, J., Wearn, A., Hobbs, F. (2002a) 'A concordance-based study of metaphoric expressions used by GPs and patients in consultation'. *British Journal of General Practice, 52*: 114–18.

—. (2002b) '"I" and "we": A concordancing analysis of how doctors and patients use first person pronouns in primary care consultations'. *Family Practice, 19*: 484–88.

Smith, D. (1983) 'No one commits suicide: Textual analysis of ideological practices'. *Human Studies, 6*: 309–59.

Smith, J. (2004) 'Adolescent males' views on the use of mental health counselling services'. *Adolescence, 39*: 77–82.

Smith, C., Mullany, L., Adolphs, S., Harvey, K. (2013) 'Spelling errors and keywords in born-digital data: A case study using the Teenage Health Freak corpus' *Corpora* (in press).

Smyth, C. A., MacLachlan, M. (2004) 'The context of suicide: An examination of life circumstances thought to be understandable precursors to youth suicide'. *Journal of Mental Health, 13*: 83–92.

Solomon, Y., Farrand, J. (1996) '"Why don't you do it properly?" Young women who self-injure'. *Journal of Adolescence, 19*: 111–19.

Sommer-Rotenberg, D. (1998) 'Suicide and language'. *Canadian Medical Association Journal, 159*: 239–40.

Sontag, S. (2002) *Illness as Metaphor and AIDS and Its Metaphors*. Harmondsworth: Penguin.

Spence, D. (2013) 'Are antidepressants overprescribed? Yes'. *British Medical Journal, 346*: f191.

Spielberg, A. (1999) 'Reply to Gurwitz'. *Journal of the American Medical Association, 282*: 730.

Stammers, T. (2007) 'Sexual health in adolescents: 'Saved sex' and parental involvement are key to improving outcomes'. *British Medical Journal, 334*: 103–04.

Stenström, A.-B. (1999) 'He was really gormless – She's bloody crap: Girls, boys and intensifiers'. In H. Hasselgard and S. Oksefjett (eds), *Out of Corpora Studies in Honour of Stig Johansson*. Amsterdam: Rodopi, 69–78.

Stenström, A., Andersen, G., Hasund, I. (2002) *Trends in Teenage Talk: Corpus Compilation, Analysis and Findings*. Amsterdam: John Benjamins.

Stewart, M. (2005) '"I'm just going to wash you down": Sanitizing the vaginal examination'. *Journal of Advanced Nursing, 5*: 587–94.

Stoppard, J. (2000) *Understanding Depression: Feminist Social Constructionist Approaches*. London: Routledge.

Strong, M. (1998) *A Bright Red Scream: Self-Mutilation and the Language of Pain*. London: Virago.

Stubbs, M. (1983) *Discourse Analysis: The Sociolinguistic Analysis of Natural Language*. Oxford: Blackwell.

—. (1996) *Text and Corpus Analysis: Computer-Assisted Studies Methods of Language and Culture*. Oxford: Blackwell.

—. (1997) 'Whorf's children: Critical comments on critical discourse analysis'. In A. Wray and A. Ryan (eds), *Evolving Models of Language*. Clevedon: Multilingual Matters, 100–16.

—. (2001) 'Texts, corpora, and problems of interpretation: A response to Widdowson'. *Applied Linguistics, 22*: 149–72.

—. (2005) 'Conrad in the computer: Examples of quantitative stylistic methods'. *Language and Literature, 14*: 5–24.

—. (2010) 'Three concepts of keywords'. In M. Bondi, and M. Scott (eds), *Keyness in Texts*. Amsterdam: John Benjamins, 21–42.

Subrahmanyam, K., Greenfield, P., Tynes, B. (2004) 'Constructing sexuality and identity in an online teen chat room'. *Applied Developmental Psychology, 25*: 651–66.

Suler, J. (2004) 'The online disinhibition effect'. *CyberPsychology and Behavior, 7*: 321–26.

Sullivan, C. (2003) 'Gendered cybersupport: A thematic analysis of two online cancer support groups'. *Journal of Health Psychology, 8*: 83–103.

Sun, P., Unger, J., Palmer, P. (2005) 'Internet accessibility and usage among urban adolescents in Southern California: Implications for web-based health research'. *Cyberpsychology and Behaviour, 8*: 441–53.

Sutton, J. (2005) *Healing the Hurt Within*. Oxford: Howtobooks.

Suyemoto, K. (1998) 'The functions of self-mutilation'. *Clinical Psychology Review, 18*: 531–54.

Suzuki, L., Calzo, J. (2004) 'The search for peer advice in cyberspace: An examination of online teen bulletin boards about health and sexuality'. *Applied Developmental Psychology, 25*: 685–98.

Switzer, J., Wittink, M., Karsch, B., Barg, F. (2006) '"Pull yourself up by your bootstraps": A response to depression in older adults'. *Qualitative Health Research, 16*: 1207–16.

Talseth, A.-G., Jacobsson, L., Norberg, A. (2001) 'The meaning of suicidal psychiatric inpatients' experiences of being treated by physicians'. *Journal of Advanced Nursing, 34*: 96–106.

Talseth, A.-G., Gilje, F., Norberg, A. (2003) 'Struggling to become ready for consolation: Experiences of suicidal patients'. *Nursing Ethics, 10*: 614–23.

Tates, K., Meeuwesen, L., Elbers, E., Bensing, J. (2002) ' "I've come for his throat": roles and identities in doctor-parent-child communication'. *Child Care Health Development, 28*: 109–16.

Telles, J., Pollack, M. (1981) 'Feeling sick: The experience and legitimation of illness'. *Social Science and Medicine, 15*: 243–51.

Ten Have, P. (1995) 'Medical ethnomethodology: An overview'. *Human Studies, 18*: 245–61.

Ten Have, H. A. (2002). Cybermedicine and e-ethics. *Medicine, Health Care, and Philosophy*, 5(2), 117.

Terrence Higgins Trust. (2007) *Understanding HIV infection: HIV?AIDS?* (5th ed). London: Terence Higgins Trust.

Teubert, W., Cermakova, A. (2004) 'Directions in corpus linguistics'. In M. Halliday, W. Teubert, C. Yallop and A. Cermakova (eds), *Lexicology and Corpus Linguistics*. London: Continuum, pp. 113–65.

Thomas, J., Wilson, A. (1996) Methodologies for studying a corpus of doctor-patient interaction. In J. Thomas and M. Short (eds), *Using Corpora for Language Research*. London: Longman, 92–109.

Thompson, S. (1990) '"Putting a big thing into a little hole": Teenage girls' accounts of sexual initiation'. *The Journal of Sex Research, 27*: 341–61.

Thornbury, S. (2010) 'What can a corpus tell us about discourse?'. In M. McCarthy and A. O'Keefe (eds), *The Routledge Handbook of Corpus Linguistics*. Abingdon, UK: Routledge, 270–87.

Thurlow, C. (2003) 'Teenagers in communication, teenagers on communication'. *Journal of Language and Social Psychology, 22*: 50–57.

Tognini-Bonelli, E. (2001) *Corpus Linguistics at Work*. Amsterdam: John Benjamins.

Tribble, C. (2000) 'Genres, keywords, teaching: Towards a pedagogic account of the language of project proposals'. In L. Burnard and T. McEnery (eds), *Rethinking Language Pedagogy from a Corpus Perspective*. Frankfurt: Peter Lang, 75–90.

Trinch, S. (2001) 'Managing euphemism and transcending taboos: Negotiating the meaning of sexual assault in Latinas' narratives of domestic violence'. *Text, 21*: 567–610.

Turan, J., Bukusi, E., Onono, M., Holzemer, W., Miller, S., Cohen, C. (2011) 'HIV/AIDS stigma and refusal of HIV testing among pregnant women in rural Kenya: Results from the MAMAS study'. *AIDS and Behaviour, 15*: 1111–20.

Turk, D., Hocking, J. (2005) 'Brief report: The effects of condom insistence on the perceptions of adolescents in first time and repeated occasions of sexual intercourse'. *Journal of Adolescence, 28*: 589–94.

United Nations Educational, Scientific and Cultural Organization (UNESCO). (2006) *UNESCO Guidelines on Language and Content in HIV- and AIDS- Related Materials*. Paris: UNESCO.

Valaitis, R. (2005) 'Computers and the internet: Tools for youth empowerment'. *Journal of Medical Internet Research, 7*: e51.

Valente, S. (1994) 'Messages of psychiatric patients who have attempted or committed suicide'. *Clinical Nursing Research, 3*: 316–33.

Van Naerssen, M. (1985) 'Medical records: One variation of physician of physicians' language'. *International Journal of Sociology of Language, 51*: 43–74.

van Roosmalen, E. (2000) 'Forces of patriarchy: Adolescent experiences of sexuality and conceptions of relationships'. *Youth and Society, 32*: 202–27.

Waldren, S., Kibbe, D. (2004) 'Email in clinical care: Best as part of an electronic record'. *British Medical Journal USA, 329*: 503–04.

Walther, J. (1996) 'Computer-mediated communication: Impersonal, interpersonal, and hypersonal interaction'. *Communication Research, 23*: 3–43.

Warner, R. (1976) 'The relationship between language and disease concepts'. *International Journal of Psychiatry in Medicine, 7*: 57–68.

Warwick, I., Aggleton, P., Homans, H. (1988) 'Young people's health beliefs and AIDS'. In P. Aggleton and H. Homans (eds), *Social Aspects of AIDS*. Falmer Press: Sussex, 59–77.

Watney, S. (1989) 'AIDS, language and the third world'. In E. Carter and S. Watney (eds), *Taking Liberties: AIDS and Cultural Politics*. London: Serpent's Tail, 182–92.

Weijts, W., Houtkoop, H., Mullen, P. (1993). Talking delicacy: Speaking about sexuality during gynaecological consultations. *Sociology of Health and Illness,15*: 295–314.

Weiss, M. (1997) 'Signifying the pandemics: Metaphors of AIDS, cancer, and heart disease'. *Medical Anthropology Quarterly, 11*: 456–76.

Weller, E. B., Weller, R. A. (2000) Depression in adolescents: Growing pains or true morbidity? *Journal of Affective Disorders, 61*: 9–13.

Wellings, K., Nanchahal, K., Macdowall, W., McManus, S., Erens, B., Mercer, C., Johnson, A., Copas, A., Korovessis, C., Fenton, K., Field, J. (2001) 'Sexual behaviour in Britain: Early heterosexual experience'. *The Lancet, 358*: 1843–50.

Whitley, R. (2007) 'Mixed-methods studies'. *Journal of Mental Health, 16*: 697–701.

Whitlock, J., Powers, J., Eckenrod, J. (2006) 'The internet and adolescent self-injury'. *Developmental Psychology, 42*: 407–17.

Widdice, L., Cornell, J., Liang, W., Halpern-Felsher, B. (2006) 'Having sex and condom use: Potential risks and benefits reported by young, sexually inexperienced adolescents'. *Journal of Adolescent Health, 39*: 588–95.

Widdowson, H. (1991) 'The description and prescription of language'. In J. Atlatis (ed.), *Linguistics and Language Pedagogy*. Georgetown: Georgetown University Press, 11–24.

—. (1996) *Linguistics*. Oxford: Oxford University Press.

—. (2000) 'On the limitations of linguistics applied'. *Applied Linguistics, 21*: 3–25.

Wight, D. (1993a) 'A re-assessment of health education on HIV/AIDS for young heterosexuals'. *Health Education Research, 8*: 473–83.

—. (1993b) 'Constraints or cognition? Young men and safer heterosexual sex'. In P. Aggleton, P. Davies and G. Hart (eds), *AIDS: The Second Decade*. London: Falmer Press, 41–60.

Williams, R. (1983) *Keywords*. London: Fontana.

Williams, M. (2001) *Suicide and Attempted Suicide*. London: Penguin.

Williams, A., Thurlow, C. (eds) (2005) *Talking Adolescence: Perspectives on Communication in the Teenage Years*. New York: Peter Lang.

Wilton, T., Aggleton, P. (1992) 'Condoms, coercion and control: Heterosexuality and the limits to HIV/AIDS education'. In P. Aggleton, P. Davies and G. Hart (eds), *AIDS: Rights, Risk and Reason*. London: The Falmer Press, 149–56.

Wisdom, J., Green, C. (2004) '"Being in a funk": Teens' efforts to understand their depressive experiences'. *Qualitative Health Research, 14*: 1227–38.

Wissow, L., Platt, R. (2006) 'Promoting adolescents' use of medical services'. *Patient Education and Counselling, 62*: 159–60.

Wittink, M., Dahlberg, B., Biruk, C., Barg, F. (2008) 'How older adults combine medical and experiential notions of depression'. *Qualitative Health Research, 18*: 1174–83.

Wodak, R. (1981) 'Problem presentation in therapy and interview'. *Text, 1*: 191–213.

World Health Organisation. (2000) *Mental Health and Brain Disorders*. Geneva: World Health Organisation.

Woollett, A., Marshall, H., Stenner, P. (1998) Young women's accounts of sexual activity and sexual/reproductive health. *Journal of Health Psychology, 3*: 369–81.

Wong, C., Tang, C. (2005) 'Practice of habitual and volitional health behaviours to prevent severe acute respiratory syndrome among Chinese adolescents in Hong Kong'. *Journal of Adolescent Health, 36*: 193–200.

Yates, S. J. (1996) 'Oral and written linguistic aspects of computer conferencing'. In S. Herring (ed.), *Computer Mediated Communication: Linguistic, Social, and Cross-Cultural Perspectives*. Philadelphia: John Benjamins, 29–46.

# Author Index

# Subject Index